Seneca by Candlelight
and Other Stories
of Renaissance Drama

Seneca by Candlelight
and Other Stories
of Renaissance Drama

LORRAINE HELMS

PENN

University of Pennsylvania Press

Philadelphia

10 9 8 7 6 5 4 3 2 1

Published by
University of Pennsylvania Press
Philadelphia, Pennsylvania 19104-4011

Library of Congress Cataloging-in-Publication Data
Helms, Lorraine Rae.
Seneca by candlelight and other stories of Renaissance drama /
Lorraine Helms.
    p. cm.
Includes bibliographical references and index.
ISBN 0-8122-3413-8 (alk. paper)
    1. English drama—Early modern and Elizabethan, 1500–1600—History
and criticism. 2. Seneca, Lucius Annaeus, ca. 4 B.C.–65 A.D.—
Influence. 3. English drama—17th century—History and criticism.
4. Classical literature—Appreciation—England. 5. Mythology,
Classical, in literature. 6. English drama—Classical influences.
7. Renaissance—England. I. Title.
PR655.H45 1997
822'.309—dc21   97-15557
                                                      CIP

For my father

Brecht, in the course of yesterday's conversation: "I often imagine being interrogated by a tribunal. 'Now tell us, Mr. Brecht, are you completely in earnest?' I would have to admit that no, I'm not completely in earnest. I think too much about artistic problems, you know, about what's good for the theatre, to be completely in earnest."

—Walter Benjamin, "Conversations with Brecht"

Contents

Prologue

> Our lives teach us what we are.
> —Salman Rushdie, *Imaginary Homelands*

ONE SPRING MORNING in 1974, I was standing in line at the Office of Human Resources in West Los Angeles. The clerk was trying to decide which among the kinds of waged work I'd done might provide a category she could use for purposes of my unemployment benefits. I was an actor who had also worked as an inventory clerk, a paralegal, the scheduler for a state senatorial campaign, a waitress, and, in my best day job, a gorilla in "The Big Show of 1936" at the Orpheum Theatre in San Francisco in 1972. ("The Big Show" had brought Jackie Coogan, Beatrice Kay, Sally Rand, and numerous others of their era out of retirement for a variety show. Before the show, I went into the house dressed in a gorilla suit, with a ticket stub in my hand, demanding that an usher show me to an already occupied seat. During the overture, I ran across the apron of the stage chasing a German shepherd, then ran back the other way, with the shepherd chasing me. For this and similar *shtick*, I was paid somewhat more each week than I'd earned each month playing Shakespeare with a small touring company.)

Realizing that even in those palmier days I might exhaust the resources of the state of California before I found such another day job, or, *a fortiori*, another Shakespeare company, the clerk decided to call me a restaurant worker. I was twenty-eight, old enough to realize that trying to convince this clerk, and the world, that I was an actor could very well end with my waiting on tables forever. At that moment and without any forethought, I decided to change my life, to

complete the undergraduate degree I'd once scorned, and become a
serviceable, or at least solvent, citizen of the republic. In my family of
doctors, lawyers, and scholars, leaving school to work in theater was
a daring and disreputable thing to do. True, my father had introduced
me to Shakespeare, telling me the stories of the plays, quoting scenes
and speeches, even teaching me the chants of *Macbeth*'s witches to
sing on Halloween. My mother had overseen my training in music
and dance. But they always assumed I would stay in school until it
was time to take a properly credentialed place in society. Waiting in
line for my unemployment insurance, I began to feel the force of their
assumptions. My status as a scion of the professional class clearly at
stake, I returned to school. Hoping to rediscover Shakespeare among
literary scholars, I became a student of English Renaissance drama.

I was delighted with my exchange. No more three-minute audi-
tions, no more two-minute rejections. No more months of enforced
leisure to corrode skill and confidence. An English major, unlike an
actor, can work all she likes. Her rewards, though slighter, are more
easily obtained. So I read and wrote, until the protocols of literary
criticism came to seem like nature methodized.

At some moment I no longer recall, I decided upon an academic
career, in the course of which I would write scholarly books. But after
wandering about, intellectually and institutionally, for several years,
I found myself en route back to the theater, where I now work in solo
performance. So I did not have a conventional academic career. Nor
did I write a conventional scholarly book. An enterprise that began
with a philological thesis and then metamorphosed into a series of
feminist essays is now a collection of something like stories I have
learned, as a scholar and an actor, about English Renaissance drama.

I have not called my chapters stories in order to proclaim the
fictionality of history, though I do acknowledge that they are my
inventions. In the rhetorical tradition that several of them examine,
argumenta and *narrationes* are often synonymous. They are discourses
designed to persuade auditors of a given interpretation of an event,
a law, a character. The usage endures in Elizabethan English, where
the summary of a play's plot is called its argument.

Modern usage distinguishes more sharply. Stories create community and arguments imply adversaries; stories acknowledge trial and error, arguments efface exploration and uncertainty; stories are creative, arguments productive. Nevertheless, in these chapters, I have tried to retrieve the rhetorical sense of *argumentum* within the conventions of the scholarly essay. My chapters do conform to those conventions. They assume the reader's specialized knowledge. They include notes. Quite a few notes. Yet once I chose to call my chapters stories, I found some freedom to articulate their autobiographical subtext, to intercalate, via narrative prologues and epilogues, the motives of my scholarly inquiries, their processes and effects in my life. So while these chapters are scholarly essays on rhetoric and theater, text and performance, gender and discourse, they are also stories shaped by my changing life as I moved from the theater to the academy and back again.

When I first chose to include this autobiographical subtext, it seemed idiosyncratic. It seems so no longer. To acknowledge (or boast of) one's idiosyncrasy by interweaving autobiography with criticism or fiction with scholarship, is, in the mid-nineties, less a quirk than a custom. The testimonial note sounded in feminist essays of the early eighties has reemerged in a fashion for "personal" or "autobiographical" or "confessional" criticism. This is, for some critics, a rejection of the sophistications of theory and, for others, a continuation of theory by other means. For some, it is a reaction to the Procrustean manipulation of the intellectual within institutional life; for others, a political action and indeed the only one available to the postmodern literary academic. Such claims have elicited counterclaims, critiques, parodic visions of libraries transformed to halls of mirrors and sable-silvered dons in the chains and leather of aging rock stars.[1]

My resort to first-person narrative originated in the less contentious (if not less competitive) context of solo performance, a world of autobiographical theater at once parallel, intersecting, and opposed to the academic enterprise. It is parallel, since both personal criticism and solo performance emerge from current celebrations of the local, the fragmentary, the anecdotal and confessional. Both involve a *faute de mieux* response to a postmodern sense of disorientation and disempowerment, though academics are rebelling against the constraints of institutional life and actors are searching for new infrastructures amid the economic disarray of this harsh time.

It is intersecting, since some academics write about performance and some performers work in academic settings, though again, among academics, at least academic literary critics, writing about performance often represents an intellectual rebellion against traditional methods, and among actors, taking a university position often represents submission, exhaustion, and defeat. And it is opposed, since the languages of those for whom the stage is a physical place of corporeal labor and those who metaphorically "stage the self" in their studies are filled with false cognates. Theater and theatricality are such a pair, and performance and performativity another. For theater and performance often are to theatricality and performativity as water is to absinthe or bread to peacock's tongues, as the essential is to the risqué or decadent.[2]

Sorting out these parallels, intersections, and oppositions is the story of my wandering life. An actor who became a philologist who became a feminist who became an actor, I am continually separating what can be packed up and taken along from what must be left behind.

As a young actor, I read Shakespeare for meter and motivation, entrances and exits. I performed in basements, storefronts, street fairs, and municipal parks; I joined bus and truck tours to hinterland high schools and colleges; and I came to know Shakespeare by heart. As an undergraduate English major, I studied the then gentle art of literary criticism, with its discourse upon naked babes and cloaks of manliness. As a graduate student, I exchanged this formalism for a philological method that sought to recover the textually transmitted influence of classical antiquity on the practices of the Elizabethan playhouse. When I came to write my dissertation, I hoped, somewhat incoherently, to unite theatrical experience, literary analysis, and historical research in a demonstration that the classical tradition was part of the theatrical and not only literary vitality of Renaissance drama.

I wanted to understand Elizabethan performance. (Thus I recreate my story of 1982: "I wanted to understand Elizabethan performance." Perhaps I should say that this is what I now wish I had then wanted.) I do not mean that I expected to discover how much blood the sheep's bladder had in it when Duncan was murdered. My hope was more intimate and more elusive. I wanted to recapture, via a historical inquiry, the ghostly affinity I remembered from a visit to the London Theatre Museum. Gazing at memorabilia from generations of actors, musicians, clowns, and mountebanks, I felt the dead alive and busy, not in yellowed playbills and worn dancing shoes, but in my own body that had once sung and danced and spoken Shakespeare's verse on stage. With a heigh-ho feeling of fellowship in every cry of players since Sophocles', I set forth on a journey that led me farther and farther from the stage.

My first chapter, "Seneca by Candlelight," recounts the beginning of that journey. Taking its title from Nashe's description of the Elizabethan playwrights who scanned translations of the Roman dramatist for purple passages, it describes my efforts to discover a historiographical method that could make sense of the resemblances I saw between the tradition of the classical *ars rhetorica* and the physical spaces of the Elizabethan playhouses. This enterprise turned on an ancient rhetorical distinction between public and private discourse, which I thought to relate to the strangely similar distinction between the public and private playhouses of Elizabethan London.

In the Renaissance rhetorical tradition, and, as I take it, in Nashe's phrase, Seneca is not only Seneca the Younger, the tragedian and philosopher, but Seneca the Elder, the rhetorician who was only differentiated from his son long after Nashe wrote. An aficionado of declamation, the elder Seneca recorded the *controversiae* and *suasoriae* he heard in the rhetors' halls, making his manuscript a gift to the son in whose tragedies the discourse of declamation was revived.

This amalgamation of father and son symbolizes the traditional relation between rhetoric and drama well. The art of rhetoric, it has long been recognized, dominates theories of language in antiquity, the Middle Ages, and early modern Europe. Its omnipresent schemes and tropes have been documented in textual analyses of English Renaissance drama. Its methods of inquiry and modes of representation have been remarked in the structural principles of comedy, tragedy, and romance. Its discussions of *actio* have been detected in contemporary descriptions of the players.[3] But it has been less often noted that the rhetoricians also examined the qualities of light and sound in forum and hall, anatomized the vagaries of different audiences, and sometimes offered rough and ready advice on the exigencies of performance.

Rhetoric set the tasks that the classics performed within the workaday world of Elizabethan theatrical culture. The accomplishment of these tasks depended not only on the transmission of texts but (*mutatis mutandis*) on the iteration of oratorical and theatrical occasions. In other words, the classical tradition concerns "candlelight" as much as it does "Seneca." Nashe's phrase, as I have adapted it, refers not only to the playwright in his study, cribbing ghosts, revenge, *sententiae*, and the five-act structure, but, *per synecdochen*, also to the subsequent performance of his play in the Elizabethan playhouse. My "Seneca by Candlelight" is about the translation of the classics into the vernacular, of rhetoric into drama, and of text into performance.

It is also about the limitations of the methods, from the stuffy to the trendy, through which I tried to bring order to this material. For no method, whether philological, theoretical, materialist, feminist, feminist-materialist, or philological-feminist, answered my questions. Instead, the questions began to change. When my dissertation was almost complete, I began studying martial arts. In confronting a contemporary rhetoric of violence, I discovered the unsuspected violence of ancient rhetoric.

So I tested my philological dissertation against materialist and feminist criticism that claimed to include the experience of the body in its survey of knowledge, and discovered that my thesis was at the same time testing my new methods. A brief history of one scholar's encounter with the critical enterprise over the last two decades, "Seneca by Candlelight" ends more as *argumentum* than argument. A work of historical scholarship, it is, finally, shaped less by its theses about English Renaissance drama than by an autobiographical plot. It is the story of a student of rhetoric who learned, via the practice of martial arts, to question the relation of discourse and violence.

From the realization that my own corporeal history illuminated the arcana of my classical education all my other stories in one way or another derive. In the next of them, I turn from the Elizabethan theater to the theatricality of everyday life among the Henrician, Edwardian, and Marian aristocracy. This is the only chapter that takes up theatricality rather than theater, and one of two that includes ritual as well as drama and declamation in its exploration of performance. "Iphigenia in Durham" anticipates several themes of later chapters —sacrifice and martyrdom, rhetoric and lamentation, kinship and memory, the anthropology of Renaissance neoclassicism, the vulnerabilities and resiliences of women's voices, the silences on the selvages of history. These are themes that have touched me more closely in the years since I began my researches, but here they are refracted through the vestigial records of the life of the Tudor noblewoman who first translated Euripides' *Iphigenia in Aulis* into English.

The next two chapters, "The Saint in the Brothel" and "Voluntary Wounds," began as scholarly inquiries into the place of rhetoric, violence, class, and gender on the Shakespearean stage. They continued as attempts to understand the force of these things in my life which is partly lived on that stage. "The Saint in the Brothel" follows a motif of rape and prostitution from the Senecan declamation of the *Sacerdos Prostituta* through medieval romance and hagiography to Shakespeare's *Pericles*. Declamation bequeathed more than its sensationalistic tales of marauding pirates, lustful tyrants, and cruel stepmothers to the Shakespearean stage. When these tales are introduced into the theatrical event that is Shakespeare's *Pericles*, they recollect the declaimer's improvisational performance and can encourage the player to resist the closure that narrative sources would otherwise impose. The chapter itself has resisted closure, opening out in its last pages to include something of my own improvisations while teaching Shakespeare.

"Voluntary Wounds," too, is a history of a classical *topos* that emerges in Elizabethan performance. Following Nicole Loraux, whose *Tragic Ways of Killing a Woman* catalogs the suicidal and sacrificial deaths of women in Attic tragedy, this chapter considers the ways in which Shakespeare's Portia, Lavinia, and Cleopatra, along with Heywood's Lucrece and Marston's Sophonisba, suffer and die. Again, I found a strain of Senecan theatricality in these plays that can enlarge the player's scope for the practice of his craft. And again, I found that my experience, here of playing Portia, reshaped my argument into a story.

"The Saint in the Brothel" and (more explicitly) "Voluntary Wounds" argue that the elite tradition of Elizabethan Senecanism, especially as reinterpreted in the private playhouses of the children's companies, partly liberated the player of women's parts from the masculinist conventions of the popular tradition. The last chapter, "Ethnicke Lamentations," makes no argument on behalf of the elite tradition of Senecan theatricality. Rather, it concerns a decidedly demotic art that recent reconstructions of early modern popular culture have not acknowledged: the mourning rituals of women in Tudor England and Ireland. Through its conscious or unconscious atavism, the Elizabethan playhouse, like the Attic theater, recovers and represents these rituals, giving women anonymous in history (and women celebrated in theater) incandescent parts to play in Shakespeare's English chronicles. This chapter was conceived in the theater where I saw Ian McKellen's *Acting Shakespeare* and developed through my study of ancient and early modern lamentation. It ends where it began, in a theater, but one where, in an epilogue, I can tell my own story of theater and scholarship, performance and bereavement.

Though the public and private discourses of the *ars rhetorica* have left traces throughout, these stories have turned out to be about women's roles in ancient and modern myths, legends, rituals, declamations, tragedies, comedies, and chronicles. And about my own exploration, as a scholar and an actor, of those roles. They incorporate the philology with which I began my academic career and the materialist feminism with which I concluded it, but I do not offer them in the service of either discourse. They are, rather, tales told by what the rhetorical tradition calls an *idiōtēs*, an amateur who is not engaged in a professional agon.

Seneca by Candlelight

> I like libraries, they contain on average one truth-
> ful book, but finding it! That's the nightmare, and
> truth's a thing you can grow out of.
> — Howard Barker, *Seven Lears*

"English Seneca read by candlelight," writes Thomas Nashe in the preface to Greene's *Menaphon*, "yields many good sentences, as blood is a beggar and so forth: and if you entreat him fair in a frosty morning, he will afford you whole Hamlets, I should say handfuls of tragical speeches" (312). In the early decades of the twentieth century, scholars of English drama often took Nashe at his word, making "English Seneca" the only begetter of Elizabethan theater. Neoclassical structure, regulating anarchic medieval narrative, resurrected true comedy and tragedy. After a dark millennium, European theaters were at last reilluminated.[1]

After World War II, when the study of classics was ceding prestige to the apparently more democratic field of English literature, a new generation of scholars produced a contrary witness.[2] Whereas Nashe chastises Latinless playwrights who must resort to translations, the character Will Kemp in the second part of *The Return from Parnassus* mocks the theatrical efforts of the learned: "Few of the university pen plays well. They smell too much of that writer Ovid, and that writer Metamorphoses and talk too much of Prosepina and Jupiter" (4.3.1766–68).

With Kemp, many scholars of the midcentury disdained the smell of that writer Ovid. Cold Warriors, liberal and democratic, they dismissed traces of classical antiquity as a superficial and elitist literariness glossing the robust popular theatricality of medieval mysteries, moralities, and mummers' plays. The literary-historical theory of classical revival gave way to the theater-historical paradigm of evolution from the medieval to the modern stage. Scholars of the classical tradition were reduced to endless reinvestigations of the grammar school curriculum or the Stoic fount of Christian thought, for neither "Seneca by candlelight" nor "that writer Ovid" now seemed to have any part to play in the theaters of early modern England.[3]

In *Shakespeare and the Rival Traditions* (1952), Alfred Harbage incorporates this opposition into his vision of antagonistic public and private playhouses. He enlists the public playhouse on the side of history, praising it as the egalitarian "theatre of a nation," where tradespeople and apprentices enjoyed wholesome entertainments that united populist and monarchical notions in patriotic chronicles, romantic comedies, and tragedies that affirm political and domestic order. The candlelit private playhouses in which children's companies performed become the elitist "theatre of a coterie," haughty, perverse, and envious. Here malcontent soldiers of fortune, landless younger sons, and alienated academics gathered to see seditious satirical comedies and arid neoclassical tragedies that nostalgically championed aristocratic privilege. The theater-historical distinction between the open-air amphitheaters and the enclosed halls was for Harbage an ethical, political, and social antithesis, raising the stakes in the War of the Theaters rather higher than those in the Wars of the Roses.

Even now, wails of protest pursue Harbage. Some of the wails come from lumpers. They observe quite accurately that Harbage ignored striking similarities between the repertories of the public and the private houses. *Bartholomew Fair*, they note, was performed at the bearbaiting Hope one day, and before King James the next. *The Malcontent* was produced by the Children of the Queen's Revels at Blackfriars and then stolen by the King's Men for performance at the Globe. "Why not Malevole in folio with us, as Jeronimo in decimo-sexto with them?" asks Condell in the Induction that is the only textual trace of the theft (104–5). Even Shakespeare, cynosure of the popular tradition, wrote for the private playhouse at the end of his career.

Others are splitters. They insist, with equally good evidence on their side, that Harbage's distinction between the adults' and children's companies is too crude. Each playhouse and each company has its own history. The Children of Paul's are not the Children of the Queen's Revels; the Rose is not the Fortune; the rowdy "tearthroats" at the Red Bull are most certainly not the up-and-coming King's Men, with their court performances and their lease on Blackfriars.

Lumpers rarely acknowledge that theatrical events, unlike scripts, cannot be transported from space to space, from amphitheater to hall or from bear garden to court; they ignore the choristers, who cling to their candlelit venues like unfledged eyases to their nests. For there can be private playhouses without children's troupes, but no children's troupes without private playhouses. Splitters often neglect the rivalries and collaborations of theatrical culture.[4] The King's Men may outclass the rowdies at the Red Bull as much as the Hazards do the Chances in Angela Carter's *Wise Children*, but they were, like the Hazards and Chances, originally a single theatrical family.

However tendentiously Harbage divides the kingdom into the theaters of nation and coterie, he nevertheless evades these errors of the lumpers and the splitters. Learned, passionate, and provocative, he acknowledges the interaction of text and venue; he respects the social energy of theatrical culture. When I encountered *Shakespeare and the Rival Traditions* thirty years after its publication, it still suggested ways to explore early modern performances.

So it seemed to me, for Harbage's theater history was the stuff of my own memories. I had played Shakespeare in the park and sung for my supper at street fairs and carnivals; I had also done experimental theater in cramped, ill-lit storefronts and basements. I had tested on my own pulse the differences between performing for distracted holidaymakers in the open air and performing in camera for a supercilious avant garde.[5] To gather my own evidence for the rival traditions, I began to investigate the physical spaces of the Elizabethan playhouses, the social occasions of performance, and the artistic credos and compromises of the players and playwrights.

Amphitheater and Hall

When Johannes de Witt made his celebrated sketch of the Swan, it was for the sake of its resemblance to the amphitheaters of the ancient world: "Since its form seems to approach that of a Roman structure, I have depicted it above" (Chambers 2:362). In 1600, another visitor also found one of the Bankside playhouses *ad morem antiquorum Romanorum constructum* (Chambers 2:366). Whether these architectural echoes are explained as survival, revival, or coincidence, the travelers' tales suggest that the large unroofed structures of the public playhouses cast a shadow of antique grandeur in the observers' minds.

Unlike the purpose-built public playhouses, the buildings that housed the private theaters—the choristers' singing school at Paul's, the Blackfriars' refectory—had no such associations. They were originally designed for communal rather than public functions, choir practice or Dominican repasts. They were neither perfectly private nor yet entirely public spaces.

Although estimates of seating capacity and stage area range widely, Jonson could call the Blackfriars stage a little "cheese trencher" (*The Devil Is an Ass*, Prologue), while the "vast stage" of the outdoor playhouses could be hard to fill, as Shirley complains in the prologue to *The Doubtful Heir*, "which should have been presented at the Blackfriars":

> All that the Prologue comes for to say,
> Our author did not calculate this play
> For this meridian; the Bankside, he knows
> Is far more skilful at the ebbs and flows
> Of water, than of wit . . .

No shows, no dance . . .
No bawdy, nor no ballads . . .
But language clean; and what affects you not,
Without impossibilities the plot;
No clown, no squibs, no devil in't. . . .
But you that can contract yourselves, and sit
As you were now in the Blackfriars pit,
And will not deaf us with lewd noise and tongues
Because we have no heart to break our lungs,
Will pardon our vast stage, and not disgrace
This play, meant for your persons, not the place.
                                        (Prologue, 1–21)

Shirley's belligerent prologue, often cited as evidence for different
popular and elite tastes during the Caroline period, also draws a contrast relevant to earlier stage conditions. All do not all things well; all
scripts are not for all venues. Jigs, duels, clowns, and squibs would
have overburdened the Blackfriars "cheese trencher," but a script that
relies on "language clean" (or even dirty) could seem dull and talky
at the Globe. *The Doubtful Heir* could be swallowed up by the space
in which it was staged, like *Madame Butterfly* at Caracalla.

Groundlings and Gallants

In *Shakespeare's Audience* (1941), almost a companion volume to
Shakespeare and the Rival Traditions, Harbage insists that Shakespeare's plays were written and performed to please the ordinary
people who dominated the audience of the public playhouses. His
egalitarianism has remained controversial, for historical questions
about Shakespeare's audience implicitly or explicitly justify topical
ones: Who is Shakespeare for? Does he "really," that is, historically,
belong to ordinary people? If so, they have been wrongfully cheated
of their bard.

    In a rejoinder to Harbage, Ann Cook argues that the patronage of ordinary Londoners was limited by lack of interest, money, and leisure. Though they attended plays "in sizable numbers" on holidays, it was "the privileged" (themselves a fairly heterogeneous group including "threadbare scholars," "wellborn apprentices," and "great merchants") who provided the players' principal support. In a rejoinder to Cook, Martin Butler defends Harbage, reiterating that plebeian playgoers were Shakespeare's true audience (293–306). Praised and blamed for insisting that Shakespeare belonged (and hence belongs) to ordinary people, Harbage, like a dream of Joe Hill, still haunts the politicized discussion of Shakespeare's audience.

The debate itself points to a heterogeneous audience in the public playhouses. So does the evidence of the Lord Mayor, with his disreputable audience of "vagrant persons, masterless men, thieves, horse stealers, whoremongers, cozeners, conycatchers, contrivers of treason and other idle and dangerous persons" (Chambers, 4:322); of Stephen Gosson, with his somewhat more respectable and more vulnerable "assembly of tailors, tinkers, cordwainers, sawyers, old men, young men, women, boys, girls, and such like" (184); of John Davies, who saw "Townsmen, gentlemen, and whores / Porters and servingmen" (Epigrams, 2:17); and of Thomas Dekker, who observes that "the place is so free of entertainment, allowing a stool as well to the farmer's son as to your Templer" (*The Gull's Hornbook*, 5). If these records reveal the recorders' prejudices about playgoing more than their powers of observation, nevertheless, taken together, they suggest a varied group of playgoers at the Fortune, the Rose, and the Globe.

This variety distinguishes the public from the private playhouse audience. It is not the presence of the privileged, argues Peter Burke, but the absence of ordinary people that definitively marks an elite entertainment in the sixteenth century (270). And their absence was conspicuous in the private playhouses. Except for an occasional "sinful six-penny Mechanick," Cook observes, the admission price "probably barred most plebeian playgoers from the private houses" (181).[6]

Since the private playhouses catered to the privileged, acquaintance with their customs could suggest a would-be gentleman's social status. In the Induction to *The Malcontent*, Will Sly, in character of a playgoer, seeks to bring his rented stool upon the stage. The tire-man tries to deter him:

Tire-Man: Sir, the gentlemen will be angry if you sit here.
Sly: Why, we may sit upon the stage at the private house. Thou dost not take me for a country gentlemen, dost?
(Induction, 1–3)

Sly's social anxiety reveals the plutocratic microcosms of both public and private playhouses. At the Globe and the other outdoor amphitheaters, "the people closest to the stage were the poorest, paying a minimal penny for the privilege of standing on their feet next to the stage platform to view the players." At Blackfriars and the other indoor playhouses, "the wealthier a patron was the closer he or she could come to the action" (Gurr, *Playgoing*, 5).

Yet once the playgoers entered, the indoor theater was less rigorously hierarchical, for the sixpence entrance fee assured every patron of shelter and a seat. The quality of being seated is an old and venerable status marker. "The seated man," observes the legal historian Frederic Maitland, "is in quiet enjoyment. We reverence the throne, the bishop's see, 'the right Reverend Bench,' the bench of judges, we obey the orders of the chair; the powers that be are seated" (88). Mercy's address to the audience in *Mankind* demonstrates the theatrical application: "O ye soverans that sitt, and ye brothern that stonde right uppe" (29).

Standing "brothern" differ from "soverans that sitt" not only in social status, but, more importantly from the players' perspective, in mood. "The unstable psychology of a standing, as compared to a seated, crowd," Chambers remarks, "must always be taken into account in estimating the temperament of an Elizabethan audience" (Chambers, 2:527). This is a truth that buskers, if not historians of Shakespeare's audience, universally acknowledge. Groundlings require lustier entertainment than gallants, not because they are tin-

kers and tailors rather than captains and courtiers, but because they
are groundlings, standing or squatting or crouching in the playhouse
yard.

Little Eyases and Great Histrionics

"O Imps of Phoebus," complains John Davies in *Wit's Pilgrim-
age* (1605), "why do you / Employ the power of your divinity . . .
Upon impeaching your own quality?"[7] Like Hamlet's "little eyases"
who exclaim against their own succession, Davies' proud "imps of
Phoebus" self-consciously separate themselves from the adult companies. Their separatism has marred their posthumous fortunes, for
they have been largely ignored in favor of the public playhouse apprentices.

Concentrating on Shakespeare, theater historians, who once argued whether Elizabethan acting was formal or naturalistic, now
ask whether the boy actor's fictitious femininity was conventional
and invisible or aleatory and open to interpretation.[8] The distinction between the adults' young apprentices and the chorister companies often disappears.[9] Yet the apprentices were "descendants of
the poor players who toured and tumbled for a living only slightly
better than vagabondage," while the choristers were "academically tu-
tored schoolchildren" (Gurr, *The Shakespearean Stage*, 95). The former
could have differed from the latter as much as the San Francisco
Mime Troupe differs from a prep school drama department.

The adult companies seem to have founded their reputations
largely on the genius of their leading players. Tradition still celebrates
the bravura effects of Burbage's Hamlet, who could "leap into the
grave / suiting the person . . . of a sad lover, with so true an eye / that
there I would haue sworn, he meant to die."[10] The names of Edward
Alleyn, William Kemp, and Robert Armin still resonate, as does that
of Nathan Field, a boy actor who grew into an adult sharer and so
achieved celebrity.[11] Otherwise, the apprentices have left few traces
in the historical record.

The choristers are even more conspicuously absent. Thomas

Clifton, impressed into the Blackfriars troupe, is known only for not performing, since his father secured a warrant for his immediate release (Hillebrand, 160–63). Salathiel Pavy owes his renown to Jonson's epitaph on his early death: at "scarce thirteen," Pavy had for three years played "Old men so duly / As sooth, the Parcae thought him one, / He played so truly" ("Epitaph on S. P.").

Though it befuddle the Parcae, Pavy's *senex* does not belong to the theatrical tradition of Burbage's tragic heroes or Kemp's clowns. The adult players, whom Hemings in the Induction to *The Malcontent* calls "folio" sized, have different resources and restrictions than "decimo-sexto" boys. The choristers were closely controlled by their "instructors," who were prototypical directors. The instructors' public playhouse counterparts, the playwrights, had far less authority, for they were the sharers' employees. Paradoxically, this authoritarian infrastructure of the private playhouse may have created a more egalitarian *mise en scène* than the adults' cooperative venture. For the instructors seem to have eschewed the incipient star system of the public playhouses. Instead, they developed ensembles to encourage the social commentary of the satires in which they specialized—a specialization that earned them the nervous censure of their contemporaries.[12]

Satirists and Balladmongers

In his voluble *Apology for Actors*, Thomas Heywood, apparently fearful that the municipal authorities, like Harbage's critics, would ignore the differences between the adults' and children's companies, lays all theatrical transgressions exclusively to the children's charge and advises the satirical rogues who write for them to mend their invidious ways:

The liberty which some arrogate to themselves, committing their bitterness, and liberal invectives against all estates, to the mouths of children, supposing their juniority to be a privilege for any railing, be it never so violent, I could advise all such to curb and limit this presumed liberty within the bands of discretion and government. But wise and judicial censures, before whom such complaints shall at any time hereafter come, will not (I hope) impute these abuses to any transgression in us, who have ever been careful and provident to shun the like. (61)

Heywood's obviously self-interested tract may protest too much. Hamlet remarks on the unfair trade practices of the "little eyases," not their perverse topicality. The legal embroilments of the children's companies, however, corroborate Heywood's complaints about their antiauthoritarianism.[13]

The *Apology* is perhaps the strongest single contemporary witness for Harbage's distinction between the civic-spirited theater of a nation and the insolent theater of a coterie. There is further, though more problematic testimony in the documents of the curious episode known variously as the Poetomachia or War of the Theaters.[14] The Poetomachia playwrights, including Marston, Dekker, and Jonson, spent their best energies caricaturing each other. On one side is the popular playwright, sometimes an illiterate balladmonger who cheerfully composes his vacuous interludes to the players' orders, sometimes a pompous "Shake-scene" or "Tamer-cham" condemned for bombast and fustian. On the other is the scholarly satirist who disdains the commercial theater from which he nevertheless hopes to make his fortune.

The first full portrait of each type appears in Marston's *Histrio-mastix*, in the vivid episodes involving Sir Oliver Owlet's Men, their playwright Posthaste, and the scholar Chrisogonus. The enterprising Posthaste does not let ignorance interfere with economic opportunity: "Let's make up a company of players, / For we can all sing and say, / And so (with practice) soon may learn to play" (p. 250, 1.2).[15] His company's offerings befit the players' rustic condition: "*Mother Gurton's Needle* (a Tragedy), *The Devil and Dives* (a Comedy), *A Russet Coat and a Knave's Cap* (an Infernal), *A Proud Heart and a Beggar's Purse* (a Pastoral), and *The Widow's Apronstrings* (a Nocturnal)" (p. 263, 1.1). Even the more charitable on-stage spectators call this "home-spun country stuff," while the critical lord Landulpho dismisses its "buzzardly simplicity" (pp. 264 and 265, 2.1).

Yet Posthaste has one great talent: "Posthaste the poet extempore can sing" (p. 265, 2.1) For Landulpho, the improvised song that concludes the performance of Sir Oliver Owlet's Men is also "base trash," but it earns Philarchus's compassionate commendation: "The Italian Lord is an ass, the song is a good song" (p. 266, 2.1). Posthaste is no poet, but his improvised song recalls the theatrical reality that his name signifies. "The plays we now regard as great literary works," Bernard Beckerman comments, "were struck off in the harassing atmosphere of a commercial enterprise" (15). Posthaste's eager compliance with this enterprise distinguishes him from the learned and rancorous Chrisogonus, who, proudly asking an exorbitant ten pounds a play, prices himself out of the market. Unemployed and unemployable, he can only rail against an age in which "every scrivener's boy shall dip / Prophaning quills into Thessaliae's spring" (p. 272, 3.1).

Despite his own affinity with the type, Marston condemns the scholarly satirist for his pride and vanity. Popular playwrights go further. In *Satiromastix*, Dekker's Horace, often thought a personal satire of Jonson, is not only envious but incompetent. First discovered "sitting in a study . . . a candle by him burning, books lying confusedly" (1.1, stage direction), he is in the throes of poetic creation:

> O me thy priest inspire.
> For I to thee and thine immortal name.
> In—in—golden tunes
> For I to thee and thine immortal name—
> In—sacred raptures flowing, flowing, swimming, swimming:
> Immortal name, game, dame, tame, lame, lame, lame,
> Pux, ha it, she, proclaim, oh—
> In sacred raptures flowing, will proclaim, not—
> O me thy priest inspire!
>
> (1.2.8–17)

Jonson responds to this caricature in *The Poetaster*. His Horace inhabits an Augustan Rome where urbane "humours, revels, and satires" are backed by the power of office. In this version of the imperial city, only suburban dullards resort to "the other side of Tiber," where the player Histrio offers a taste of his quality:

> O doleful days! O direful deadly dump!
> O wicked world! And worldly wickedness!
> How can I hold my fist from crying, thump,
> In rue of this right rascal wretchedness!
>   (3.4.210–13)

By 1600, such thumpingly alliterative decasyllabics, a parody of what J. V. Cunningham calls "the moral style," were long outmoded.[16] Yet the Posthastes and the Histrios still purveyed their wares in the public playhouses, ignoring the sophisticated "humours, revels, and satires" of the literati.

The consequent frustration of this literati is the theme of the Cambridge *Parnassus* plays. Refugees traveling in the opposite direction from the way that twentieth-century actors and directors must often take, the young scholars Philomusus and Studioso find themselves driven from the academy to the stage to earn a living:

> [I]s't not strange these mimic apes should prize
> Unhappy scholars at a hireling rate?
> Vile world, that lifts them up to high degree.
> And treads us down in grovelling misery.
>   (2 *The Return from Parnassus*, 5.1.1918–21)

Their audition for Kemp and Burbage is disastrous. In Kemp's eyes, learning and laziness are all one. Studioso is "Master Otioso" (1845), one of the university men who "smell too much of that writer Ovid" to "pen plays well."

In most of the Poetomachia texts, the balladmongers come off rather better than the satirists. Even in Jonson's additions to *The Case Is Altered*, the foolish and complacent Antonio Balladino, apparently a caricature of Anthony Munday, is an articulate spokesman for the public playhouse:

Why look you sir, I write so plain, and keep that old decorum, that you must of necessity like it; marry you shall have some now (as for example in plays) that will have every day new tricks, and write you nothing but humours. Indeed, this pleases the gentlemen; but the common sort they care not for't, they know not what to make on't. They look for good matter, they, and are not edified with such toys . . . and they'll give me twenty pound a play, I'll not raise my vain . . . Tut give me the penny, give me the penny, I care not for the gentlemen I, let me have a good ground, no matter for the pen, the plot shall carry it.

(1.2.58–77)

Balladino, unlike Posthaste, is neither grasping, presumptuous, nor hypocritical. His belief that a strong narrative takes precedence over stylistic refinement gives him a respectable aesthetic; his insistence that the common sort go to plays more for edification than for amusement wins him the dignity of his own stodgy integrity. He is an upholder of traditional morality whose plays are meant to teach the citizenry. The style he admires, if not attains, may fairly be described in the terms George Hunter uses to describe Shakespeare's: "It is rhetorical, easily intelligible in general drift, powerfully expressive of large, extroverted emotions, unconcerned with the details of velleities of the poet's private emotional state, content to echo generalized assumptions about religion or patriotism and to stimulate a fair number of stock responses" (*Dramatic Identities*, 287).

Yet finally, Balladino, like Posthaste, is only a conventional hack with no more literary éclat than a writer of sitcoms. Horace and Chrisogonus are pretentious, vainglorious, supercilious snobs, endlessly revising what they have not yet written. On the one side are stolid ignorance and the rustic traditions of itinerant players; on the other, the fractious egotism and chic neoclassicizing of the upwardly mobile academic. Though the Poetomachia portraits flatter neither balladmonger nor satirist, they do argue, as do the documents of amphitheater and hall, groundlings and gallants, adults and little eyases, that there were indeed two theatrical traditions in early modern England.

Tamquam Explorator

Thus far Harbage brought me on the way. Now I turned toward
antiquity, seeking, with the playwrights themselves, a tradition that
was both classical and popular. For not only truculent Chrisogonus
and costive Horace, but also the Latinless Posthastes and Balladinos,
who read English Seneca or none at all, fell under the spell of Greece
and Rome. The staunchly egalitarian Heywood, hoping to dignify
the public playhouses, compares them to Roman amphitheaters,
and likens Elizabethan players to Greek "Magi and Gymnosophis-
tae" (*Apology*, 25, 27). For the playwrights, fantasies of antiquity, so
variously luminous and tenebrous, ethereal and carnal, amiable and
ardent, are entwined into their theatrical representations, rituals, and
rhetoric. For the players, neoclassicism is Caesar, Brutus, Cleopatra—
roles to be inscribed on the body, inspired through the breath. Taking
from Harbage his distinction between popular and elite theaters, I
relocated it in continuous traditions that were at once ancient and
medieval, textual and theatrical.

The Ancient Dilemma

In *Muses of One Mind*, Wesley Trimpi traces the history of an epistemological problem he calls "the ancient dilemma of knowledge
and representation." Originating in Attic philosophy, rhetoric, and
drama, the most poignant version of this dilemma is found in Plato's
dialogues, the most exacting in Aristotle's *Rhetoric*, and the most
amusing in Aristophanes' *The Frogs*.[17]

   In *The Republic*, Socrates asks, "would it not be absurd to strain
every nerve to attain to the utmost precision and clarity of knowledge
about other things of trifling moment and not to demand the greatest precision [*akribeia*] for the greatest matters?" (504e). Adimantus
readily agrees, but *akribeia* is not easily attained. For a contradiction
lies within Socrates' question, which the companion dialogues, the
Timaeus and the *Critias*, reveal. Timaeus, speaking of the divine creation of the cosmos, can offer only *skiagraphia*, a rough sketch of

half-glimpsed gods. Critias, whose subject is civic life and institutions, complains that his is the more arduous task. Those who paint the heavens content us "with even a faint degree of resemblance." Having no exact knowledge about such objects, we do not criticize the paintings, but accept "a dim and deceptive outline." The painter who represents the human body, however, leaves himself open to criticism from everyone, for "daily familiar observation makes us quick to detect shortcomings and we show ourselves severe critics of one who does not present us with full and perfect resemblance." The same thing, Critias adds, occurs in discourse: "Where the subjects are celestial and divine we are satisfied by mere faint verisimilitudes; where mortal and human, we are exacting critics" (107c–e).

Plato's dilemma reemerges in the third book of Aristotle's *Rhetoric*, where it is resolved into the hierarchy of discourses known as the *genera dicendi*. The most noble and hence most elusive subject within this hierarchy is politics, and its method of inquiry is deliberative oratory, in which a speaker attempts to persuade an assembly of citizens to pursue or to abandon a certain course of action. Like Timaeus's representation of the cosmos, deliberative oratory is inherently obscure, for it concerns the future, which allows us only guesses and glimpses. The orator, lacking demonstrative proof, must resort to rough and approximate *exempla* drawn from history or legend.

The deliberative orator faces not only the epistemological dilemma of representing the unknown future, but the practical problem of addressing the entire citizenry in an open forum. The physical distance between the speaker and the majority of his auditors, as well as their ignorance of economics, diplomacy, warfare, and statecraft, require him to chose simple, repetitive exhortations over subtle, intricate arguments.

Less noble and less obscure in subject, the next branch is forensic rhetoric, which poses legal and ethical questions before a judge or jury. Whereas deliberative oratory deals with the political future of the community, forensic rhetoric takes the past for its domain, deciding the legal significance of events that have already taken place. Although the past has its own kind of obscurity, forensic rhetoric nevertheless lends itself more readily to *akribeia* than the future

(3.17.5–10). Again, decorum depends on the practical circumstances of performance as well as the epistemological dilemma of representation. Since a jury is smaller than an assembly and physically closer to the speaker, it may grasp more subtle arguments than a larger gathering. The judge, a single auditor trained to understand legal technicalities, can follow still greater subtlety.

The third branch of rhetoric, the epideictic art of praise and blame, is the most precise of all, sometimes approaching the *akribeia* of the written word. Its audience gathers not in an open forum but in a private venue set aside for aesthetic rather than political or judicial decisions. These are leisured listeners who enjoy a discourse without concern for its practical consequences. As tragedy, with its vast crowds, open-air performance, and communal agon resembles deliberative rhetoric, closet drama shares the methods and purposes of epideixsis (3.12.2).

The distinction between agonistic and epideictic representation sometimes appears as a battle of ancients and moderns. Moderns mock the crude simplicity of skiagraphic sketches and colossal statues, while ancients condemn the effete decadence of laboriously polished miniatures. In the celebrated agon of *The Frogs*, Aristophanes represents a contest for the throne of tragedy. Aeschylus, spokesman for the militaristic ethos of the old *paideia*, must defend his title against Euripides, an unsavory upstart with dangerously radical views. The conservative Aristophanes is always at his exuberant crankiest when Euripides is his target. In *The Frogs*, the younger tragedian is a sincere but misguided revolutionary whose artistic innovations are designed to subvert the state. Whereas Aeschylus has cheated playgoers into patriotic passion, Euripides hopes to reason them into philosophical truth. He will replace his predecessor's heroic colossi with domesticated deities, the notorious "private gods" (*idiōtoi theoi* [891]) of the Euripidean pantheon. He will exchange grandiloquent choral odes for rational dialogue, and mystifying pomposity for meticulously constructed "scenes of common life" in which the entire audience may immediately detect any "blunder" (959–60).

Like later theorists of the left, Euripides is driven toward ideological incoherence by the intelligentsia's uneasy relation to the pro-

letariat. His tragedies are too elitist for the public theater of democratic Athens, since only trained philosophers can follow their eristic
debates. At the same time, they are too radically egalitarian, for even
women, slaves, and foreigners are given speaking parts. And to give
voices to the disenfranchised, to place a Medea, a Phaedra, or an Iphigenia at the center of a tragedy is to move from the *polis* to the *oikos*,
from the public to the private, from the skiagraphic to the akribeic,
from the noble to the trivial, from the masculine to the feminine.[18]

Thus Euripidean tragedy, the original *belle monstre* of the Western theatrical tradition, mounted its campaign against orthodoxy,
militarism, and half-glimpsed gods. The ancient dilemma of knowledge and representation, elegantly articulated in Platonic epistemol-
ogy and methodically organized in Aristotelian rhetoric, became, in
Aristophanes' critique of tragedy, a vigorous statement of the politics of discourse. Thereafter poets and orators were confronted with
a somewhat melancholy choice: on the one hand, the Aeschylean
aesthetic that is robust and egalitarian but grandiloquent and dema-
gogic, and on the other, the paradoxes of the Euripidean alternative,
at once radical and elitist, adversarial and aloof, supercilious and
compassionate.

The Rival Traditions in Rome

Roman rhetoric at once conserves and transforms the ancient dilemma. From the early *De inventione* to the late *De optimo genere oratorum*, Cicero insists that the nobility of political oratory demands
clarity and fullness rather than the *skiagraphia* of the Greek tradition. Nevertheless, he affirms Aristotle's belief that a large audience
of ordinary people (*mediocres homines*) is the indispensable precondition for agonistic discourse: "[T]his oratory of ours must be adapted
to the ears of the multitude, for charming or urging their minds to
approve of proposals, which are weighed in no goldsmith's balance,
but in what I may call common scales" (*De oratore*, 2:159). Though
Cicero demands expansive lucidity rather than the elliptical majesty
of *skiagraphia*, these are still the "common scales" on which Aeschy-

lean grandeur weighs more heavily than Euripidean subtlety. The
noblest rhetoric is still political, its venue open-air, its audience popular, and its method agonistic.

All this distinguishes oratory from the philosophic, sophistic,
and literary discourses of the learned among themselves. Associated
with these discourses are propaedeutic exercises that train the orator
for the forum. "Set apart for the gymnasium and the palaestra," such
exercises allow the fledgling orator a sophist's freedom to experiment
with diction, rhythm, and syntax (*Orator*, 42).

The Roman rhetorical tradition also maintains the Attic association of oratory and drama. Although Cicero sometimes contrasts
theatrical representations and oratorical realities, his analogies affirm
the Aristotelian association between rhetorical and theatrical agons.
The art of the greatest orator, an *actor veritatis*, has in it something tragic and divine, earning him the title *tragicus* (*Brutus*, 203).
Cicero distinguishes the orator's probity from the player's suspi-
ciously meretricious art, yet his ideal orator works the crowd just as
the great comic actor Roscius does. As he speaks, the audience falls
silent, assents, laughs, or cries "so that a mere passer-by observing
from a distance, though quite ignorant of the case, will recognize
that . . . a Roscius is on the stage" (*Brutus*, 290). Finally, things are
much of a muchness on stage and in the forum: "*Ut in scaena, sic
etiam in foro*" (*Brutus*, 116).

Under the empire, Cicero's ideals and exemplars were out of
date. Tacitus's *Dialogus* commemorates the Republican eloquence
that vanished, along with political liberty, into the imperial maw. The
dialogue is a dispute between the ancients who lament the passing
of the grand old *tragicus orator* and the moderns who rush to replace
him with the *novus rhetor*. Aper, Tacitus's spokesman for the moderns, comes to bury the simplicity Cicero had praised. The sophisticated audiences of the present day, he argues, "will no more put up
with sober, unadorned old-fashionedness in a court of law than if
you were to try to reproduce on the stage the gestures of Roscius"
(20.3). Born into a belated age when the only agons were trivial cases
argued in recitation halls and record offices, the moderns created a
new rhetorical culture based on declamation.

Declamation, a schoolboy's practice in the Republic, had by Tacitus's time become a fashionable entertainment. The halls or schools where it was performed became the haunts of aficionados who gathered to hear celebrated rhetors imitate the forms of deliberative and forensic oratory, adapted to provide epideictic pleasures. In the deliberative *suasoria*, the rhetor takes on the persona and the problem of a historical or legendary character: "Agamemnon deliberates whether to sacrifice Iphigenia" (3) or "Alexander the Great, warned by an augur, deliberates whether to enter Babylon" (4).

In the forensic *controversia*, the rhetor is given a statute, real or fictional, and a *narratio*, an outline of the events in the case. The *narratio* is designed to expose potential conflicts and contradictions in the statute by creating a case that the law had not anticipated and cannot easily resolve. The rhetor chooses one side of the case to argue, and then invents rhetorical *colores*, glosses that specify motive and circumstance, to support that side. Thus adding an internal structure to the *narratio* of external events, *colores* enable a judge to reach a just — or at least justifiable — decision. In the *controversia* of the *Raptor Duarum*, the statute reads, "A girl who has been raped may choose either marriage to her ravisher or his death." The *narratio* reads: "On a single night a man raped two girls. One demands his death, the other marriage." Seneca reports that Porcius Latro, speaking for the prosecution, demanded the rapist's execution to rid the state of such cruel and insatiable lust, while Pompeius Silo, as the rapist's advocate, insinuated that only jealousy motivated the second victim to ask her assailant's death (1.5).

Protected from the heat and dust of the forum, unconstrained by the exigencies of actual cases, and heedless of the expectations of *mediocres homines*, the rhetors devised sensational themes and peopled them with marauding rapists, clever poisoners, wicked stepmothers, and lustful tyrants. They competed for the most extravagant *colores* and the most ingenious *sententiae*. For this, Quintilian, Tacitus, Pliny, Petronius, and Juvenal all condemn them. "The declamations," Quintilian complains, "which we used to employ as foils wherewith to practise for the duels of the forum," now composed only for pleasure, "have become flaccid and nerveless: indeed, declaimers are guilty of exactly the same offence as slave-dealers who castrate boys in order to increase the attractions of their beauty" (5.12.17). Devalued as effeminate and puerile, a declamation was a "mimic battle" (*pugnae simulacrum*) whose combatants, unlike the true agonists of the forum, did not possess the manly ability to stand and fight.

In Rome as at Athens, the rhetorical distinctions between force and elegance, agon and declamation, popular and elite audiences pervade drama. Ancient (and eventually Renaissance) *paragones* of Plautus and Terence restage *The Frogs*' battle of ancients and moderns and reassign the victory. Plautus pleases the crowd with theatrical noise and bombast, the commentators say; he relies on exaggeration, incongruity, and improbability; he incorporates tragic diction into bawdy farces. Terence's *elegantia* has a philosophical cast only the learned appreciate; he experiments to refine plot and characterization; his *bona meretrix* is a daring innovation, a comic analogue of Euripides' tragic adulteresses and murderesses.[19]

Yet Terence, like Plautus, writes for the open-air theater of the Republic. The truly umbratical Roman drama is Senecan tragedy, in which the declamations live a lurid half-life. Like the rhetors, the tragedian privately offered *sententiae* and sensationalism to a sophisticated coterie for whom the luxuries and terrors of the Neronian court were the stuff of daily experience.[20] In adapting tragedy to this venue, Seneca completed the process that Aristophanes accused Euripides of initiating. He transplanted a sunlit spectacle to the shade of an imperial garden, refining tragedy's skiagraphic sketches of the *polis* into anatomies of tortured subjectivity for an etiolated closet drama.

In Saecula Saeculorum

Throughout antiquity, rhetorical, philosophical, literary, and theatrical culture reiterate the ancient dilemma of knowledge and representation, translating it into their own terms of art. When Plato's epistemological distinction between the skiagraphic sketch of the divine and the akribeic representation of humanity is assimilated into the *ars rhetorica*, it serves to separate the agonistic from the epideictic, force from elegance, the heat and dust of the forum from the shaded refuge of the school. The philosophic dignity of representing the gods skiagraphically becomes the rhetorical power of manipulating the multitude agonistically. The akribeic inquiry into mundane life, cherished among philosophers for its rigor yet suspect for its requisite attention to minutiae and ephemera, is in the rhetorical tradition sometimes valued as the leisure discourse of the cultivated few, but more often disdained as puerile, effete, and unworthy of the political classes. Through these transformations, the epistemological dilemma became a starkly and sometimes stridently ideological antithesis: public and private discourse was characterized, respectively, by catholic versus coterie audiences, universal versus trivial subjects, and, baldly enough, good and bad art.

In such guises, the ancient dilemma permeates Renaissance rhetoric and poetics. Erasmus, Elyot, Heinsius, Hoskyns, Wilson, Puttenham, Webbe, and many others adapt it to "open assemblies and ladies' chambers," "narrow schools and spacious temples," "the bench and the bar," "the stage and the study."[21] Such phrases, drawn from rhetorical, religious, legal, and literary traditions, may testify to the intellectual power of the classical paradigm, but their omnipresence depends upon the often wearying repetitiveness of the textual tradition, the legacy of generations of orators, philosophers, dramatists, preachers, lawyers, and poets following closely in each other's footsteps. I set forth after them, marching through the long centuries from the Silver Age of Roman letters to the building of the Theatre in Elizabethan England. Rhetoric was my scarlet thread through the labyrinth of the "dark ages." The Ariadne who offered it was Saint Augustine.

Egyptian Gold

Like the Israelites who refashioned the gold they took from Egypt, Augustine's *De doctrina Christiana* reshapes the wealth of pagan discourse for a new currency (4.40.60). It is, as Marc Fumeroli remarks, at once the last ancient and the first ecclesiastical rhetoric (*L'âge de l'éloquence*, 73), uniting the biblical distinction between Christ's exoteric and esoteric teachings with a classical hierarchy of genres. "There are some things," he argues, too difficult for popular audiences to understand, "no matter how eloquently they are spoken, or how often, or how plainly." Such things must be left to books and learned conversation (4.9.23). Augustine's popular audience, the Christian congregation, is, like Aristotle's deliberative assembly, the antithesis of the curious reader or philosophical interlocutor. It is also like Aristotle's deliberative assembly in its resemblance to a theater audience:

If in the idle following of the theatres, a man loves a certain actor and enjoys his art as a great good or even as the greatest good, he loves all those who share his love for the actor, not on their own account, but on account of him whom they love together. . . . Does not this pattern of behavior befit the action of us who are united in the brotherhood of the love of God? (1.29.30)

And thus, Jonas Barish remarks, "from this nettle, the theatrical audience, Augustine plucks this flower, the Christian congregation" (58).

For later clerics, Augustine's comparison between congregation and audience suggests that Christ's ministers are, like Cicero's *tragicus orator*, actors. In the tenth century, Honorius of Autun writes,

It is known that those who recited tragedies in the theatres represented to the people, by their gestures, the actions of conflicting forces. Even so, our tragedian [the celebrant] represents to the Christian people in the theatre of the church, by his gestures, the struggle of Christ, and impresses upon them the victory of his redemption.[22]

Thus subsequent centuries spent Augustine's Egyptian gold. And thus I, inverting Augustine's method, plucked from the nettle of religious rhetoric the flower of theatrical experience.

Haec ad Negotium cum Agitur

The later tradition of the *ars praedicandi* elaborates on and eventually codifies Augustine's distinction between the learned and unlearned audience. It becomes a constant motif and often a complaint in the self-reflexive *sermo ad clerum*. With its intricate structure of theme, protheme, division, and subdivision, the *sermo ad clerum*, developed for scholastic audiences in university halls, shifts the focus from exhortation to display—a shift that taught preachers, like ancient sophists and rhetors, the dangers of a hypercritical audience.[23]

Conversely, the *sermo ad populum*, descended from the old homilies and revived by Franciscan and Dominican friars, relies on the rough and ready methods of public debate. The friars, who sally forth to preach "in the street, at public fairs, in churchyards, wherever crowds are found," mock cloistered monks as ancient orators did sophists, for their otiose discourse that cannot stand and fight.[24] Properly agonistic sermons, the friars insist, are at once earthy and elliptical, built, like deliberative orations, on *exempla* drawn from history, legend, nature, or daily life. They are simple, practical, and urgent: *Aliae artes ad ingenium pertinent, haec ad negotium cum agitur*. "Leave ingenuity to other arts," warns Humbert of Romans, mid-thirteenth century master general of the Dominicans, "here it is a question of souls" (18.100; trans, 44).

Where it is "a question of souls," the visceral power of the spoken word matters more than the cerebral pleasures of written discourse. A treatise once attributed to Thomas Aquinas and called the Aquinas-tract by its translator Harry Caplan insists that the preacher must "preach vigorously, so that his utterance may . . . abide in the listener's heart":

Sometimes he must speak with grief and lamentation, as in: "O my son, Absalom! my son, my son Absalom!" Often with horror and agitation . . . At times with irony and derision . . . [T]he preacher's gesture should conform to that which he must believe Christ used when He said: "Destroy this temple," by placing his hand above his heart and looking at the temple. (56)

Such instructions enable the preacher to transform his text, through gesture and inflection, from biblical narrative into contemporary theater. The skill he acquires thereby will eventually guide the player, when the popular sermon is adapted for an open-air theater where it is also "a question of souls."

Sermon and Drama

The Hundred Merry Tales of 1526 records the story of a Coventry preacher who advised his skeptical congregation to attend the Corpus Christi play. The play, he tells them, will demonstrate the doctrine he has preached to them "with more surete and sufficient auctorite." Sermon and drama are for this preacher alike in their hortatory purpose, though the drama offers more persuasive proofs.[25] Indeed, the Wakefield Resurrection play closes with a sermon, as Christ preaches to the playgoers from the cross:

> Erthly man, that I have wroght,
> Wightly wake, and slepe thou noght!
> With bitter bayll I have the[e] boght
> To make the[e] fre.
> Into this dongeon depe I soght,
> And all for luf of the[e].
>
> (226–31)

This is not dramatic closure but a hortatory expansion into the lives of the playgoers. Similarly, the Chester Expositor and the Doctor of the Brome *Sacrifice of Isaac* close their plays by pointing the moral to an audience they treat as a congregation. The Hegge *Death of Herod* ends with Death's warning and the second half of the Wakefield *Raising of Lazarus* is Lazarus's own sermon on repentance.

Like the Franciscan and Dominican *sermones ad populum*, the Corpus Christi drama deploys, with joyous opportunism, whatever rhetorical, poetic, and theatrical devices come to hand: vivid *exempla*, colloquial diatribes, impassioned lyrics. In the ensuing gallimaufry, the Annunciation may provoke an old man's jealousy, the Passion occasion a game of hot cockles, shepherds clumsily imitate the songs of angels, and God himself come on stage to speak with extravagant Latinity of his inscrutable work:

> I am greate God gracious,
> which never had begyninge.

The wholl foode of parente is sett
in my essention.
I ame the tryall of the Trenitye
which never shal be twyninge,
pearles patron ymperiall,
and Patris sapiencia.[26]

(1.5–12)[26]

This speech, David Mills remarks, "though meaningful, is unlikely to have been readily intelligible delivered from a wagon in a Chester street on a Monday morning" (73). Other cycles, without resorting to such grandiloquence, also offer evocative, symbolic, and almost incomprehensible openings: a mysterious figure, masked and enthroned, at length breaks silence to utter a few portentous words.

This is essentially the same *coup de théâtre* for which Euripides, praising his own philosophical didacticism over his predecessor's mystifying *psychagogia*, criticizes Aeschylus's prologues in *The Frogs*: a mournful figure sits, veiled and silent, until at last the chorus begins to intone its obfuscating ode (910–15). Like the mourner in the Aeschylean prologue, the deity of the Chester Creation play is a valiant response to the ancient dilemma of knowledge and representation, an epistemological and aesthetic achievement won from the tragic limitations of mind and the churlish resistances of matter.[27]

A Marvelous Convenient Place

Like the Corpus Christi cycles, the morality play is a popular dramatic form, indebted to the sermon and responsive to the exigencies of open-air performance. But unlike the cycle plays, it could, Glynne Wickham observes, be "borrowed from the Church and tailored to fit the Hall" (*Shakespeare's Dramatic Heritage*, 26).

Among the extant moralities, *The Castle of Perseverance* is the most spectacular, with its panoramic view of heaven, hell, and earth, and its great battles between the Virtues and Vices for the soul of *Humanum Genus*. *Tunc pugnabunt diu*, reads a repeated stage direction, "Then they will fight for a long time." The spectacle implied in this action lends *The Castle of Perseverance* some of the schematic grandeur of the cycle plays. But while the latter encompass history from creation to judgment, the former focuses on the soul of the character *Humanum Genus*.

Intended to represent all humanity, *Humanum Genus* gives *The Castle of Perseverance* a claim to universality and at the same time belies it. Despite the play's communal auspices, its dramaturgy asserts a melancholy individualism. Besieged by enemies, protected by the Virtues who keep the Castle of Perseverance, companioned by Good and Evil Angels, still *Humanum Genus* remains a lonely figure on a vast stage, without social affiliation or historical place. Death comes for Everyman and finds a solitary creature, desolate and alienated.

This isolation enables the morality to adapt its religious *argumentum*, as the Corpus Christi cycles could not, to smaller scale performances in guildhalls, colleges, manor houses, and palaces. In these settings, the morality play was at once secularized and gentrified. John Skelton's *Magnificence* (ca. 1516) turns the allegorical structures of the morality into a mirror for magistrates rather than a *memento mori* for Everyman. John Rastell's *The Four Elements* (ca. 1520) transfers them to natural philosophy. Since, the prologue insists, "man to know God is a difficulty," the subject of the interlude is "light matters here below." John Redford's *Wit and Science* (ca. 1530–48) reduces allegory and homily to leisurely digressions and embellishments that may inculcate pedagogical principles into schoolboys. As the morality is transformed into interludes for schoolroom and banqueting hall, the moderns' *otium* supersedes the ancients' *negotium*, the skiagraphic representation of the divine gives way to the akribeic representation of "light matters here below," and the ancient distinction between public and private discourse enters Tudor theatrical culture.

The Blason of Ancient Armory

Within that culture, Lyly's mythological fantasies and allegorical pastorals continue the sophistic tradition of private discourse. Contrasting Lyly's comedies with popular Elizabethan drama, George Hunter reiterates the ancient distinction between a "laboriously polished masterpiece" and a "spontaneous, unfinished sketch or fragment" (*Lyly*, 9). The venerable metaphor is especially apt here, for the playwright himself had resort to it.

In *Campaspe*, the painter Apelles contrasts his art with his predecessors':

Alexander: Methinketh four colors are sufficient to shadow any countenance, and so it was in the time of Phidias.
Apelles: Then had men fewer fancies, and women not so many favors. For now, if the hair of her eye brows be black, yet must the hair of her head be yellow: the attire of her head must be different from the habit of her body, else must the picture seem like the blason of ancient armory, not like the sweet delight of new found amiableness. For as in garden knots diversity of odors make a more sweet savor, or as in music diverse strings cause a more delicate consent, so in painting, the more colors, the better counterfeit, observing black for a ground, and the rest for grace.

(3.4.86–96)

The heraldic blazon, limited by rule to a few bright tinctures visible in sunlight and at great distances, cannot make a good counterfeit when sophistication (with its root sense of mixture) is the aesthetic criterion. It is the criterion of a worldly artist with a fashionable public—an artist like Lyly himself, in whose image the Apelles of *Campaspe* has been cast.

Lyly drew his information about Apelles mostly from Pliny's *Natural History*, which includes the description of an inimitable innovation, a "black varnish" (*atramentum*) that subtly muted Apelles' paintings, "so that the brilliance of the colors should not offend the sight" (35.36.97). Like his historical prototype, Lyly's Apelles also uses "black for a ground." But in Pliny, the *atramentum* makes Apelles' colors more subtle; Lyly's "black ground" reveals luster by contrast. The playwright consistently changes Pliny's text to emphasize the delicacy, sophistication, and *curiositas* of Apelles' work. He transforms the Hellenistic painter into a Tudor court dramatist, identifying Apelles' black background with the chiaroscuro of the candle-lit hall in which Lyly's own *colores* find their proper setting.[28]

The Closure of a Golden Ball

While Lyly's chorister company confronted "the blason of ancient armory" with "the sweet delight of new found amiableness," Marlowe too was engaged in reforming the drama. Vigorously experimental and resoundingly theatrical, Marlowe's plays were with one exception produced in the public playhouses. *Dido, Queen of Carthage* was printed in 1594 "as played by the Children of the Chapel." Like other plays of the children's companies, it smells, in Kemp's synecdoche, too strongly "of that writer Ovid, and that writer Metamorphoses" ever to serve the public playhouse repertory. The play's long Vergilian passages, sometimes translated and sometimes in Vergil's own Latin, are designed for the gallants, not the groundlings. But unlike other chorister plays, *Dido* retains the sapor of the poetic, theatrical, and erotic pleasures that the children's troupes gave Elizabethan audiences.

Of all the world's poetic tragedies, *Dido* is surely the funniest. And *Dido*, as several commentators have remarked, *is* funny.[29] Though it is not quite a parody, burlesque, or travesty, drolleries stipple its heroic theme. In the Induction, Jupiter dandles a petulant Ganymede on his knee:

Jupiter: Come, gentle Ganymede, and play with me.
I love thee well, say Juno what she will.
Ganymede: I am much better for your worthless love,
That will not shield me from her shrewish blows.
Today, whenas I filled into your cups,

And held the cloth of pleasance whiles you drank,
She reached me such a rap for that I spilled,
As made the blood run down about mine ears.

(1.1.1–8)

Like Euripides' "private gods," the gods of Marlowe's pantheon bicker and grumble, flirt and fornicate. Euripides' contentious deities, however, were adults. Marlowe's Olympus is a clubhouse for quarrelsome, clever, sexually precocious children, rather like the theater in which it was represented.

Heroes as well as gods are given their comic turns. At the tragedy's climax, Dido plunges into the pyre quoting Vergil:

> *Litora litoribus contraria, fluctibus undas*
> *Imprecor, arma armis; pugnent ipsique nepotes!*
> Live, false Aeneas! Truest Dido dies;
> *Sic, sic juvat ire sub umbras.*

(5.1.310–13)

A solemn moment, but within five lines, Iarbus, then Anna, have so precipitously followed Dido into the flames that they invite if not command the playgoers' laughter. Laughter spoils the solemnity, but not the moment itself, which estranges heroics through absurdity, lyricism through buffoonery.

Dido refracts tragedy through a poetic prism that offers the sophisticated playgoer pleasure in the theatrical artifact itself. "O that I had a charm to keep the winds / Within the closure of a golden ball," laments Dido, as she determines to confiscate Aeneas's oars and tacking (4.4.99–100). And so she has, for *Dido*'s verse, like that of *Hero and Leander*, creates a miniature world of wit, paradox, hyperbole, and allusion, of exquisite joys and delicious sorrows. Like winds enclosed in a golden ball, Marlowe's poetry gives breath of life to the niello artifice of court drama.

The winds range more freely in the public playhouse. In *Tamburlaine*, Marlowe fashions a warrior in the image of a colossal statue from "the time of Phidias":

Of stature tall, and straightly fashioned,
Like his desire, lift upwards and divine,
So large of limbs, his joints so strongly knit,
Such breadth of shoulders as might mainly bear
Old Atlas' burthen.

(Part 1, 2.1.7–11)

Like a colossal statue or heraldic blazon, Tamburlaine is designed to dominate the daylit landscape. He fills the open-air amphitheater with his progress from kingdom to kingdom, evoking, as the prologue promises, exotic wonders in "high astounding terms."

During the decades that Marlowe's colossus held the popular stage, parodies and satires such as Joseph Hall's pay unwilling tribute to the "huff-cap terms and thundering threats" that "ravish the gazing scaffolders" (Satire 3, lines 17, 28). In *Discoveries*, Jonson castigates the "*Tamerlanes* and *Tamer-chams*" that had only "scenical strutting and furious vociferation, to warrant them to the ignorant gapers" (8:587). Although "scenical strutting and furious vociferation" be the defects of the virtue at which popular discourse aims, they have always stood open-air performers in good stead, from the time of Aeschylean *onkos* through Ciceronian *gravitas* and the Latinity of the Chester Creation play to Marlowe's mighty line. As Marlowe brought elegance to court drama, so he brought magnificence to popular theater, evoking "the stately tent of war" in *Tamburlaine*, the psychomachia of the old morality play in *Doctor Faustus*, and the pageant of English history in *Edward II*.

Marlowe's achievement at once affirms and denies the rival traditions. For the differences between *Dido* and Marlowe's public playhouse tragedies corroborate Harbage's distinction between popular and coterie drama, but not the pride of place, the aesthetic and ideological preference he gives the public playhouse—unless the episodic mayhem of *Tamburlaine* and the doctrinal terrorism of *Doctor Faustus* must always be preferred to *Dido*'s polymorphous perversity.

De Te Fabula Narratur

While I was tracing the rhetorical agon of public versus private, popular versus elite, and ancient versus modern, the American academy had been engaged in its own battle of the ancients versus the moderns. As a graduate student in the early 1980s, I had rather unwittingly enlisted on the side of the ancients who were in possession of the classical texts, the languages in which to read them, and the theater history that the erudite generations of Chambers and Bentley had unearthed. The moderns, as far as I could then see, had only comic books, horror movies, and the incomprehensible ravings of an arrogant clerisy.

Eventually I discovered that they also had a political agenda to which I owed allegiance. My discovery took place, not in seminars or at conferences, but in the dojo where, while I was completing my dissertation, I had begun to study martial arts.

When I began my training, I had had some nine years of ballet. I had wept, sweat, and bled in those pretty, tormenting satin shoes and learned that one practices a corporeal art only at the risk of one's tendons and ligaments. I had some sense too of what it was to be a victim of street violence, to be accosted in alleys by drunks with broken bottles in their hands. But I did not understand the intersection of art and violence, the usable graces and unrehearsed dangers, the terrifying and exhilarating exigencies of a martial art. I now entered a world in which I needed the earthbound athleticism of Arlecchino rather than the ethereal elegance of Pierrot: a lower center of gravity, a foot flexed rather than pointed, upper body strength, muscles rotated inward rather than turned out, soft places protected rather than vaunted, a fist.

Despite my adventures in touring companies and street theaters, the practice of art had for me remained a carelessly elitist and at least quasi-feminine activity. The karate I now studied (whatever its origins among the warrior castes of China and Japan) was a masculine and a plebeian art. Its adepts were men who had been drafted for the Vietnam War twenty years earlier, who had returned to train bodies broken and sometimes maimed by the war. They knew that the body is compelled to tell stories—of injuries, illnesses, and insults suffered; tasks achieved or abandoned; love won or lost; bread and meat eaten; beer, wine, and water drunk. They submitted to the discipline of a harsh and exacting art so that their bodies might tell these stories with grace and strength and wit.

They did not think altogether well of women, though they paid grudging respect to those who endured the hazing of the white belt, and respect without grudging to the ten or twelve women among them who held black belts. Their misogyny was jokey, nimble, and assured. It was cruder, but no more peremptory, than that of the actors and musicians I had once known or the scholars with whom I now spent my time. Perhaps less, for in the dojo, misogyny consistently confronts another, conflicting value. Ruthlessly hierarchical, this subculture is also adamantly meritocratic. The social insecurity that breeds swaggering belligerence on the street (and in the lecture room) here submits to a simple and explicit measure of worth: skill in combat, and especially, skill to refrain from combat, which is earned at a yet greater cost. As a traveler learns the customs of her own country from seeing others' ways, I learned from these martial artists that my ballet training had given me strength and turned it to display; that my education had given me discipline and turned it to quietism. I learned that I had mistaken my class privileges for rights and my acquired frailty for an ineluctable femininity.

Acknowledging these lessons, I sought another way to do a scholar's work. I began, belatedly, to study the literary and cultural theory I had neglected. Simone de Beauvoir articulated the significance of my confrontation with violence, and Raymond Williams taught me to perceive the ideology of what I called tradition. From Walter Benjamin I learned that in reading the rhetorical tradition as a history of civilization, I had ignored the history of barbarism on the verso of each page.

I began to understand that both my rival traditions, public and private, popular and elite, ancient and modern, consisted of the chatter of the chattering classes. What the rhetorical tradition calls public or popular discourse is the propaganda through which ancient democracies and republics maintained social hierarchy. What it considers private, scholastic, and otiose is the poetry and philosophy the elite produced for its own leisured consumption. I had followed Aristotle, Cicero, and Quintilian when they praised the agonistic orator who enters the arena and conquers his audience through the force of his eloquence. I had followed them when they condemned the declamatory exercises of schoolboys and the domestic speech of women and servants as irenic and self-indulgent, vulnerable and voluptuous. I had not realized that the violence of rhetoric comprises not only the protocols of the arena but also the butcheries of the abattoir.

Hic Labor Est

As I reconsidered the politics of my own historiography, I turned toward a *marxisant* criticism, hoping that a feminist materialism would enable me to find a more truly popular discourse in the public playhouses, one that would illuminate the history of the gender- and class-linked violence that I had discovered in the dojo. I began by comparing *The Roaring Girl*, performed at the Fortune, and *The Silent Woman*, performed by a children's company at Whitefriars. Delighted with the heroic Moll Cutpurse, I credited the representation of her wild autonomy in part to the open Fortune stage and its popular displays of swashbuckling swordsmanship. Dismayed by Epicoene's harassment of the androgynous collegiate ladies, I partly blamed the rank domestic *mise en scène* that the indoor playhouse encouraged Jonson to thematize.

An inquiry into theatrical venues and repertories could not rest on two productions, nor a quest for traditions on synchronic methods. Foraging further, I found in Robert Weimann's *Shakespeare and the Popular Tradition in the Theatre* an alternative classical tradition that was both popular and theatrical. Emphasizing the dynamic relation between actor and auditor, Weimann distinguishes between the locus on which homiletic, tragic, or romantic actions are staged and the *platea* from which the Shakespearean clown addresses the playgoers. The *platea*, he argues, resurrects not only the morality Vice but the shadowy figure of the antique *mimus*. Weimann dissents from

Harbage's belief in radical differences between the public and private playhouses, yet shares Harbage's preference for the former (247). Rather than its emerging democratic liberalism, however, Weimann celebrates its residual plebeian resistance to the dominant culture: the popular tradition empowers the clown, speaking from the *platea*, to articulate a "countervoice" from "outside the representative ideologies" (157–59). In his discussion of Henry Medwall's 1497 *Fulgens and Lucrece*, Weimann praises the interlude's use of this plebeian countervoice to challenge "the moral authority of the ruling class" (110).

Fulgens and Lucrece is descended directly from the *Controversia de vera nobilitate* of the Italian jurist Bonaccorso.[30] Despite its origin in an elite rhetorical genre and its performance in a great hall, this interlude is, as Weimann notes, not an exclusively elite entertainment. Designed for professional players, it embraces the dramaturgy of the popular tradition, employing the servants A and B to comment directly to the audience on the actions of the aristocratic characters. And, as Weimann also argues, this earthy and sometimes scatological commentary belies the chivalric idealism of the aristocratic characters. But, as he neglects to observe, it also parrots misogynist truisms about women's shrewishness and lechery: "He is well at ease that hath a wife / Yet he is better that hath none, by my life" (1.785–86); "The chief means of their living / Is lechery—leech-craft I would say— / Wherein they labor night and day" (1.800–802); and "[O]f wedded men there be right few / That will not say the best is a shrew" (2.857–58).

A and B, like many other clowns before and since, resist class domination through gender oppression. The "plebeian countervoice" does not speak for Joan any more than for my lady. Meanwhile, my lady, in this interlude at least, has much to say for herself. When Lucrece's two suitors debate whether true nobility lies in virtue or in aristocratic birth, it is Lucrece who is given the power to judge:

> [S]ith the choice of this matter is mine,
> I can be content under certain protestation,
> When that I have heard you, to say mine opinion.
> Lo, this wise I mean and thus I do intend,

That whatsoever sentence I give betwixt you two,
After mine own fantasy, it shall not extend
To any other person, I will that it be so,
For why no man else hath therein ado:
It may not be noted for a general precedent.

(2.424–32)

After the debate, Lucrece chooses her virtuous suitor over the one who is merely well-born. A dangerous precedent, but this is a judgment in equity, as Lucrece later remarks. Equitable judgments "may not be noted for a general precedent;" they do not enter the case record of the common law.

It is appropriate that Medwall's female *iudex* preside over an equity court, for in England, these courts traditionally protected women (at least women of property) from the more patriarchalist provisions of the otherwise more egalitarian common law. Hence equity enables a brotherless woman to inherit her father's property without jeopardizing the laws of primogeniture.[31] And hence Lucrece's judgment has no political significance. However brave and just, it is literally inconsequential. Like Euripides couching his subversive notions in a discourse only trained philosophers could follow, the Roman rhetors exposing the law's carious skeleton to their coterie audiences, or Thomas More writing the *Utopia* in the language of scholars, Medwall restricts his arguments for a meritocracy to the individual edification and moral improvement of "gentlemen of name" (2.891–94).

Weimann's magisterial work is among the few historical studies that reward the theater practitioner as well as the scholar. Yet my feminist inquiry fared no better with his materialism than with Harbage's liberalism. Whereas Harbage argues with somewhat condescending chivalry that the wholesome representations of the public playhouse tend to ameliorate women's lot, Weimann simply neglects the misogyny of the popular tradition. Humanist criticism tends to assume that the public theater is good to the extent that it is Shakespearean, while materialist criticism tends to assume that Shakespeare is good to the extent that he draws on plebeian culture. Whether subversion or orthodoxy is considered the source of theatrical vitality and social merit, the same plays and playhouses are privileged. The deity is new, yet the same angels sing in the choir. The same devils are cast into a different outer darkness.

The Children's Crusade

Fulgens and Lucrece scumbled my design for a feminist version of the rival traditions. It suggested a heterodox hypothesis: perhaps the much sought "site of subversion" in Elizabethan theatrical culture was not located in its popular, but its elite traditions; not in its public, but its private playhouses. Perhaps there was an Elizabethan analogue to what Howard Barker, defending his own dark and sullen art against "the tin crusaders of the new populism," calls "radical elitism."[32] For ever since Euripides, "radical elitism" has been the political stance of artists and intellectuals marginalized by the dominant culture. Even now, postmodern exposés of compulsory heterosexuality are more common in lesbian cabaret than in regional repertory theater; performers who gnaw the heads off mice and spit their carcasses into the audience are evidently not ambitious to appear on network television.[33]

In early modern England, too, the adversarial politics of the aristocratic Henrician, Edwardian, Marian, and early Elizabethan drama contrast with the less polemical public stage of the later Elizabethan era. The most radical (and most truly Senecan) political drama of the English Renaissance is the closet tragedy of the courtier-poet Fulke Greville. Even within the celebratory conventions of the Jacobean court masque, Queen Anne and her ladies produced theatrical experiments that could surprise and shock the spectators.[34]

The private playhouses of the children's companies, with their historical associations of leisure and license, extend this elite privilege into commercial theater. As Heywood laments, they mock and curse and grumble audibly against the dominant culture of the city. They are skeptical, sometimes cynical, and, from the perspective of the authorities, up to no good. Their seating and *mise en scènes* enshrine social subordination less rigorously than the public playhouses. Their large casts of pubescent and adolescent boys offer more, and more varied, women's roles than the public playhouses.

This is not to say that the transgressions of the private playhouses deserve to please the political critics of the twentieth-century academy, aesthetically or ideologically, any better than they did the Elizabethan city fathers. I will suggest, in "The Saint in the Brothel" and "Voluntary Wounds," that the elite tradition of Senecan rhetoric liberalizes Shakespeare's representation of gender in *Pericles*, *Titus Andronicus*, and *Antony and Cleopatra*. Yet Moll remains more congenial to a twentieth-century feminist than the collegiate ladies, and there is little reason to prefer Marston's virulent *Dutch Courtesan* to Dekker's repentant *Honest Whore*.

The social contexts of the public playhouse seem more volatile, but the theatrical strategies of the private playhouse more venturesome. The Children of the Revels, playing at Blackfriars, might present an elitist, misogynist, and yet thoroughly antiauthoritarian performance, while at the Globe, the productions of the King's Men (to say nothing of the raunchy tear-throats at the Fortune and the Red Bull) might be populist and yet relentlessly androcentric and jingoistic. The critical adjectives will not line up; the Elizabethan endeavors of art will not be drafted for contemporary academic armies.

Trusting the historical authenticity of the rhetorical tradition, I had adopted its categories—*skiagraphia* versus *akribeia*, the agonistic versus the epideictic, *negotium* versus *otium*, the heat and dust of the forum versus the umbratical shelter of the school. But while I stood on the shoulders of giants, I could not see historical conflict and change, nor the opportunism of ancient elites. I had trusted my *auctores* too far and had turned historiography into epideixis.

Later, maintaining the political significance of contemporary Shakespeare criticism, I drew on its categories—subversion versus containment, elitism versus egalitarianism, androcentrism versus feminism. But these categories, especially subversion and containment, which had first seemed so fascinating, soon became as reductive as my rival traditions. Essay after historicist essay split into a dexterous examination of the geographical location of the public play-

houses, say, or the presence of women in the audience, followed by a
literary-critical interpretation of a play text that ignored the theatrical
circumstances just examined. The "subversion-containment debate,"
which had aimed to discover whether Elizabethan theatrical representations exposed the inequities of the early modern status quo in
a way that its victims could have perceived, enjoyed, and responded
to, came to mean little more than a hermeneutics of "what we're for."
Following my neoteric *auctores*, I had once again turned historiography into epideixis, rashly allocating plays and playwrights praise or
blame for the fancied good or harm they had done city wives, prostitutes, apprentices, and choristers.

What this good or harm may have been, I do not know. My
popular and elite traditions are, in Williams's phrase, "not the past
but an interpretation of the past: a selection and valuation of ancestors, rather than a neutral record" (*Modern Tragedy*, 16). Except as I
select and evaluate my ancestors, I no longer expect political help or
hindrance from the public or private playhouses.

I am then left with other terms, common to the rhetorical tradition and contemporary criticism—popular versus elite, public versus private, ancients versus moderns—that remain provocative, yet
vague and mercurial. They seem to illuminate, then to obscure the
theatrical culture of early modern England. They seem sagacious,
then maladroit; rapiers of analysis, then clumsy blunderbusses. Perhaps, like blunderbusses, they are accurate only at close range, for
they now seem to illuminate the institutional history I lived more
clearly than the cultural history I hoped to write. During the 1980s,
while reactionary pundits were calling for conventional pieties in
straightforward prose, leftists in the academy embraced an impene-
trably scholastic style. On the humanist right, a dominant discourse
claimed to be populist, despite its collusion with the holders of
power, because it was accessible to the plebs. On the poststructuralist
left, an elite discourse also claimed to be populist, despite its obscur-
antism, because it challenged authority. Humanists versus theorists,
inheriting the *pugnae simulacrum* of orators versus sophists, friars
versus monks, and balladers versus satirists, wrangled in an Aristo-
phanic agon for our times.

It is the agon itself that has been so troublesome to me, and the adversative conjunction that left its Manichean mark on both my scholarly inquiry and my academic career. Yet even now, as I try to erase that mark, I still find arguments and even stories in the categories of the rhetorical tradition. In telling them, I have tried to distinguish where, like Timaeus, I must be content with a shadowy sketch and where, like Critias, I may insist that the rendering be exact.

Iphigenia in Durham

Qui vulnera spectavit, vulnus habet.
— Ovid, *Ars Amatoria*

CONFOUNDED IN MY SEARCH for more supple distinctions between the rival traditions, I set my work on the public and private playhouses aside for awhile. I retreated from the contentions of "Bardbiz" to a quiet archive where I could privately reconsider the traditions of public and private discourse. I began to experiment with a new, feminist philology that would link those traditions to the questions of gender and violence that now engrossed me.[1] My subject was Lady Jane Lumley's mid-sixteenth-century version of Euripides' *Iphigenia in Aulis*, the first translation of a Greek tragedy into English.

Sacrificial Epithalamia

When Euripides' *Iphigenia in Aulis* opens, Iphigenia's father, Agamemnon, the commander of the Greek army, has sent for her to come to Chalcis, where the Greek army has camped, to be married to the hero Achilles. The marriage is a fiction, a ruse to lure Iphigenia to the death that is the price the goddess Artemis demands for the winds that will carry the Greek warships to Troy. Agamemnon, fumbling remorsefully, tries to rescind his orders, but Iphigenia and her mother, Clytemnestra, have already arrived at Chalcis. Menelaus, who had insisted on the sacrifice, also changes his mind, now that he has "looked close to see what slaying children means" (lines 489–90). It is too late to deflect the army's demands for the sacrifice. Recognizing that her death is inescapable, Iphigenia goes heroically to the slaughter with patriotic slogans in her mouth.

Throughout the tragedy, as throughout the later tradition of European literature, the language of marriage and sacrifice are intertwined.[2] This analogy, Helene Foley argues, enables the final resolution: Euripides' "emphasis on the shared aspects of the rituals ultimately uncovers an intrinsic harmony in the structure and purpose of marriage and sacrifice that makes possible the final transformation" (69).[3]

Perhaps. But perhaps this dark tragedy, which ends with a word that means booty, spoil, or prey, rather validates Jean-Pierre Vernant's uncompromising judgment. Human sacrifice, he insists, is in Greek art always "a deviant or corrupted sacrifice, a monstrous offering" (295). For Iphigenia is not only the victim of sacrifice; the deceitful imagery of the epithalamion makes her also the victim of a rhetoric of sacrifice. "By sacrificing the virginal blood of his family to the divine will," Lynda Boose argues, the father "ensures the success of the cultural project. . . . But through the father's participation in his daughter's blood, the exogamous model leads back to the incestuous one in which it is anyway implicit" (40). In consenting to her own sacrificial death, the daughter transforms murder into martyrdom and incestuous rape into symbolic marriage.

Desunt Nonnulla

The story of Iphigenia has borne many interpretations, as Renaissance humanists, neoclassical dramatists, and modernist poets have all embraced the clouds that Euripides' elliptical ironies did not dispel. Like the Hebrew folktale of Jephthah's daughter and later Christian legends of virgin martyrs, Iphigenia's tragedy has become part of an omnipresent cultural narrative of the sacrifical daughter.

I came upon this narrative, and upon my own version of Iphigenia's tragedy, while seeking the story of Lady Jane Lumley among the sparse and cryptic records of the women of Tudor England. The daughter and wife of noblemen prominent in Tudor political life, Lumley lived in neither the obscurity of ordinary people nor the illumination of independent achievement. Her translation of Euripides' *Iphigenia in Aulis*, written in the early 1550s and unpublished until 1909, is, and is not, part of the classical tradition of English Renaissance literature. It has earned few editions and commentaries; I found myself working with a fragmentary archive of library catalogs and estate inventories, manuscripts and marginalia, family portraits, formulaic elegies in English and Latin, and occasionally letters that, like the Lisle letters, plead with Secretary Cromwell for a favorable settlement in disputes over dowries, jointures, entails, purchases, and fines. This wilderness of documents brought me to wonder, as the well-cultivated garden of Shakespeare studies had not recently done, what questions I might hope to ask a Renaissance text.

Like others investigating the history of women in early modern England, I entered the archives with a zeal that both fortified and burdened me. I demanded of myself both meticulous empiricism and unabashed speculation; I chid myself for both doddering antiquarianism and the slithery maneuvers of postmodern historiography. Eventually, I learned to ask the question that Janet E. Halley asks in regard to Anne Donne: "Can we respect the subjective, historical existence of Anne Donne not only by recognizing her presence in history, but also by acknowledging her absence to us? Is it possible to hear her silence?" (191). In the silence that I now identify with Lumley, I learned that hers was not only a different story of the Renaissance but a story that I must tell differently. Issuing from the solitary labors of the translator rather than from the boisterous conviviality of theatrical collaboration, Lumley's text never entered the arena where Shakespeare and his contemporaries are continually recostumed in changing fashions. It has not been subdued to the service of the literary critic. Stark, alien, and unannotated, it is like those early modern maps on which unexplored lands are inscribed only with the phrase *Ubi dragones*.

The Doing of My Lady Lumley

Lumley's *Iphigenia*, Royal manuscript 15.A.ix in the British Library, bears the inscription: "The doing of my Lady Lumley dowghter to my L Therle of Arundell." Its contents, "The Tragedie of Euripides called Iphigeneia translated out of Greake into Englisshe," with three orations of Isocrates translated from Greek into Latin, are New Year's gifts to Lord Arundel, accompanied by dedicatory letters *ad dominum patrem*. The text of *Iphigenia* is much abridged, deleting the choral odes altogether. It relies on Erasmus's Latin version of the tragedy as much or perhaps more than the Greek text, following him into grammatical errors as well as translating his prefatory *Argumentum* from Latin into English. It is written in the recalcitrant English prose of the mid-sixteenth century.

This holograph has rarely been mentioned in twentieth-century discussions of the classical heritage of English literature, but it did earn its author a place in George Ballard's 1752 *Memoirs of Several Ladies of Great Britain Who Have Been Celebrated for Their Writings or Skill in the Learned Languages, Arts and Sciences*. Acknowledging the silences and absences that surround Jane Lumley, Ballard remarks: "What other things this learned lady may have translated or written herself or when she died, I know not. But I find by her father's will, dated December 30, 1579, that she was then dead" (144).

Subsequent notice of the manuscript includes Harold H. Child's edition for the Malone Society in 1909; a philological debate between two classicists in a learned journal during the 1940s; scattered references and listings in surveys of Tudor women; and several pages in a recent study of women writers in the English Renaissance.[4]

In his introduction to the text, Child observes that the signature "Lumley" dates it after her marriage, which had taken place in 1549 or early 1550. Although the manuscript cannot be more precisely dated, the dedication of John Lumley's translation of Erasmus's *Instruction of a Christian Prince* in 1550 to his father-in-law, Henry Fitzalan, suggests to Child "that husband and wife pursued their classical studies concurrently, and that the present play was translated at no long period subsequent to their marriage" (vii).

In the early 1940s, David Greene and Frank Crane debated the merits of the translation in the pages of *The Classical Journal*. For David Greene, "Lady Lumley's play is extremely important if we realize the unfortunate state of Greek scholarship in sixteenth-century England" (537). He iterates Child's argument for dating the text to the early 1550s and, with less caution regarding both Lumley's birth date and the date of composition, concludes, "We are then faced with the unusual situation of attributing the first English translation of Greek tragedy to a thirteen-year-old girl" (539).[5]

While Greene does not argue for the translation's fidelity or literary merit, he endeavors to demonstrate that Lumley translated Euripides' Greek, not merely Erasmus's Latin text. He adduces the placement of lines 117–18 before lines 115–16 as the earliest example of an emendation that has since become standard. Like Samuel Johnson, who so memorably compared women preachers to dogs walking on their hind legs, Greene finds that the wonder is not that it is done well. He is surprised to find that it is done at all: "Lady Lumley's total lack of taste and critical ability is evident in her exclusions. . . . But when one considers that not only did her attempt stand alone in her age but was the first in the English language, no little honor and credit are hers" (542–43).

Her honor and credit did not long go unchallenged. Three years later, *The Classical Journal* published Crane's response to Greene's article. Crane details Lumley's errors. Some reveal her dependence on Erasmus's Latin version; others reveal that "even Latin was often too difficult for her" (226). He demolishes Greene's argument for her emendation: "She does no transposing; she merely omits lines 115 and 116 entirely, as she admits some hundreds of others" (225). Her infelicities are also grave: "'Troble' is Lady Lumley's favorite word. There is hardly a page of her version on which someone (usually Agamemnon) is not 'in troble,' or 'wonderfully' or 'mervelousely trobled'" (224). Crane finds not only that it was not well done, but that it was not done at all: "Lady Lumley shows no knowledge of Greek, and none of poetry in any language; her version succeeds only in reducing high tragedy to a mediocre tale of 'troble'" (228).

With tepid praise or cordial condemnation, both Greene and

Crane ask the question that classicists still ask of outsiders: How much Greek does she know? With kindly condescension or savage indignation both answer, as classicists still often do: Not enough. Crane's philological argument does for the most part withstand the test of time, and (having myself once received undeserved credit in an undergraduate Latin class for a learned emendation that was in fact an ignorant error) I am inclined to his side in that aspect of the dispute.

Yet if Erasmus was Lumley's untrustworthy *arbiter elegantia-rum*, she also pondered the Greek text, comparing it with Erasmus's Latin. Among the Lumley Library copies of Euripides is a 1519 Louvain edition of the Greek *Iphigenia* and *Hecuba*, bound together with Aristophanes' *Nubes*. The hand of Royal manuscript 15.A.ix has annotated both Euripidean texts with words from Erasmus's Latin versions.

For Greene and Crane, Erasmus takes his place in a classical tradition established through a dominant discourse that transcends historical difference. Even though Erasmus's Euripides cannot be granted the independent literary value of Pope's Homer or Dryden's Vergil, it nevertheless holds an honored place in the history of classical scholarship.[6] But not Lumley's. Her discursive world is to these twentieth-century classicists more alien than either Euripides' Greek or Erasmus's Latin. Lumley's *Iphigenia*, irrelevant to the tradition of "high tragedy," is, Crane insists, a "childish performance" (227), which should remain abashedly silent in the presence of its elders.

The very "childishness" of the performance suggests a different line of inquiry. Taking Lumley's text as a schoolroom exercise, one could also ask what she might have learned in translating Euripides. One could even ask what, along with Euripides, she might have translated.

In her survey of women writers of the English Renaissance, *Re-deeming Eve*, Elaine V. Beilin asks such questions. Beilin is content to concede the inadequacy of Lumley's Greek. A feminist scholar of early modern literature, she approaches Lumley's text as a structure of intentions, asking not what Lumley did to Euripides, but what Erasmus did for her. Like Child, Beilin links Lumley's work to her husband's 1550 translation of Erasmus's *Instruction of a Chris-*

tian Prince, which describes patriotic self-sacrifice and the Christian virtues of the Renaissance ruler. She observes that Jane Lumley's *Iphigenia* also tells of patriotic self-sacrifice and the virtues of a crypto-Christian heroine: "By choosing a play about a heroic Greek woman and by selecting those passages from Erasmus with Christian resonance, Lumley composed a play which would pay tribute to a woman's Christian spirit, courage, and eventual sanctification" (157). Lumley's *Iphigenia*, then, is the feminine counterpart of an Erasmian enterprise in which Lady Lumley followed her husband's lead (153, 156).

Like Beilin, I want to explore the domestic and religious resonances of Lumley's text rather than pounce upon her philological faux pas. Yet I am unconvinced that John Lumley's translation deserves so much credit for inspiring his wife's work. Nor would I rush Iphigenia to a Christian rest without bearing witness to the mortification that precedes sanctification. Pebbles cast into the still pool of this text form circles that ripple past the protocols of Erasmian pedagogy toward Euripidian memories of sacrificial violence. Lumley's text testifies to Renaissance theories of education and translation; it resonates with popular and elite variants on the story of the sacrificial daughter; it hints at the domestic duties that shaped Lumley's daily life; it whispers of the court politics in which her family was often embroiled. Each of these is a sound that makes the silences of Lumley's *Iphigenia* a little more audible.

Lost in Translation

In *The Schoolmaster*, Roger Ascham recommends a program of rhetorical education that begins with *translatio*, which "is most common and most commendable of all other exercises for youth" (83). The student's translations become less and less literal until he is ready for *imitatio*, "a faculty to express lively and perfectly the example which ye go about to follow" (114), and eventually for *declamatio*, or original composition on a traditional theme—such as Agamemnon's decision to sacrifice Iphigenia. Ascham's pedagogical method distinguishes

productive stages in a continuous process. It may deceive the critic
who judges the product without reference to the process. For Greene
and Crane, Lumley's text is self-evidently a *translatio* undertaken at
an early stage of her education and must be judged for fidelity to its
source. For Beilin, it takes on some attributes of *imitatio* and an implicitly agonistic motive is added to the criteria of evaluation. For
me, it is both of these and a *declamatio* as well, a discourse on the
theme of the sacrificial daughter that emerges from an individual sensibility confronting a complex literary inheritance.

In interpreting this text so polyphonously, of course I blur the
boundaries of Ascham's careful pedagogy. I transform a Tudor exercise into a text that I can, following Jane Gallop's strategy of interpretation, read "either as body (site of contradictory drives and heterogeneous matter) or as Law" that reproduces the symbolic realm of
the fathers (62). I do not want to presume too far on this Lacanian
language, but I find in it a reminder that Royal manuscript 15.ix.a is
part of the corpus of Jane Lumley, the literary remains of a female
body bred in a noble household of mid-sixteenth-century England
for dynastic marriage and childbearing; a body that enjoyed the cod-
dling and endured the constraints of her sex and status. When Greene
and Crane chide the silences and absences of Lumley's text as flaws
and errors, they castigate this body for its symbolic wounds and fancied frailties.

This somatic register is not entirely anachronistic: an association of bodies and texts, gender and language, is present in the Renaissance rhetoric of translation. Throughout early modern Europe,
Latin was, Walter Ong remarks, a "puberty rite" for elite males (*Presence*, 249–52). Latin and the *Romanitas* that it enshrined participated
in the hurly-burly of political life in the Renaissance court. Greek language and culture, as locutions like "Greekling" and "merrygreek"
suggest, could by contrast seem decadently mired in the illicit and
sensual world of whores and cony-catchers. More often, however,
Greek takes on the ambivalent connotations of scholarly *otium*.[7]

Unserviceable in the public realm, Greek was a language of the
academy, for intellectual display rather than political use. From the
scholar's perspective, Greek is the privileged and prestigious achieve-

ment of advanced students. It stands at the valued extreme of a continuum which ranges from the ancient tongues of prophets, poets, and philosophers to the despised domestic vernaculars of women, children, and servants. Yet from an extramural perspective, Greek is otiose and effeminate. Its scholarly possessors are not always good members of the commonwealth: More's philhellenic Hythlodaeus shirked his duty when asked to serve as counselor to a king. Like the skillful speaking of Shakespearean verse in Hollywood, the knowledge of Greek in early modern Europe seems to be at the same time an admired achievement and a risible idiosyncrasy that may hinder its possessor from the serious business of getting and spending, and even the less urgent enterprise of showing and telling.

Within the early modern hierarchy of languages and linguistic forms, a translated text might also be suspected of effeminacy. The act of translation raises questions of confidence and creativity, silence and alienation, authority and submission that Renaissance writers answer with metaphors of gender and violence. So John Florio suggests in the dedication of his translation of Montaigne's *Essayes* to the countess of Bedford:

To my last birth, which I held masculine (as are all men's conceits that are their own thought but by their collecting; and this was to Montaigne like Bacchus, closed in, or loosed from great Jupiter's thigh). I the indulgent father invited two right honorable godfathers, with the one of your Noble Ladyship's to witness. So to this defective edition (since all translations are reputed females), delivered at second hand; and I in this to serve but as Vulcan, to hatchel this Minerva from that Jupiter's big brain. (A2) [8]

The violence of "hatchelled" translation is not Florio's idiosyncrasy, but a philological phenomenon that gathered extensive commentary within the rhetorical tradition. For Tudor rhetoricians, *translatio*, Quintilian's Latin term for the Greek *metaphora*, implies an "improper" and even violent use of language. In *The Arte of English Poesie*, Puttenham calls it "a kind of wresting of a single word from his owne right signification to another not so natural" (37–38). [9]

Despite, or perhaps because of this suggestion of violence, *trans-*

latio was less grudgingly allowed to women than *imitatio* and *declamatio*. Perhaps, as Mary Ellen Lamb observes, women's translation of men's works did not threaten the literary establishment as original composition might have done (116). Perhaps *translatio*, which is for rhetorical education a merely propaedeutic stage of the creative process, is more easily relinquished to women because it is associated with children, as grammar school teaching seemed a suitable career for women at times when university posts were exclusively occupied by men. In any event, learning classical languages and translating texts was so often associated with women in Tudor England that even late in the following century, William Wotton found it worth comment. A classical education, he observes, had formerly been "so very modish that the fair sex seemed to believe that Greek and Latin added to their charms; and Plato and Aristotle, untranslated, were frequent ornaments of their closets. One would think by the effects, that it was a proper way of educating them, since there are no accounts in history of so many truly great women in any one age, as are to be found between the years 15 and 1600."[10] What seemed to Wotton a great throng now seems a sparse population indeed. Classical languages, and literacy itself, were privileges accorded to very few women during the sixteenth century.[11] Those who wrote about women's education were entitled to assume that, far from translating classical texts, those women who could read at all could read only translations:

She may read (seeing at this present they are translated) besides the books of holy scriptures, . . . the words of Plutarch written touching women of renown, who in times past lived in the world. . . . She shall read of and admire the women of the Trojans, Sabines, Phociens, Argives, and the virgins of Rome. And shall learne a singular example of piety towards her country, by Megistone, Aretaphile, Policrite, and of those godly women Judith and Hester, and of love towards their husbands, by Lucretia and Portia, and the Barbarian Camma, that at one instant became a glorious revenge both of her honesty and the injury of her slain husband. And to conclude (that I may make an end of rehearsing strangers) she shall find examples of all virtues, religion, holiness and loyalties, in so many sacred virgins whose names are renowned among us, as in Cecile, Agathe, Theodore, Barbara, and infinite others, who both by shedding of their blood and losing of their lives, enduring most incredible and accustomed torments, have given unto the world most certain testimonies of their faiths and made our religion as at this day we find it.

Thus Thomas Salter, in *The Mirrhor of Modestie*, a 1579 translation of Giovanni Bruto's treatise on the education of noblewomen.[12] Despite Salter's distinction between "strangers" and the "sacred virgins whose names are renowned among us" his *exempla*, like Ernst Curtius's medieval *auctores*, "belong to no period and are all equally good" (267). The patriotic zeal of Romans, barbarians, and Jews and the religious fervor of Christian martyrs may all serve the Renaissance noblewoman in the presumably less exigent circumstances of her daily life.

Like those who believe pornography's harms exist only if they are statistically correlated with rape, Salter seeks an implausibly predictable heuristic effect between cultural expression and individual experience. Still, these reiterated stories of martyred heroines could indeed have helped to shape the lives of the Renaissance women to whom they were recommended. They may have done so in mysterious, clandestine, vulgar, and uninvited ways that neither Salter then nor I now can articulate truly.

One Fair Daughter

Among these stories of martyred heroines is the biblical analogue of the tragedy of Iphigenia, the narrative of Jephthah's daughter in Judges—a motif for the "high tragedy" of elite drama and for popular "tales of trouble" as well. The popular tradition is familiar from the ballad that found its way into *Hamlet*: "When Jeptha was judge of Israel, / He had one fair daughter and no mo, / The which he loved passing well." Such ballads retain or retrieve Hebraic motifs of the biblical narrative: the daughter dies by fire rather than the cutting of her throat, and the sacrifice is contrasted with rather than compared to a wedding.[13]

The elite tradition includes the *Liber Antiquitatum Biblicarum*, attributed to Philo. Like the Hebrew narrative, Philo's contrasts the death of the daughter, here named Seila, "she who was de-manded," with marriage: "my hunger for my bridal bed has not been quenched, / nor am I sated with wedding-garlands" (10–11).[14] Yet one stark phrase reveals the persistent presence of Death the bride-groom: "hell has become my bridal bed" (*factus est infernus thalamus meus* [16]).

Eleven centuries later, Abelard's *Planctus Virginum Israel super Filia Jepte Galadite* elaborates on the infernal *thalamus*. The virgins of Israel adorn Jephthah's daughter with jewels and unguents, prepar-ing her for death as if for her wedding (*tamquam nuptiis morti se pre-parent* [119–20]). At last, she rejects the analogy between sacrifice and marriage as emphatically as Seila had affirmed it. Repelling attempts to adorn her further, she cries, "Enough for a wedding; for death, it is too much" (*Que nupture satis sunt, / periture nimis sunt* [137–38]).[15]

In Philo's contrast, the similarity between death and marriage will out; in Abelard's comparison, the difference. In acknowledging both similarity and difference, each text bears witness to the interrela-tion of death and marriage as a tragic fact and cultural dilemma. Con-versely, in the version intercalated into the *Confessio amantis*, Gower offers neither comparison nor contrast. His character complains only "That sche no children hadde bore" (4.1587).

Sixteenth-century school and university drama, imitating Eu-ripides, emphasizes the Greek motif of the fatal marriage. In John Christopherson's Greek *Jephthah*, performed at Cambridge about 1544, Jephthah, like Agamemnon, speaks of sacrifice in terms that allow his daughter to believe that he describes her marriage, and her death takes the Greek form of throat-cutting.[16] George Buchanan's neo-Latin school drama on the same theme is also an *imitatio* of Euripides, in which Iphigenia becomes Iphis and Clytemnestra takes the symbolic name of Storge, "love between parents and children." Unlike Christopherson's, Buchanan's Jephthah does not delve into the ironies that link marriage and death. The erotic resonances of the daughter's sacrifice nevertheless reemerge when the Messenger brings the tale of the daughter's death to her waiting mother:

As the maiden now stood, an imminent victim, before the grim altar, her virginal modesty spread a crimson blush over her white countenance, for she was unaccustomed to gazing upon bands of men. It was as if a man were staining Indian ivory with crimson, or intermingling roses with snowy lilies (92–93) [17]

The Messenger's descriptive tour de force continues for thirty-four lines. Then Storge interrupts him to insist that he describe the manner of the crime (*modus facinoris*) itself, "and do not spare a mother's ears. You can report nothing so grim that my mind does not pose before itself a grimmer scene" (93). In the Messenger's aestheticized answer, lamentation is turned to praise:

The priest, overwhelmed with weeping, could scarcely loose the passage of her breath, and the hushed crowd was for long numb in sorrowful silence. But when a way lay open for their voices, there was none of the usual groaning nor the din of grief and wailing customary at such times. Instead there was a confused din, a buzz from the assembly felicitating you and praising you as a woman who, amidst the hostile wounds of a harsh fate and happy gifts of a pandering fortune, was unique in the heights of both blessedness and utter misery. For though the blow has entered deep to your innermost bones, you have a great consolation in your great grief. (94) [18]

But such solace is for Storge rather sorrow's crown of sorrow:

This consolation is more painful than the ill itself; with its soft touch it irritates the long-standing sore. It renews continually the recollection of bitter grief, and it forces the wound which had closed to break open afresh. The braver the spirit with which my daughter bore her death, the sorer the anguish which gnaws my heart. (94) [19]

This response to the Messenger's offered consolation ends the play. Confronted with Storge's lament, the ecphrastic roses and lilies with which the Messenger has decorated Iphis's body seem obscene, like a plastic bouquet in the hands of a corpse.[20]

    As Hebraic rite and myth persist in the popular ballads, so Buchanan's neo-Latin school drama preserves the harrowing anthropology of Attic tragedy. In *Tragic Ways of Killing a Woman*, Nicole Loraux observes that the female characters of Attic tragedy almost always die of neck wounds. Not only are the throats of sacrificial vir-

gins slit by priests or patriarchs, but wives, like Jocasta, Evadne, and
Deineira most often die by hanging themselves from a rafter of the
marriage chamber. The sacrificial knife testifies to the dangerous limi-
nality of virginity, but wives also come at last to an infernal thalamus.

Buchanan too associates the vulnerable organs of women's
voices with the matron Storge as well as the maiden Iphis. Storge
does not hang herself, but her opening speech is characterized by an
ominous breathlessness:

My heart trembles, my voice cleaves to my very throat, my mouth offers no
open passage for words; for the specters of the night terrify me repeatedly in
my wretchedness. (65)[21]

Storge's fears recall the vulnerability of women's voices, not metaphorically but anatomically, with the force of the simple truth that
breath is life. Freeing her own windpipe from forebodings of her
daughter's severed throat, Storge's breath gives life to the archaic customs, rites, and symbols that mingle with the Christian dreams and
desires of Buchanan's tragedy.

The Lives of the Saints

Even when, with Salter, we "make an end of rehearsing strangers," the
father who sacrifices his daughter remains to trouble legend and history. Christian hagiography tells of many beautiful and nobly born
virgins who die at the command of a father or his surrogate: Barbara,
whose father Dioscorus locked her in a tower to keep her from her
suitors and who, after she became a Christian, first tried to kill her
and then turned her over to a hanging judge; Agatha, whose death
under torture was accompanied by marvelous signs and portents;
Cecilia, a patrician convert who refused to consummate her marriage
to the pagan Valerian; Ursula and the eleven thousand virgins who
shared her death; Agnes, who chose death rather than the loss of her
virginity; Christine, whose legend conflates those of several other
saints.[22]

These virgin martyrs of bloodstained memory are also of dubious historicity, for they are, as the generically named Barbara and Christine suggest, feminine exemplars of the tamed barbarian and the virtuous Christian. Their legends reveal cultural desiderata rather than record historical events, often echoing ancient entanglements of sacrifice and marriage. For the Christian saints, however, the sacrificer is no longer a grieving father who must himself submit to divine commands, but a rebel against them. The earthly father murders; the heavenly father receives the daughter's dismembered flesh and celebrates her undaunted spirit.

Like Euripides' Iphigenia and Buchanan's Iphis, however, the Christian saints strive against the slaughter that is human sacrifice by claiming the greatest benefit for themselves. They are "brides of Christ," as Iphigenia is the "bride of Greece." Unlike sacrifices, their deaths are not ordained to grant victory, fecundity, or stability to the community in which they die. Yet the sanctity of the martyrs does bring their worshipers tangible benefits, on which foundation the medieval cult of the saints is erected. Thus, Brigitte Cazelles argues, a sacrificial stratum emerges in the lives of the virgin martyrs whose "heroism is the result of a process of victimization in which one individual must die for the others to survive" (16–17). As the stories of the virgin martyrs are told and retold, they sometimes seem victims and sometimes victors; they become variously avatars of submission, defiance, reconciliation, or transcendence. But always, the part they play comes out of the old sacrificial script, with its inexorably iterated action. Martyrs make their own history, but they do not make it just as they choose.

Iphigenia in Durham

Nor do scholars make their historiography without constraint. Like Ballard, who found only "by her father's will" that Jane Lumley was dead by 1580, I have had to look to the records of the political activities, financial transactions, book collecting and connoisseurship of Henry Fitzalan and John Lumley for my story of Jane Lumley's *Iphigenia*, since it is the father and husband whose lives have entered the historical record.

The Life of Henry Fitzalan, Twelfth Earl of Arundell was written by his chaplain and published by John Gough Nichols in *The Gentleman's Magazine* in 1833. The anonymous chaplain's laudatory sketch claims that Henry Fitzalan "did exceed others, the time of his life, in calling and true nobility. He feared God, did good to many, and was not the harmer of any. . . . He was in mind of the noblest sort, rather to be wished for in a king, than to be found almost in any subject, and yet ordered in such manner, as both his humor in that regard was bountifully supplied, and such as he left for heirs nobly remembered" (11).

Posterity has judged the earl less charitably, beginning with Webster and Dekker's *The Famous History of Sir Thomas Wyatt*, in which Arundel appears as a character. The *dramatis personae* of this 1607 text display an unyielding opacity more often found in the pre-Shakespearean chronicle. Even among these unpsychologized figures, the earl of Arundel conspicuously lacks ethical *colores*. Other characters can at least be designated honorable or dishonorable, but as Arundel moves from one scene of political crisis to another, seizing the options his interlocutors offer, his conniving seems too motiveless even for malignity.

Recent commentators have been still less flattering. They have found in the earl's career a series of stratagems and betrayals that place him among the more prevaricating and venal politicians of the Tudor court.[23]

Henry Fitzalan's first wife was Catherine Grey, the daughter of Thomas Grey, duke of Suffolk. She died May 21, 1542, leaving three children, Henry Lord Maltravers, Jane, and Mary. Each of these children, as well as John Ratcliff, Arundel's stepson by his second marriage, and his son-in-law John Lumley left exercise books of classical translations. Preserved among the royal manuscripts, these books are, like Jane's translations of Euripides and Isocrates, dedicated to Arundel as *dominus pater*. Jane and Mary were especially celebrated for their knowledge of the classics. Educated at home, they used the excellent library that Arundel had collected.[24]

Sometime in 1549 or 1550, Jane married Baron John Lumley, who had lately matriculated at Queen's College, Cambridge, along with her brother Lord Maltravers. John Lumley was not only a student of the classical languages and of Erasmus but an antiquarian, bibliophile, and connoisseur. He inherited Arundel's library and added to it until, at his death, it was the largest in the country. He also collected paintings, especially portraits. Although the collection included several fine Holbeins, these portraits were apparently valued rather for the sitters' celebrity or relation to the owner than artistic merit. For John Lumley was a fantastical genealogist of his own house, and decorated Lumley Castle with the arms and achievements of imaginary ancestors tracing his line to Adam via Charlemagne.[25]

In 1556, Jane's brother Maltravers died in Brussels "through a hot burning fever." The following summer, her younger sister Mary died in childbirth at the age of sixteen. That autumn, Jane's step-mother, Mary Arundell, also died. Now her father's sole heir, Jane returned with her husband to her father's house, where she spent the rest of her life, "as [her father's] nurse and dear-beloved child" (Nichols, *Life*, 214).

Other anecdotes corroborate the close relationship between father and daughter. Writing in about 1630, the Jesuit hagiographer of Jane Lumley's nephew, Philip Howard (sainted as a Catholic martyr in 1970) and his wife Anne Dacres, reveals something of their relationship in recounting Howard's adolescent behavior toward his aunt: he

was induced by the bad counsel of some he met with at court, set on secretly, as was thought, by higher power, to neglect his duty in a manner wholly to the Earl his grandfather, and to behave himself in such manner towards his aunt the Lady Lumley, as caused much grief to her, and much disgust to the Earl her father, who much loved and esteemed her as she well deserved for her virtue and discretion and by that means they were both so averted from him that they alienated unto others a great part of their estates which otherwise would have come from them to him. (Henry Graville Howard, 14–16)

The same source offers one other glimpse of the mental life of Jane Lumley: the author attributes Anne Dacres' return to Catholicism in part to "her living afterwards with the Lady Lumley daughter to Henry Fitzalan Earl of Arundel, and aunt to her husband: for she was not only a good Catholic, virtuous and discreet, but also well learned and could speak much in defense of her religion" (177).

This record of Philip Howard's youthful churlishness and Anne Dacres' wavering faith were the work of a later generation than Jane Lumley's. Few events of her life were noted contemporaneously. She is mentioned twice in real estate transactions.[26] Her name also appears as the subject of a letter from a "Mr Doctor Halle," revealing that she and John Lumley traveled to Padua, where they both fell ill.[27] She is mentioned once in the history of the political events of the day: dressed in crimson velvet, she attended the coronation of Mary Tudor, riding with five other baronesses in the third coach of state (Nichols, *Life*, 493).

Of her intellectual activities after the translation of Euripides and Isocrates, there is little more. Several volumes of the Lumley Library are inscribed with her name: some theology, some Italian history, a volume of the *Ad Herennium*. Perhaps she shared not only her husband's intellectual interests, but his genealogical obsessions as well: the library catalog indicates that she was the owner of several unidentified heraldic manuscripts, including "a roll containing a memorial of certain of Jane Lumley's kindred living in her own time, being not under the degree of a baron or baroness, neither nearer to her than cousin germans, nor further off than cousin german's children, with their arms."[28]

She also reappears once more in literary history, shortly before her death, as the dedicatee of Nicholas Bacon's *Great House Sententiae*: "Sir Nicholas Bacon Knyghte to his very good ladye the Lady Lumley sendeth this." The manuscript, prepared about 1575, is a collection of maxims for Renaissance statesmen, mostly from Seneca and secondarily Cicero. The relationship with Bacon recorded in the dedication suggests, as Nichols remarks, that Lumley's "taste for letters and learning" continued throughout her life.

It also suggests another lacuna within the historical record. Only the dedication of Bacon's *Sententiae* remains to suggest that Lumley was also acquainted with Bacon's wife, Anne Cooke, the translator of Jewel's *Apologia Ecclesiae Anglicanae*.[29] There is no suggestion of collegiality or rivalry between these learned ladies; Lumley's conversion of Anne Dacres remains her only documented relationship to another woman.

Yet Lumley's *Iphigenia* evokes such a relationship. Within her "tale of trouble" lies a high tragedy of her own time, in which a young woman's sacrificial marriage entered the history of the royal succession.

Jane the Queene

On May 21, 1553, Jane Grey was forcibly married to Guildford Dudley, the son of the duke of Northumberland. On July 10, she was proclaimed queen. She reigned for nine days. Then Mary Tudor was proclaimed queen, and Jane Grey was committed to the Tower of London, where, in response to Wyatt's Rebellion, she was beheaded in February 1554. Like Euripides' Iphigenia, Jane Grey unites in one persona the martyr and the scapegoat. She was a zealous Protestant, and her zeal, her biographers often remark, might have made her a religious martyr had her place in the succession to the throne not made her a political victim.[30] For Lady Jane's Protestant contemporaries, the roles were identified. In Foxe's *Acts and Monuments*, the sober ecclesiastical history that was the Protestant successor to Caxton's fanciful legendary, the entry for Lady Jane Grey inherits its themes from the stories of Agnes, Barbara, and all the lovely ladies of patrician birth who died for their faith.[31] Even Judge Morgan, who pronounced Jane Grey's death sentence, suffers retribution as mysteriously as the pagan judges and bureaucrats who were punished for persecuting Christians: "shortly after he had condemned her, he fell mad, and in his raving cried out continually to have the Lady Jane taken away from him; and so ended his life" (Foxe, 425).

The pathos of Grey's brief life and reign have encouraged artists to characterize her as childlike in retellings of her story from Webster and Dekker's chronicle play through Victorian narrative paintings to twentieth-century films. The conventional use of her family name seems to suggest not a queen regnant but a daughter who died within her father's house. For not only was Jane Grey's marriage arranged by her father; so in effect was her death. Henry Grey's participation in Wyatt's Rebellion was the direct cause of his daughter's execution, which, Holinshed writes, was "the more hastened for fear of further troubles and stirs for her title, like as her father had attempted" (23). She herself recognized his responsibility, and wrote to him the night before her execution to extend her forgiveness:

Father although it hath pleased God to hasten my death by you, by whom it should rather have been lengthened, yet I can so patiently take it, that I yield God more hearty thanks for shortening my woeful days, than if all the world has been given into my possession, with life lengthened at my own will. And albeit I am very well assured of your impatient dolors, redoubled many ways, both in bewailing your own woe, and especially as I am informed, my woeful estate; yet my dear father, if I may, without offence, rejoice in my own mishaps, herein I may account myself blessed, that washing my hands with the innocence of my fact, my guiltless blood may cry before the Lord, Mercy to the innocent . . . And thus good father, I have opened unto you the state wherein I presently stand, my death at hand, although to you perhaps it may seem woeful, yet to me there is nothing that can be more welcome than from this vale of misery to aspire to that heavenly throne of all joy and pleasure, with Christ my Savior: in whose steadfast faith (if it may be lawful for the daughter so to write to the father), the Lord that hath hitherto strengthened you, so continue to keep you, that at the last we may meet in heaven with the Father, Son, and Holy Ghost. (Nicolas, 47)

It was not only or even primarily her own father, however, but her father-in-law, the duke of Northumberland, who had created "Jane the Queene." Another patriarchal figure too had played a part in the elevation and execution of Jane Grey. An uncle, a member of the council that had affirmed Jane's sovereignty on July 9, betrayed the oath of allegiance he had sworn to her and delivered the seal of England to Mary Tudor. That uncle was Henry Fitzalan, the earl of Arundel.

Jane Grey and Jane Lumley were cousins. Lady Jane Grey's father was the brother of Catherine, Jane Lumley's mother.[32] There is no record, as far as I know, of their relationship, certainly no likelihood of the intimacy that existed between Jane Lumley and the docile Anne Dacres. The 1590 inventory of Lumley Castle includes a portrait "Of the Lady Jane Grey, executed" (Cust, 26), but nowhere is there a hint of the esteem or affection that the portrait's owners may have felt for its subject. I have found only one reference to a possible public meeting between the cousins. In November of 1551, the queen dowager of Scotland, whose ship was driven by a storm to land at Portsmouth, received Lady Jane Grey, the countess of Arundel, and a hundred other ladies and gentlemen (J. G. Nichols, *Chronicles*, xxiv). Perhaps the countess's stepdaughter, Jane Lumley, was among the hundred unnamed attendees. Otherwise, only genealogical charts document the relationship between these cousins.

They were born within a year or so of each other and were, Retha Warnicke suggests, both named for the then queen consort Jane Seymour (99). Both were celebrated for their classical learning and their religious devotion. As these religions differed, so their fates diverged in the early 1550s. While one cousin was proclaimed queen, imprisoned, and finally executed, the other, then living in Durham, far from her father's lethal politics, studied Greek and Latin, returning south for the coronation of Mary Tudor. Both Jane Grey and Jane Lumley came to know something of the ritual affinities between marriage and death, which the former endured and the latter articulated when she translated the story of the sacrificial daughter into English prose.

A Tale of Trouble

Buchanan's Storge elegantly expresses the terror that deprives her of speech, but Lumley's gauche, unstriving rhetoric stands between her characters and their speech, turning Euripides' tragedy into what Crane calls "a tale of trouble." For Crane is right: Lumley's resort to the word "trouble" does come to seem obsessive. It appears, as noun or adjective, sixteen times in a text of slightly more than fourteen hundred lines. Agamemnon is "wonderfully troubled" (330), and shortly thereafter "in trouble" (450). Iphigenia asks, "How should I suffer this trouble?" (920) and later answers her own question in counseling Clytemnestra: "Suffer this trouble patiently, for I must needs die" (1171–72). The chorus, listed in the *dramatis personae* as "a company of women," praise her who "can suffer so patiently all this trouble" (1211).

Perhaps, as Crane has it, Lumley's reiterated "trouble" reveals her lack of literary skill. Or perhaps it seems obtrusive only because it no longer does the work that Lumley's text requires of it. Perhaps it was the word she needed, the word that clung and swarmed within her thought. Its antecedents and analogues include the Latin verb *turbo* and its adjectival form *turbulentus*. Turbulence, the *Oxford Latin Dictionary* notes, originally means a whirlpool, an eddy, a storm, an object spinning; it soon becomes metaphorical, to describe violent language; it becomes psychological, to describe a disturbed spirit. In Estienne's 1536 *Dicionarii sivi latinae linguae thesauri* and Cooper's 1578 *Thesaurus Linguae*, *turbulentus* is documented, especially in Ciceronian usage, as a term for anxiety, confusion, distress, and grief: *animus turbulentus, mens turbulenta*.

In English, "to trouble" is to disturb, to stir up or muddy, to harm, injure, molest, or oppress. The meanings gather force from the religious contexts in which the word so often appears. The *Oxford English Dictionary* cites Tindale, "For an angel went doune . . . and troubled the water" (John 5.4); Dunbar, "I am trublit with gret seiknes"; Tindale again, "Why trouble ye the woman?" (Matthew 26.10); and Milton, "God looking forth will trouble all his Host" (*Paradise Lost*, 12.209). The noun too has strong religious connotations: "In the tyme of my trouble I call upon the" (Coverdale's Bible, 1535). The religious resonance that extends back to Tindale also extends forward to African-American spirituals: "Nobody knows the trouble I see"; "Soon I will be done with the troubles of the world"; "God's gonna trouble the water." Even today, "the Troubles" can describe the plight of Northern Ireland or, in Tony Kushner's *Angels in America*, the symptoms of AIDS.

Like Tindale's, Lumley's resort to the word trouble registers an attempt not only to find modern English phrases for ancient and sonorous words of grief, but also to discover a spiritual significance in worldly sorrows, to translate pain into the language of religious supplication. It is this language that fills the prayer book of the Lady Jane Grey, Harleian manuscript 2342, which she used while imprisoned in the Tower. There is "A prayer for patience in tribulation" and, in another hand, "A Prayer in adversity and grievous distress" and "A prayer in trouble." Again and again, "trouble" is a word to evoke the deepest grief and the gravest dread: "I was overwhelmed in innumerable troubles," "My spirit is sore troubled," "I am full poor and full of trouble," "Go not far from me, for my trouble draweth nigh," "Bring my soul out of trouble," "Give me help in my trouble," "Show thy self in the time of our trouble," "Let them not take their pleasure upon me who are my troublous enemies." In the prayer Jane Grey composed shortly before her execution, she writes,

O Lord, thou God and father of my life, hear me, poor and desolate woman, who flyeth unto thee only, in all troubles and miseries. Thou, O Lord, art the only defender and deliverer of those that put their trust in thee; and there-fore, I, being defiled with sin, encumbred with affliction, unquieted with troubles, wrapped in cares, overwhelmed with miseries, vexed with temp-tations, and grievously tormented with the long imprisonment of this vile mass of clay, my sinful body, do come unto thee. (Nicolas, 49)

In the lexicon of prayer and lamentation, the word "trouble" de-scribes an agitated spirit within an imprisoned body. In the superfi-cially Senecan stillness of Jane Lumley's text, it is a Euripidean move-ment, a disturbance, a contingency of grief and a gasping for breath. "Trouble" troubles the quiescence with which patriarchy's daughter accepts the sacrificial wound.

How Shall We Lament?

The rest is an unsettling sort of silence, as if a child crying in another room fell suddenly and inexplicably still. The chorus had at first com-mented boldly: "It is meet, O Agamemnon, that you should follow your wife's counsel, for it is not lawful that a father should destroy his child" (1023–26). After Iphigenia's death, they can only ask "How shall we lament, since we cannot show sadness at the sacrifice?" (1305). Euripedes' chorus had directed this question to Clytemnestra (*potnia mater*) and called the grief hers; Erasmus had translated the Greek phrase as *veneranda parens*.[33] Lumley's "company of women" has, it seems, no mistress or mother to whom this question can be ad-dressed, no one to whom the grief chiefly belongs. Instead, it hovers in unmoving air; every member of the company of women shares the silent sorrow of Iphigenia's death.

Like Iphigenia, Jane Grey refused to lament her own fate. "As for my heavy case," Foxe has her telling the priest Fecknam, "I thank God I do so little lament it, that rather I account the same for a more manifest declaration of God's favour towards me than ever he showed me at any time before. Therefore, there is no cause why either you or others, which bear me good will, should lament or be grieved with a thing so profitable for my soul's health" (303). In Jane Grey's death and in Jane Lumley's text, there are losses one may not or cannot mourn.

I draw these parallels between Lumley's text and her cousin's death without knowing whether the fate of the zealous Protestant Grey grieved the devout Catholic Lumley, or whether she acknowledged that her father had betrayed her cousin. Henry Fitzalan supported Mary's accession and Jane Lumley wore crimson velvet to ride in state in Mary's coronation parade—an occasion at which sorrow for the then imprisoned Lady Jane was unfitting and perhaps unfelt.

Mary's coronation was neither the first nor last occasion in Lumley's life in which her family's political rewards and punishments so jostled each other. Toward the end of Edward's reign, she had seen her father, then lord chamberlain, placed under house arrest and fined for embezzlement. He was later imprisoned in the Tower for felony and treason, then fined again, and at last restored to favor. She had seen her husband serve as juror at the treason trial of her uncle Henry Grey and then, under Elizabeth, his own long imprisonment in the Tower while her father was under house arrest at Nonsuch. Both were accused of involvement in the Ridolfi plot that aimed to marry the duke of Norfolk, the widower of Jane Lumley's sister, to Mary, Queen of Scots. What such giddy turnings of fortune's wheel, such handy-dandy reversals of the roles of prisoner and judge, meant to Jane Lumley she did not record, even when she accepted the dedication of the Gorhambury *sententiae*.

Jane Lumley died in 1577, at the age of forty-two. Her funeral is among those illustrated in the British Library manuscript *Funeral*

Processions, 1557–1603 (Add. MS 35324). The pictorial record is prefaced by her husband's elegy for her, composed in English and Latin "The lady was uprightly bent to all that good was," he writes, "One whom some violence might move, but none much trouble / Whom fortune when she forced with her most hurtful weapons did prick but not wound." She was "A dear and most obedient daughter to her father" and "A wife without all spot, careful, tender, and loving, Whose usual behaviour (in joining all modesty with that which was due to her birth and calling) was very rare. / In good learning both Greek and Latin none did exceed of her sex."

This invincibly lackluster elegy is not the last of her husband's tributes to Jane Lumley's dutiful fulfillment of social and familial responsibilities. He erected a monument to her at Cheam in Surrey "in which she is represented kneeling, with small figures of her three children below, and the pediment adorned with the horse and oak branch of Arundel, the popinjays of Lumley, accollated or collared and the frets of Maltravers" (Nichols, *Life*, 496). There is also a curious portrait listed in the 1609 Lumley Castle inventory of "my Lord Lumley in armour, with his two wives," living Elizabeth and dead Jane, along with Jane's dead son Charles and "the old Earl of Arundel" (Hervey, 42). Like the well-known Saltonstall portrait and John Souch's *Sir Thomas Aston at the Deathbed of His Wife*, this iconographic union of the living and the dead, with its plangent declaration that the dead are not dead, commemorates a woman's service to her widower's house.[34]

Neither elegy, monument, nor portrait relates what the fear was that did not dismay Jane Lumley, or the violence that might have moved her, or the trouble that could not. No memorial describes the ordeals that include the deaths of her mother, sister, brother, stepmother, and three children; her illness in Italy; the trials in which her uncle and cousin were condemned; those in which her husband and father were variously judge and defendant; or the imprisonments in which they were sometimes jailed and sometimes jailer.

Even so, the record suggests that Jane Lumley had, by the end of her lifetime, lived her own "tale of trouble." I find myself wondering whether, had she returned to the translation of Greek tragedy at the end of her life, she would have chosen the *Hecuba* that she had once annotated, in which the narrative of a virgin's sacrifice is only one episode in the tragedy of a woman who, like Lumley, survived to become the chief mourner at many funerals. But the extant record of Lumley's intellectual life in fact closes with a faint and fortuitous echo of the sacrificial daughter. The last *sententia* of Bacon's Gorhambury collection is from Ennius's *Iphigenia*, by way of Aulus Gellius's *Attic Nights* (90). Whatever the course of her irretrievable experience, the record of Lumley's intellectual life ends as it began, intermingling humanist learning with court politics, mythic sacrifices with domestic duties, and dynastic marriages with judicial murders. At the conclusion of the journey, the figure of Iphigenia recedes into shadow.

Lacrima Rerum

In Webster and Dekker's *Sir Thomas Wyatt*, Suffolk and Northumberland are repeatedly blamed for the deaths of their children Lady Jane Grey and her husband Guilford. The play closes with Norfolk's aphoristic restatement of this accusation: "The fathers' pride has caused the children's fall" (62).[35] Although the text restricts the moral to the would-be royals Northumberland and Suffolk, the powers of sixteenth-century fathers over their children were more pervasive, although usually less lethal.

So the case of Thomas More and his daughter Margaret suggests to Jonathan Crewe. Evoking the image of Margaret More Roper as she stood waiting to receive her father's blessing when he was led to the Tower, Crewe argues that her devotion signifies a "daughterly absolution" for and "ultimate reciprocation" of an incestuous desire that "paradoxically transforms the daughter from the victim into the legitimating conservator of patriarchy" (94–100).

Such desires are not the stuff of historical record, yet Margaret Roper's devotion to More, like Jane Lumley's return to the house of her *dominus pater* and the forgiveness that Jane Grey granted to Suffolk, occurred within social structures that make incest endemic. Where marriage is predicated on bloodlines, inheritance, and dynasty, prohibited degrees of relationship must be both explicit and negotiable. Moving through a maze of alliances secret and unsecret, licit, questionable, and forbidden, the endogamous Tudor aristocracy continually readjudicated incest with reference to canon law and the biblical injunctions on which that law is founded. In such a world, the notorious omission of father-daughter incest from the prohibitions of Leviticus becomes the most eloquent silence of all those patriarchy has produced. Severe, ardent, and unresolved, Tudor relations between fathers and daughters, even as they are dedicated to dynastic aggrandizement, evoke something primitive, oneiric, and perilous. The early modern father, choosing among his daughter's suitors, no longer elects the priestly sacrificer, yet the severed throat, the infernal *thalamus*, the martyr's dismemberment, and the stifled lament are literary relics of a larger *patria potestas*.

Lumley's *Iphigenia*, poised as it is between the humanists' program for the acquisition of classical learning and the obsessive genealogies of the Tudor nobility, at once recalls ancient articulations of sacrifice and anticipates dilemmas of the modern family, where the daughter's departure to death or marriage is still "a tale of trouble."[36] It also inaugurates a women's classical tradition, less agonistic than the Erasmian, and more patient.

Many generations after Lumley's translation, the choral odes missing from her text at last appeared in the work of another woman. In 1919, H. D., translating only the choruses from Euripides' *Iphigenia in Aulis*, ends the silence of Lumley's "company of women" who could not lament:

> But still we lament our state,
> The desert of our wide courts,
> Even if there is no truth
> In the legends cut on ivory
> Nor in the poets
> Nor the songs.

After the *auctores* who find in Lumley's text only a curious sport of Renaissance classicism, after the missing manuscripts and irretrievable responses, after the lacunae and the silences that are the story of Lumley's life, I have come to a writer who acknowledges the omissions of the archivists and the partiality of the poets, and insists that women's narratives continue in their despite: still we lament our state, still we seek breath to tell our ancient tale. For such are the stories of women—whether Iphigenia or Lady Jane Grey—and the stories of women who tell woman's stories—whether a Tudor baroness, a modernist poet, or a late twentieth-century scholar seeking her way through the nostalgic pleasures of philology to the querulous consolations of feminist criticism.

The Saint in the Brothel

Celui qui souffre, c'est le tronc et ce sont les bras
qui se plaignent.
—Etienne Decroux, *Paroles sur le Mime*

JANE LUMLEY'S MANUSCRIPT TRANSLATION is the most private of
the private discourses about which I have written; Jane Grey's political career, the most public of the public performances. Together they
had led me through cobwebby archives to estate inventories, library
catalogs, and county surveys; to watermarks, holographs, ciphers,
and glosses; to ancient deeds, dowries, petitions, and prayers. They
had opened a historical record at once sparse and dense, eloquent
and elusive. They had enthralled me in the pastness of the past.

But they had taken me further from the world of the theater
than I could have imagined when I first decided to study rather than
play Shakespeare. Even when I began to work with rhetorical theory,
I expected it to yield a phenomenology of Elizabethan performance.
(That, at least, is how I phrased it later, hoping such a formulation
would lend more luster to my apprentice work.) But I had already
spent long years in departments of English and had come to mistake
the interpretation of texts for the knowledge of theatrical practices.
Unlike Antony's Hercules, Thalia and Melpomene depart silently.

Only when I began teaching did I discover at what cost I had
replaced theater with criticism. My study of Shakespearean imagery,
then of the classical tradition, and finally of the textual representation
of class and gender had each seemed in its turn an intellectual adven-
ture. Once in my own classroom, each sounded hollow, customary,

ncreative. Not false exactly, not trivial or irrelevant, but not the one hing I had to teach.

That one thing was the pleasure of playing Shakespeare. So I ocused increasingly on student performance, and eventually, while eaching in a small and adamantly antitheatrical college, I introduced or, rather, insinuated into the curriculum some courses that were all performance and no literary criticism at all.

These acting courses were as amateurish as anything Posthaste's players could have devised. I was myself only half-trained and had not cted in years. But my students were true novices. They were attendng a college where theater had never been part of the curriculum. 'or several years it had not been available even as an extracurricular ctivity. Some of them had never seen a play. So, one-eyed, I led my lind charges in a journey through fear, resistance, confusion, and oy. I began to think about the theater again and began once more to eek a phenomenology of Elizabethan performance in the rhetorical raditions of the public and private playhouses.

The Rhetoric of Rape

The fifty-third declamation in Lazarus Piot's 1596 translation of *The Orator* tells a tale "Of her who having killed a man in the stews, laimed for her chastity and innocency to be an Abbess." The declanation begins with an imperative statement in the guise of a law: 'The order of religious women is such, as they must be pure, chaste, nd free from all crime, but the Abbess must be the chastest of all the est." The narrative that follows challenges the definitions of chasity and purity implicit in this fictive law: "It chanced that a certain oung nun of Naples was to sail into Sicily to be an abbess there." But en route she was captured by pirates, who sold her to a brothel. When clients were brought to her, she persuaded them to treat her s a suppliant. A soldier who could not be so persuaded tried to rape er. She killed him with his own sword. She stood trial for murder nd was acquitted. At last she sailed on to Sicily, where she seeks to ecome abbess.

Piot's declamation, printed as an analogue to Shakespeare's *Pericles* in Geoffrey Bullough's *Narrative and Dramatic Sources of Shakespeare*, is part of the legal, religious, literary, and rhetorical prehistory of the brothel scenes in *Pericles* (6:546–48).[1] It was originally gathered among the declamations of Seneca the Elder as the *controversia* of the *Sacerdos Prostituta*. In this *controversia*, the statute reads: "A priestess must be chaste and of chaste [parents], pure and of pure [parents]." The accompanying narrative states:

A virgin was captured by pirates and sold; she was bought by a pimp and made a prostitute. When men came to her, she asked for alms. When she failed to get alms from a soldier who came to her, he struggled with her and tried to use force; she killed him. She was accused, acquitted, and sent back to her family. She seeks a priesthood. (*Contraversiae*, 1.2)

Like the aspiring abbess of Piot's declamation, the Senecan character of the Prostitute Priestess has been abducted by pirates, sold to a pimp, and held captive in a brothel. She has defended herself against rape, first with her eloquence and then through homicide, killing the soldier who assaulted her. The narrative ends inconclusively as the Prostitute Priestess petitions a court empowered to determine her fitness for the order of the vestal virgins (*Controversiae*, 1.2).

The *narratio*, with its exaggerated imitation of life's infinite variety and messy materiality, puts the idealistic and inflexible rule to the proof. The rhetors, having created a conflict between a statute of religious chastity and a narrative of abduction, attempted rape, and homicide, now turn law and narrative into performance. Improvising arguments for or against the candidacy of the Prostitute Priestess, they test their rhetorical skill before an elite audience of aficionados in the halls of declamation.

Like many of the *controversiae*, the declamation of the Prostitute Priestess is a misogynistic tale of terror. It takes place in a rhetorical heterocosm peopled by pirates, kidnappers, rapists, cruel stepmothers, poisoners, and tyrants. Yet its improvisational theatricality complicates and to some extent compromises its misogyny. Composed, as Quintilian complains, "solely with the design of giving pleasure" (5.12.17), the ludic agon fragments forensic argument and denies juridical finality. By asking whether there are any circumstances in which an enslaved prostitute can legally become a holy virgin, the declaimers disturb conventional definitions of female chastity and purity; their narrative deliberately blurs cultural distinctions between virgin and whore.

At the center of this declamation lies the question of sexual pollution. The prosecutor Cestius Pius insists that the Prostitute Priestess has incurred the *stuprum* of illicit sexuality. Even if she has retained her virginity, her experience has irrevocably defiled her:

> You offered yourself, a girl in a brothel. Even if nobody outraged you, the place itself did so (*locus ipse violavit*). You offered yourself with harlots, beautified to please the populace, dressed in the clothes the pimp had provided. Your name hung at the door; you received the wages of sin (*pretia stupri*) . . . the hand that aspired to sacrifice to the gods took immoral gains. (*Contraversiae*, 1.2.7)

For the prosecutors, *stuprum* is a material contagion transmitted through "the place itself." "Pollution rules," writes Mary Douglas, "by contrast with moral rules are unequivocal. They do not depend on intention or a nice balancing of rights and duties. The only material question is whether a forbidden contact has taken place or not" (130).

Pollution rules divide the pure from the defiled body without questioning motive and intention. Publius Asprenas quarantines the polluted body of the Prostitute Priestess by policing the boundaries between the sacred space of the temple and the profane space of the brothel: "Once you enter a brothel, all temples are closed to you" (*Contraversiae*, 1.2.10). Publius Vinicius alludes to her motives only to dismiss their significance: "Do you regard yourself as chaste just because you are an unwilling whore?" (1.2.3).

The advocates of the Prostitute Priestess, however, posit an internal purity that eludes *stuprum*: "I guarantee," swears Pompeius Silo,

> a priestess whom no bad fortune can make unchaste. Some women can be forced to it by slavery: she served barbarians and pirates, remaining inviolate in their hands. Some women can be depraved by the evil habits of a decadent

age . . . she will remain chaste to the end. You may put her in a brothel: even through this she managed to carry her chastity away untouched. (1.2.20)

While the prosecutors equate the woman's defilement with the material circumstances of her imprisonment, the advocates stress the discrepancy between her invincible chastity and the physical conditions of the brothel. By insisting on internal purity, they create a precondition for an argument based on rules of morality.[2]

For the prosecutors, pollution is pollution *tout court*. In interpreting her act of homicide, Publius Asprenas argues, "You consorted with men who were murderers, smeared with human blood. Hence, of course, your ability to kill a man" (1.2.9). Rather than survive by killing, a woman so defiled "could," Publius Vinicius insinuates, "do nothing more upright (*nihil honestius*) than to die" (1.2.3). While her survival demonstrates the *audacia* of sexual license, her act of homicide convicts the Prostitute Priestess of unchastity. The rapist then is innocent, and his intended victim becomes the criminal: "*Was* she justified in killing an innocent man who wanted to employ the body of a prostitute?" asks Latro. Although she was acquitted of homicide, her trial "showed not that she was pure but that the law could not touch her" (1.2.14).

Again, her advocates distinguish between her internal purity and the material circumstances of her captivity. Albucius presents the homicide in these *colores*:

There came a man of fierce and violent temperament, sent, I believe, by the gods themselves to put on display the chastity of one destined to be priestess, not to violate it. She told him to keep his hands off her holy body: "You must not dare to harm chastity that men preserve and gods look forward to." When he came rushing to his doom, she said, "Look, your weapon—you do not realize that it is in the cause of chastity that you carry it." And seizing the sword she drove it into her attacker's breast. Those same immortal gods took care that this deed of hers should not go unnoticed; an accuser turned up to bear witness to her chastity in the courts. No one could believe a man had been killed by a woman, a youth by a girl, one armed by one unarmed. It was too great a feat for it to be supposed to have taken place without the aid of the immortal gods. (1.2.18)

The Prostitute Priestess acts forcefully by seizing the soldier's weapon. With it, she appropriates a phallic power to penetrate another's body. But Albucius's *color* denies her agency. Crediting the gods with the defense of her chastity, he validates the survival of the Prostitute Priestess without bringing the vulnerability of ordinary women into question.

Albucius resolves the paradox inherent in the figure of the Prostitute Priestess, but when the declamation was performed, his was only one among many rhetorical *colores*. The purpose of declamation was not to hold the mirror up to nature but to argue *in utramque partem*. In order to construct a narrative which pushes the legal dilemma to its most sensationalized extreme, the rhetors forgo conventional criteria for the realistic representation of women. They endow the Prostitute Priestess with the ability to speak eloquently and the ability to kill ruthlessly. Eloquence and courage, arts and arms, Mercury and Mars: the Prostitute Priestess challenges the male monopoly of these qualities, endeavors, and symbols, and it is for this that she stands trial. The rhetors may call her speech either divine eloquence or meretricious wheedling, her martial skill either miraculous or murderous, and her survival either a triumph or a transgression. The open structure of the declamation subversively suggests that a woman can confound even the worst circumstances that the male imagination can devise for her. Consigned to the brothel, she retains a state of holy chastity; elected to the priesthood, she retains a sordid history in the stews. The rhetors cannot debate their conflicting interpretations of their character's status without raising the question of her self-interpretation.

The Case Is Closed

The motif of the Prostitute Priestess proved as resilient as the character herself, outlasting the legal and religious institutions in which the declamation originated. It endures in two major forms, each with many variants. One is the figure of the virgin martyr from Christian hagiography; the other is the kidnapped princess of Greek romance. As the hagiographers and romance writers adapt the rhetors' scenarios to narrative structures, they jettison the *argumentum in utramque partem*. Saints' lives and romances present only one side of the argument, exerting authorial privilege to close the case of the Prostitute Priestess.

The virgin martyrs, all beautiful and wellborn, are enslaved in brothels for refusing to worship pagan idols or for rejecting pagan suitors. *The Golden Legend* tells the tale of Agnes, who, at the age of thirteen, was sought in marriage by the son of the prefect of Rome. She refused the offer. She was sent to a brothel for punishment. But an angel surrounded her with a bright light. When men entered the brothel and perceived this radiance, they offered her reverence. The son of the prefect, like the soldier in the declamation, came to the brothel and tried to rape her. He dropped dead at the edge of the holy light. When Agnes's prayers resuscitated her would-be rapist, the pagan priests insisted she be burned as a sorceress. But the fire would not burn her, for she prayed, and as she prayed, the flames lost their heat. Finally a lieutenant commanded that she be stabbed with a sword, and thus Agnes achieved her martyrdom (Caxton, 2:245–52).

Agatha too was "right fair, noble of body and heart, and . . . rich of goods." Quintianus, the provost of Sicily, "being of a low lineage, avaricious, and a miscreant and paynim," became enamored of her. Hoping to destroy her chastity by destroying her faith, he tried to induce her to sacrifice to his idols. He put her into the hands of the infamous bawd Aphrosidia, who sought day and night to persuade Agatha to prostitution and idolatry. When Aphrodisia acquainted Quintianus with her failure, he had Agatha scourged, burned with red-hot irons, and torn with sharp hooks. Her breasts were cut off. She was "rolled all naked upon burning brands, and anon the ground . . . began to tremble like an earthquake." When she was returned to the prison, she prayed to God to release her and so died (Caxton, 3:32–39).

Lucy, self-consciously modeling herself after Agnes and Agatha, was brought before the judge Paschusius, who condemned her to a brothel. Unintimidated, she replied, "The body may take no corruption but if the heart and will give thereto assenting . . . if thou make my body to be defouled without mine assent, and against my will, my chastity shall increase double to the merit of the crown of glory." But her body could not be so fouled without her consent, for "the Holy Ghost made her so pesant and heavy" that even a thousand men and oxen could not move her thence. So Paschusius had her tortured with pitch, resin, and boiling oil. She prayed and preached in the fire, and continued to speak to the people even after "they roof a sword through her throat." She died only after a priest had come to give her her last sacrament (Caxton 2:130–36).[3]

In telling these tales of virgin martyrs, the hagiographers incorporate the rhetors' arguments into their narrative premises. Like Pompeius Silo, they find that physical contact with the brothel and its inhabitants need not constitute loss of chastity. They also take up Albucius's hint that divine aid rather than her own strenuous efforts enables the Prostitute Priestess to avoid rape. But they also use the prosecutors' arguments. Like Publius Vinicius, they find that when placed in a brothel, a woman can do nothing more upright than to die. When this premise is incorporated into the narrative structure, the mortification of the virgin in the brothel becomes the foundation for her sanctification. There is here an implicit response to the Augustinian argument against the suicide of rape victims. In *The City of God*, Augustine condemns Lucretia for choosing suicide as proof that she had not consented to Tarquin's rape. He argues that Christian victims of rape need not die, for they "have within themselves the glory of chastity, the witness of their conscience. They have it also in the presence of their God and need nothing more" (1.19).

Were the witness of conscience and the presence of God sufficient, Lucy's legend might have concluded with her insistence that she could not be defiled against her will. But hagiography must demonstrate the chastity of its subjects, not for the witness of conscience, not before God, but in stories that will persuade readers who require more emphatic closure. The chastity of the living Prostitute Priestess raises a legal debate; that of the dead saints resolves a narrative dilemma.

When the Prostitute Priestess's aggressive self-defense has been transformed into the Christian virtue of passive endurance, the narrative need no longer ask whether killing one's would-be rapist is justifiable. The Christian martyrs lack the martial skill which made the homicide possible. They lack this skill, at any rate, in the tales of *The Golden Legend*. But there is at least a partial exception among the earliest stories.

Thecla, whose history appears in the apocryphal *Acts of Paul*, is the prototype of the androgynous saint who exchanges a woman's status for spirituality. To follow Paul, Thecla cut her hair. She abandoned her family and her fiancé. In the course of her wanderings, she was imprisoned and tortured. She was condemned to be burned in the theater at Iconium and threatened with wild beasts in the arena at Antioch. When an official of Antioch attempted to embrace Thecla in the marketplace, she "ripped his cloak, took off the crown from his head, and made him a laughingstock." Unlike other virgin martyrs, Thecla went on from Antioch to a full career of preaching in Seleucia, at last ending her life in "a noble sleep" (Schneemelcher, 445–63).

The unorthodox legend of Thecla, John Anson notes, "possesses at least the verisimilitude of what might be described as a historical fiction," while the legends which emerged from a later monastic culture take place in "a world of pure erotic romance" (11). Unlike the "erotic romance" of orthodox hagiography, the apocryphal history of Thecla (for which its author, a presbyter of the second century, was expelled from the church) remains on the margins of Christian narrative. Like the Prostitute Priestess, a saint who inhabits those margins need not die to defend herself against rape. Thecla's legend incorporates the subversive survival of the Prostitute Priestess into its fictive premises. Like later hagiographies, however, it concludes emphatically with the sanctity of the saint. It is not a rhetorical agon to be interpreted in performance. To recover the theatrical risks and rewards of the rhetors' improvisations, the story of the saint in the brothel must be enacted rather than narrated.

The Case Is Altered

Death concludes the history of the virgin martyr. In the romance sources and analogues of Shakespeare's *Pericles*, from *Historia Apollonii Regis Tyri* to the *Gesta Romanorum*, Gower's fourteenth-century *Confessio amantis*, and Twine's *The Patterne of Painefull Adventures*, the story of the eloquent virgin ends in marriage. In all these romances, a princess is kidnapped by pirates and sold to a pimp who places her in a brothel. Like the Prostitute Priestess, she persuades the clients to give her alms. The narrators, like the advocates of the Prostitute Priestess, praise her eloquence as miraculous. Her oratory not only preserves her virginity, it reunites her with her royal father and gains her a husband as well.

These narrative romances, like the saints' lives, take up only one side of the argument the declamation raises. Their *colores* offer only one interpretation of the negotiations between the prisoner and her clients. As a virgin in a brothel and a princess among bawds, the heroine is a woman displaced downward. Her royal marriage, like the saint's martyrdom, restores order by ceremonially reintegrating her into her proper social status: as in the tragedy of Iphigenia, though without Euripidean irony, marriage and death are structurally equivalent.[4]

The romance tradition takes the brothel scenes from juridical contexts of violence and death to economic contexts of money and marriage. In the *Historia Apollonii Regis Tyri*, the princess Tharsia, like the Prostitute Priestess and the saints, is forcibly abducted and held in a brothel against her will, but the *Historia* emphasizes commercial exchange, partly obscuring the violent exchange of women in the declamation and the saints' lives. Physical force merges into symbolic violence; sexual domination becomes a strategy for economic exploitation.[5]

Like the romances and saints' lives, *Pericles* presents only one side of the declaimers' argument, theatrically representing a valiant virgin whose eloquence and courage are rightly rewarded. Following the romance tradition, the opening lines of *Pericles*' brothel scenes emphasize not the violation but the commodification of the female body:

Pander: We lost too much money this mart by being too wenchless.
Bawd: We were never so much out of creatures. We have but poor three, and they can do no more than they can do; and they with continual action are even as good as rotten.

$$(4.2.4-9)$$

They later specify the means through which Marina too will become the bawds' commercial property. Her body will be verbally anatomized for a pornographic advertisement:

Boult, take you the marks of her, the color of her hair, complexion, height, her age, with warrant of her virginity, and cry, "He that will give most shall have her first." Such a maidenhead were no cheap thing, if men were as they have been.

$$(4.2.57-61)$$

The flesh peddler's cry threatens further material harm. In the brothels of Mytilene, the "continual action" of the whores is a kind of military action. Sex has become a war of attrition:

Bawd: The stuff we have, a strong wind will . . . blow it to pieces, they are so pitifully sodden.
Pander: Thou sayest true, there's two unwholesome, a' conscience. The poor Transylvanian is dead that lay with the little baggage.
Boult: Ay, she quickly poop'd him, she made him roast-meat for worms.

$$(4.2.18-25)$$

The bawds' metaphoric configuration of military action and venereal disease evokes the historical conditions of the sixteenth-century syphilis epidemic. Syphilis, a disease of early modern naval exploration and military conquest, reanimated the ancient fear of physical pollution that underlies the Roman idea of *stuprum*. It transferred the corporeal pollution of illicit sexuality from the realm of ritual dread into the world of early modern medical discourse. In times of plague, *stuprum* regains its primitive material foundation; contamination supersedes Augustinian shamefastness.

As our own time of plague sadly shows, fear of contagion can be exploited ideologically. Syphilis, explains the London physician William Clowes, arose from "the licentious and beastly disorder of a great number of rogues and vagabonds, the filthy life of many lewd and idle persons, men and women." Although, as Clowes admits, "some other of better disposition are many times infected," the syphilitic became an underworld figure, for the primary carriers of the disease, prostitutes and discharged soldiers, were socially vulnerable and readily marginalized (149).[6]

Since venereal infection and social marginalization are reciprocal, the bawds' threat suggests a terrorist tactic of germ warfare: to threaten a princess with the occupational hazards of prostitution is to marshal the hierarchy of gender against that of rank. When prostitution has destroyed the dynastic value of a princess's hymen, the fragments of the pornographic image will be grotesquely reunited in the diseased flesh of the syphilitic whore: Marina will become another "little baggage."

Like the Prostitute Priestess, Marina converts her clients through the power of eloquence: "Come," says one who has heard her sermon in the stews, "I am for no more bawdy-houses. Shall 's go hear the vestals sing?" (4.5.6–7). The gentlemen of Mytilene move between the brothel and the temple. These *loci*, which homologously represent the bodies of the prostitute and the priestess, are landmarks in the symbolic geography of what Peter Stallybrass calls "patriarchal territories" (123–42). Marina's eloquence, like that of the Prostitute Priestess, reconfigures those territories, exposing the motives of those who draw the boundaries.[7]

Marina resembles the Prostitute Priestess in her eloquence, but not in her homicidal fervor (a trait unlikely to increase one's value in the marriage market). Only verbal suggestions of the earlier character's androgynous power remain. The "sweet harmony" of her eloquence "make[s] a batt'ry through [Pericles'] deafen'd parts" (5.1.47), and he tells her "Thou art a man, and I / have suffered like a girl" (5.1.136–37). For Bawd and Pander, Marina's rhetorical victory over her hopeful clients is "virginal fencing" (4.6.57). When they send their servant Boult to rape her and break her to the trade, she responds with ferocity:

> Thou hold'st a place for which the pained'st fiend
> Of hell would not in reputation change.
> Thou art the damned door-keeper to every
> Custrel that comes inquiring for his Tib.
> To the choleric fisting of every rogue
> Thy ear is liable; thy food is such
> As hath been belch'd on by infected lungs.
>
> (4.6.163–69)

Marina's pugnacious oration is a vestige of the Prostitute Priestess's martial art, but it is not in itself sufficient to convert Boult. For those employed in the whorehouses of Mytilene, economic need is impervious to the persuasive powers of a moralizing rhetoric:

> What would you have me do? Go to the wars, would you? where a man may serve seven years for the loss of a leg, and have not money enough in the end to buy him a wooden one?
>
> (4.6.170–73)

An excellent question, to which Marina's eloquence cannot find a practical answer:

> Do anything but this thou doest. Empty
> Old receptacles, or common shoures, of filth.
> Serve by indenture to the common hangman:
> Any of these ways are yet better than this.
>
> (4.6.174–77)

At last, confined rhetorically to the marketplace, she gains her freedom through barter instead of force:

If that thy master would gain by me,
Proclaim that I can sing, weave, sew, and dance,
With other virtues, which I'll keep from boast,
And will undertake all these to teach.
I doubt not but this populous city will
Yield many scholars.

(4.6.182–87)

The art of eloquence, extended into music, weaving, and riddle lore, purchases Marina's release from the brothel. Unlike the Prostitute Priestess or the saints, she need neither kill nor die to avoid prostitution; her art preserves her chastity without bloodshed. Her most characteristic combat takes a form more appropriate for preparing a trousseau than repelling a rapist. When embroidering, Gower as chorus tells us, Marina "would with sharp needle wound / The cambric, which she made more sound / By hurting it" (act 4, lines 23–25).

The practice of embroidery requires costly leisure, and Marina's proficiency testifies to an aristocratic education. Embroidery, the 1596 preface to Giovanni Battista Ciotti's *A Booke of Curious and Strange Inventions* argues, is suitable for women who are either "of a high degree" or who hope to elevate themselves socially: "For many maidens but of base degree . . . / With noble ladies oft companions be / Sometimes they teach the daughter of a king."[8]

This advice for displaying or acquiring status is doubly significant for a princess imprisoned in the material circumstances of a prostitute. Like the enterprising dukes who turn their ancestral estates into theme parks, Marina joins entrepreneurial ability to the advantages of her patrician upbringing. Although a princess may, like a prostitute, be a commodity, the princess's price includes the charges of her birth and breeding, a higher rate than pimps and bawds can pay.

As the declamatory technique of speaking *ethicos* ("in character") constructs the Prostitute Priestess from the rhetors' discourse, the theatrical convention of the boy actor encodes Shakespeare's Marina as feminine. Yet Shakespeare's script, relying on the corporeal presence of the sexually ambiguous boy actor, must work harder to create femininity than the rhetorical fiction of the androgynous Prostitute Priestess. Eloquence and embroidery, not the Prostitute Priestess's martial prowess, allow Marina to return to her rightful place in a patriarchal world where fathers and husbands are a woman's best protection against pirates and pimps. Hence no verbal or visual cue need suggest that the boy Marina could defend himself physically against an attempted rape by the adult Boult.

While the character's sexual vulnerability, and its economic value, underscore the player's precarious position as the demimondaine of the playhouse, the dynamics of performance continue to disturb the complacencies of the romance narrative.[9] In introducing each act, the choral figure of the poet Gower attempts to "stand i' th' gaps" of the story (4.4.8). Still the play of *Pericles* remains open. Gower cannot defeat theatrical indeterminacy through his narrative strategies because it is not Gower, the representative of ancient poetic authority, but the actor playing Gower who will "stand i' th' gaps," and no actor can control the performance when he is not on stage. Gower's commentary may be charming or irritating, but it cannot authorize either Marina's version or the bawds'. Like the rhetors whose *argumenta in utramque partem* reveal the limitations of statutory law, the antagonistic characters of the brothel scenes reveal ideological interests underlying the dramatic conflict.

The bawds, like the accusers of the Prostitute Priestess, trivialize rape and prostitution. Neither, they assume, can occur without the implied consent of lascivious and greedy women. Shakespeare's dramatization of this attitude produces a crudely comic *mise en scène* for the brothel at Mytilene. When Marina is introduced into this setting, her repugnance at once exposes the economic motive of the bawds' assumption and ironically heightens its theatrical vitality. The more zealously Marina cherishes her maidenhead as a pearl beyond price, the more energetically they appraise its market value. While her rage embarrasses the prurient laughter with which misogyny greets the sexual exploitation of the unprotected, their hard-boiled pragmatism mocks the horror with which patriarchy greets the violation of aristocratic virginity. The case, argued *in utramque partem*, is altered.

Pericles does not explicitly reopen the *controversia* of the Prostitute Priestess. Restored to political and domestic authority as king and father, Pericles ratifies the marriage of Marina and Lysimachus: "This prince, the fair betrothed of your daughter," he announces to Thaisa, "Shall marry her at Pentapolis" (5.3.71–72). Yet eloquent Marina, like Isabella, the eloquent virgin of *Measure for Measure*, responds silently to the announcement of her marriage.

Marina's silence, like Isabella's, is audible in the playhouse.[10] Through it she may articulate joy, dread, or confusion. She may ratify Pericles' pronouncement or rebel against it. She may uphold the notion that romance ends in reconciliation or suggest that Lysimachus's loving voyage is but two months' victualed. For this freedom to intervene in the dénouement, the player is indebted to the theatrical ellipses of Senecan declamation, surfacing from another stratum of storytelling than the narrative tradition of medieval romance and hagiography.

From romance, *Pericles* derives a plot which permits Marina to escape the brothel, but not to evade the marriage which reinserts her into the social structures of Mytilene. When that plot is adapted for theatrical representation, however, its ending becomes less conclusive. Gower's poetic authory, the bawds' mocking of maidenheads, and Marina's prenuptial silence must all be performed, and the contingencies of performance, mediating between the text and the playgoer's response, may expose the improvisational (and hence provisional) quality of the drama's resolution. Actors' choices for inflections and gestures, directors' decisions about dynamics and stage images, the extradramatic relation which a strong performer may establish with the audience, even the danger of a missed cue or a bumbled exit may, in various ways, defeat dramatic closure, evoking instead an open-ended *controversia*. The Prostitute Priestess is not only Marina's literary precursor, passing through classical and medieval discourses of gender and violence en route to the Shakespearean play text. She is the survivor of an agon through which the rhetoric of rape is debated whenever *Pericles* is performed.

Institutio Orationis

Among these performances, some take place in the private playhouse of the classroom, where student actors and directors may experiment with the Shakespearean text. There they may, as my students have done, present the brothel scenes both from the bawds' perspective and from Marina's. My students had difficulty with half the task: they could make strong, theatrically interesting choices favoring only one side (usually Marina's, for they were young, middle or upper middle class, and either female or too self-consciously liberal to joke publicly about rape). Their choices on behalf of the bawds were hesitant and lackadaisical, for they were unwilling to claim the desires of such unsavory characters as their own.

Learning to make such claims is a purpose of the training of the contemporary actor, as it was of the ancient orator. Both actor and orator must suspend judgment, playing with possibilities, making up stories to interpret stories. In literate, or postliterate culture, this theatrical significance of the *ars rhetorica* has long been obscured. For the residually oral culture of the Renaissance, however, words are events and characters the result of *ethopoesis*.[11] Senecan declamation, which so vividly records rhetoric's contribution to Renaissance drama, preserves a Shakespearean characterology that is at once historically appropriate and theatrically viable. As such, it may adjudicate between the twentieth-century actor's process of characterization and the questions of early modern subjectivity that literary scholars of Renaissance drama have recently raised.

Habeas Corpus

The revisionist "history of the subject" elaborated in the work of Catherine Belsey, Francis Barker, Jonathan Dollimore, and others argues that the intricate interior life of the modern psyche, with its memory, desire, ambition, and repression, is merely emergent in early modern Europe, and that, as a corollary, the recognizably modern rondure of Shakespeare's characters is only anachronistically read into his play texts. Shakespearean character is fragmented, discontinuous, made from the shreds and patches of social categories through which premodern subjectivity was constructed. Although Hamlet, if no other, prefigures the modern subject, interiority remains rough-hewn until the nineteenth century smooths it into Romantic sensibility. Largely innocent of the universalist claims of bourgeois humanism, Shakespearean character seems fully psychological only because modern interpreters have made Shakespeare's characters virtually indistinguishable from Chekhov's.

This poststructuralist valediction to the early modern subject, or at least to conventional Shakespearean characterology, may already lie amoldering, rotten before it was half ripe. Since it has come to the attention of cultural historians who read medieval religious as well as early modern literary texts, the revisionist history seems itself to require revision. For it neglects the many works, from Augustine's *Confessions* through Chaucer's *Troilus and Criseyde* and *The Book of Margery Kempe*, that reflect the troubled and divided self in late antiquity and the Middle Ages.

Nor do the revisionists' political intentions weather this critique. Lee Patterson condemns their *soi-disant* radicalism for reproducing a blandly Burckhardtian paradigm; David Aers detects a reactionary Robertsonian strain; Debora Shuger argues that they have missed the revolution in Shakespearean characterization, where innovative poetic techniques transform religious radicalism to create the new sense of selfhood in a king whose hand smells of mortality or a prince who behaves like a rogue and peasant slave ("Subversive Fathers").

From a perspective less attentive to intellectual history but more responsive to the theatrical structures of Shakespearean and other play texts, Edward Burns disputes the revisionists' analogies between pre- and postmodern characterologies. He insists that the fragmentary and nonnaturalistic characters of early modern drama no more resemble the deliberately fragmented and antinaturalistic characters of modernist and postmodernist theater than they do the humanist subject. It is finally meaningless to refer to a subject as "decentered" before it has been "centered."[12]

The argument that reinterpreting Shakespearean character as

fragmented and discontinuous will restore a historical radicalism begins to seem as redolent of postmodern fictions and fixations as
the girlhood of Shakespeare's heroines is of Victorian values. The
revisionist history, insisting that Shakespeare's characters resemble
Brecht's rather than Chekhov's, has inadvertently made them over in
the image of Beckett's.

In denying modern subjectivity to Shakespearean character, the
history of the subject has become a new weapon in the interminable
war of the stage and the study. Although postmodern artistic practices are as common in current Shakespearean performance as poststructuralist theories are in academic Shakespeare studies, literary
critics see as little innovation in the former as theater practitioners
hear in the latter.[13] Certainly, the waggish directors who shoe fairies
in hightops and relay Caesar's assassination over closed-circuit television do not strive to present the historicized subjects of the critics'
supposings. For most players and playgoers still insist that the plays
are about Hamlet and Lear and Othello, our contemporaries. While
producers want to see money up there, and Shakespeare scholars (as
Barbara Hodgdon once reminded me) want to see text up there,
people want to see people up there. Even the most experimental
players and sophisticated playgoers seem to find the poststructuralist
insistence that characters are not people merely churlish.[14]

Performance and Pedagogy

The call to historicize the subject has therefore not much influenced
those who teach Shakespearean performance. For many acting teach-
ers, as Erika Fischer-Licht remarks, "history is but the overlay of
'period styles,' which a costume, a few gestures, and some quickly
learned methods of walking and sitting take care of" (21). Nor
have many Shakespeare scholars who practice performance pedagogy
joined the vociferous contests between formalism and historicism,
criticism and theory, bardolatry and bardicide.[15]

It is not evident what they would gain thereby. In departments
of English, where the *arrière-garde* teaches that a Shakespeare play

is a long lyric poem with people in it and the *avant-garde* teaches that plays are texts no more (and no less) yielding than a dream, a pamphlet, or the *Calendar of State Papers*, performance is condemned equally by right and left. Lusting, it seems, after *Lebensraum*, professors of all persuasions scour theatrical weeds from their literary gardens and construct impenetrable walls between their spacious vistas and the dark and narrow quarters of the players: "Our business is finally critical and scholarly and analytic, not technical and professional" (Edward Partridge, 6). Although one can no more argue with those who prefer reading to performing than with those who prefer masturbation to intercourse, such separatism sanitizes the academic study of Shakespeare. The theatrical pleasures and dangers lost to formalist and historicist criticism are also largely missing from theorizations of performance and performativity, where critics, relying on antitheatricalism, may flout conservative colleagues without actually having to do anything that is not "critical and scholarly and analytic."

In this antitheatrical climate, practitioners of performance pedagogy defend methodologically radical departures from both formalism and historicism with claims that performance is a more effective means to critical and theoretical ends. Some, like Ellen O'Brian, recommend performance to achieve the "traditional goals" of poetics, textual criticism, and theater history. Others, such as Simon Shepherd, use it to subvert those goals. Inventing exercises and improvisations to "deprivilege," "problematize," and "interrogate" character, Shepherd hopes to reveal the historical categories of race, class, and gender that subtend Cleopatra, Shylock, or Mistress Ford.

While a performance pedagogy predicated on traditional criticism may silently reinforce a humanistic status quo, politicized stances may reduce the exploration of character and language to pedagogical (as they have become critical) shibboleths. They may assume too quickly that the uses of subtext are invariably anachronistic or reactionary. Ironically, these assumptions especially impoverish the characterizations of woman and workers, who, with far fewer lines than the lunatic king or the roguish prince, must rely on extratextual techniques to assert their theatrical presence.

Subtext, Burns has it, is the illusion of characterological depth that emerges from the "clash" of the playwright's text with the personal desires and memories that Stanislavskian actors bring to their characters (13). Bearing theatrical witness to the psychopathology of everyday life, subtext assumes that characters do not say what they mean and cannot mean what they say. Since Shakespeare's characters, unlike Chekhov's, do say what they mean, subtext is an actorly excrescence, an anachronism in the premodern play text.

Often it is. Yet even a Hamlet or Iago may not say everything he means. For Elbow and Mistress Overdone, for the citizens who hear Brutus's and Antony's orations, the peasants who follow Jack Cade, and the eloquent virgins about to become *femes covertes*, subtext may stand for unauthorized desires that can fill their silences with theatrical significance. Counting Lady Macbeth's children has long served to mock naive responses to Shakespearean characterization, but players who are to stage the food riot in *Coriolanus* can work toward a political as well as psychological understanding of the scene by answering these questions for themselves: How many children do you have? When did they last eat?

Whether the exercises of performance pedagogy are designed to teach students to appreciate Shakespeare's imagery or to problematize his characters, they derive from the methods and purposes of literary criticism. Sighting a cultural monument to be revered or demolished rather than a job of work to be done, both use performance to teach Shakespeare rather than Shakespeare to teach performance. Neither would enable my students to grasp the *argmentum in utramque partem* that is the historical and theatrical heart of the brothel scenes in *Pericles*.

Shakespearean Declamation

In the *suasoria*, in which the rhetor portrays a legendary or historical character at a moment of crisis, subjectivity is rooted in social and political questions: "Should Agamemnon sacrifice Iphigenia?" The arguments seek out an intersection of language, character, and society, drawing on historical context as it impinges on a character's subjectivity. As the Senecan rhetor, speaking in the persona of Agamemnon, debates the politics in his ethical choice, a student actor may debate whether, as Isabella, she should submit to Angelo; or whether, as Helena, she should use the bed trick to win Bertram. As Cressida, she may weigh the consequences of resisting Diomedes; as Emilia, those of stealing Desdemona's handkerchief.

The Stanislavskian actor playing Emilia may motivate her theft of Desdemona's handkerchief privately, through her own memories. To invent a *suasoria* that articulates arguments for and against the theft, however, involves the reasoning (and the rationalizations) of a social consciousness as it debates the conflicting demands of duty to one's husband and one's mistress. This Shakespearean subtext is not discovered when the actor's own memories "clash" with the playwright's text, but when she incorporates the Renaissance anthropology only adumbrated in the tellingly elliptical conclusion of Emilia's brief soliloquy: "I nothing but to please his fantasy" (*Othello*, 3.3.299).

Shakespearean subtext might better be called "intertext," for it is located not beneath the surface of the lines but within them, like drawings in which a careful observer can detect seven elephants although the casual eye sees only four. In Chekhov or Ibsen, subtext enlarges the space between words and meaning, while Shakespearean intertext diminishes it. Verse imps the wings of words with the signifying force of rhythm, rhyme, alliteration, assonance, repetition. Thus meaning, conveyed as much by sound as by sense, is also conveyed by sound's cessation. The caesura in "What should Cordelia speak? Love and be silent" (*King Lear*, 1.1.62) contains an entire unspoken *suasoria*. Though the words of the actor's *suasoriae* must be confined to the rehearsal room, their meaning, conveyed through gesture and inflection, may be comprehended on stage. After the scene in Diomedes' tent, whether it is staged as rape or seduction, Cressida must say,

> Troilus, farewell! one eye yet looks on thee,
> But with my heart the other eye doth see
> Ah, poor our sex! this fault in us I find,
> The error of our eye directs our mind.
>
> (5.2.107–10)

A Cressida who had discovered, among the arguments for submission, that only the poltroon Calchas and marauding Diomedes stood between her and the Greek army, need not perform this speech in the posture of a whore. Turning her head toward Diomedes' tent, but her body toward Troy and Troilus, she can physically express division between a cerebral acceptance of the soliloquy's misogynist clichés and an elegiac yearning of the torso, breast, and pelvis. Then it is indeed the error, the wandering, of the eye and the rationalizing mind that capitulates, while the torque of the body expresses the dislocation, alienation, and constraint of what she must perforce call choice.[16]

While the *suasoria* maps the social boundaries that constrain personal choice, the *controversia* constructs a forensic conception of intention and responsibility, the *mens rea*. Unlike a guilty conscience, the *mens rea* originates in what, in *Doctor and Student*, Christopher St. Germain calls a forum of the soul (*forum interius*). The law of this interior tribunal coincides with the divine and positive law interpreted in the *forum exterius* (29). For both the Roman rhetors and the early modern legal theorist, guilt depends on the relation between the exterior and interior courts, between the *actus reus* and *mens rea*. The play is the thing wherein Hamlet can catch the king's conscience because a "thing," in its original meaning, is a court of law.[17]

Pericles is only one of many Shakespearean plays to use the rhetors' forensic methods. Lurking in the prehistory of *Hamlet* is a statute that reads: "A suicide may not be buried in consecrated ground," with a *narratio* that states, "A young woman has been ordered by her father to leave her lover. She does so. He apparently goes mad and kills her father. She herself goes mad and subsequently drowns. Her brother requests that she be buried in consecrated ground." The *controversia* requires arguments for and against Ophelia's burial in the churchyard.

These arguments may include a hypothetical reconstruction of Ophelia's state of mind at the time of death. Gertrude's monologue, "There is a willow grows askaunt the brook," which some have found too mysteriously clairvoyant, is one such hypothesis. The fictive color she gives to Ophelia's death argues for innocence by reason of insanity, releasing Ophelia from the legal penalty for suicide, "As one incapable of her own distress" (4.7.178).

The gravediggers argue the other side of the case: "If this had not been a gentlewoman, she should have been buried out of a Christian burial" (5.1.23–25). Class conscious and gender blind, they assume a gentlewoman's guilt, and, muttering over her expected acquittal, anticipate the resentments that centuries later would condemn Patricia Hearst.

Speak That I May See You

Senecan *ethopoesis* is a process of characterization in which character is an epiphenomenon of speech, the end of which is persuasion of others, not revelation of the self. Even when a speech begins "Now I am alone," it remains a formal rhetorical structure, publicly purposeful.[18] Yet *ethopoesis* does not simply corroborate poststructuralist arguments for premodern *personae* uncluttered with psychological paraphernalia. The creatures of the declaimer's art—the saint in the brothel, the man who raped two women in one night, the madman who demanded his own daughter's execution—are precursors to the ravenous protagonists of Senecan tragedy, with their slavering interiority that gnaws and munches and finally gobbles up the world. They are also, as a few days' reading any metropolitan newspaper will confirm, all too obviously our contemporaries. But we cannot recognize them as such without a salutary shock.

Senecan declamation is extravagant, precious, and cruelly prurient. But its open structure exposes the conflicts and contradictions that were present at the making of the stories. It retrieves moments in which character and action are still taking shape; it explores the realm of change and choice as it exists in the world of the play. Declamation can, then, be a historical analogue of Augusto Boal's Forum theater. In Forum theater performances, the audience (the spect-actors, as Boal calls them), having seen a play performed once, can intervene during a second showing, trying out their own ideas for a better solution to the characters' dilemmas. "Forum theatre is always possible when alternatives exist." Where there are no alternatives, "it becomes fatalist theatre" (Boal, 226).

The plot of a Shakespeare play, not only complete but familiar, is in Boal's sense fatalistic. Hamlet, Lear, and Cleopatra must die, Hermia and Rosalind (though perhaps not Isabella) must marry. Still, the playwright's apparently finished product need not, should not foreshorten the players' imaginative and exploratory process. If that process includes the *argumenta in utramque partem* from which the now inexorable action grew, unscripted possibilities may be restored to the performance through the players' subtext, intertext, gesture, and inflection, chosen from among the political and juridical alternatives of the rhetorical tradition that also shaped Shakespeare's choices.

Voluntary Wounds

L'individu seul est esclave; l'espèce est libre.
—Buffon, *Histoire Naturale*

SEVERAL TIMES OVER THE PAST twenty-four years I have had occasion to consider the role of Portia in *Julius Caesar*, and especially these lines:

> I have made strong proof of my constancy,
> Giving myself a voluntary wound
> Here, in the thigh. Can I bear that with patience,
> And not my husband's secrets?
> (*Julius Caesar*, 2.1.299–302)

The first time, in 1972, I was rehearsing for a workshop production in a small basement studio in San Francisco. Brutus and I were too young and inexperienced for our roles, but we worked well together, and I remember the pleasures of discovery during rehearsal.

Among these discoveries was the force of the word "here" in the phrase, "Here, in the thigh." I had begun rehearsing with very little understanding of my "voluntary wound." I did not see or feel the wound there, until I learned to confront the specific images and sensations of the lines and so understand that "Here, in the thigh" means here and now. Here and now while blood flows and I am feverish with the pain of it; here and now that I have just set down the ivory-handled knife with which I inflicted this unanswerable wound. "Here" means that here on stage is an event, a revelation, a crisis.

My discovery seemed self-evident once it occurred. But the process of incorporating self-evident truths into performance is arduous and exhilarating. The player at first blunders about, clumsy and
resistant. She often hesitates and is often lost as she faces the fear
that while enduring Portia's wound, she may encounter a pathos of
her own.

Pathos and Praxis

For the next seventeen years, I forgot how Portia's blood had flowed
down my thigh, until one day when I wanted to return, as a scholar,
to the moment I had lived as an actor, and to understand the meaning of Portia's wound when a boy actor displayed it in Shakespeare's
playhouse.

Some of the practices of that playhouse—soliloquies, asides,
prologues, and epilogues—have left obvious textual traces. Others—
the resonance of voice and the nuance of gesture, the spectacle of
a bleeding thigh or a severed hand, the intermittent sunlight and
shadow of an open-air amphitheater or the deeper chiaroscuro of a
candlelit hall—have vanished. Still others—the restless groundlings
and the arrogant gallants, the rouged and petticoated body of the
boy actor—are inscribed paradoxically in the play texts. The texts
too belong among the playhouse practices, for, unlike their narrative
sources, they contain entrances, exits, and cues. They imply crosses,
pauses, and gestures. They are parsed into actions performed before
sullen, boisterous, or enthusiastic spectators and into scenes played
with congenial, indifferent, belligerent, or seductive partners, partners who step on one's skirts or one's lines, who smell of garlic or
owe the cat too much perfume. The ephemera of the stage, thus ma-
terializing the minutiae of the script, submit cultural narratives to the
players' sometimes opportunistic and often fortuitous interventions.

Variously constrained and enfranchised by these and other contingencies, the players produce the dramaturgical meaning of the
play for the spectators as they renegotiate the social meanings of the
theatrical occasion for themselves. For those who play Portia and

Brutus, the textual and subtextual resonances of Portia's wound may participate in an offstage dynamic in which status depends on skill or seniority. As the characters negotiate their roles, the players negotiate theirs. The blood that is shed on stage also flows through the corporate body of the troupe, carrying alliances, rivalries, flirtations from player to player. The wound an apprentice actor reveals to a shareholder may reverberate with the master's legal power to punish the servant. Or it may signify the boy's initiation into the quality, ushering a momentary egalitarianism into the *mise en scène*. The systematic and institutionalized vulnerabilities that resonate in Portia's words shape both the dramatic fiction of a woman's injury and the theatrical occasion for an actor's discipline. That discipline may transform the pain of Portia's wound into the player's pleasure and triumph.

Shakespearean Ways of Killing a Woman

While Portia's voluntary wound gives her the victory in the conflict of the orchard scene, it also foreshadows her suicide. It is one of what, following Loraux's *Tragic Ways of Killing a Woman*, I have called Shakespearean ways of killing a woman. Shakespearean ways are far more various than the sacrifices and suicides of Attic tragedy.[1] Suicide remains a frequent cause of death, but women also die by homicide, assassination, execution, and accident; they are hanged, drowned, poisoned, strangled, stabbed, and burned; they die at home and abroad, in public, in private, on stage and off.

These deaths too reveal subtexts of sacrifice and suicide. Shakespearean spectacles of the female body in pain also emerge from the protocols of a patriarchal society and testify to the resilience of an ancient discourse of gender and violence. In Shakespeare's Roman tragedies and those of his contemporaries, the old motifs of sacrifice and suicide emerge starkly from narrative and poetic sources. Resistant to Christianized folklore and humanist reinterpretations, Plutarch, Seneca, Ovid, and even the anonymous *Tragical History of Titus Andronicus* reiterate the old imperatives. They lead from Stoic resolution and Epicurean *urbanitas* toward a polis of furtive gods and mortified cannibals, where the tragic mask discloses the sources of its anguish. There, hymeneal blood at once guarantees and threatens the laws of exogamy, and so the sacrifice of a daughter can still structure a tragic action. Marriage and death are intertwined through the dangers of childbirth and through the entombing silence, chastity, and obedience legally enjoined on the feme covert, and so the suicide of the wife remains a resonant theme.

Ars Moriendi

Unlike the wound located "here, in the thigh" and displayed on the stage, Portia's suicide offers the player no opportunity to exercise his craft. Shakespeare's source, North's translation of Plutarch's narrative *Life of Marcus Brutus*, delineates her self-destruction: she "took hot burning coals and cast them into her mouth, and kept her mouth so close that she choked herself" (Bullough 5.133–34). In *Julius Caesar*, too, Portia devours her death: "[S]he fell distract, / And, her attendants absent, swallow'd fire" (4.3.155–56). But it is Brutus's quarrel with Cassius that engulfs her body:

Brutus: Portia is dead.
Cassius: Ha? Portia?
Brutus: She is dead.
Cassius: How scap'd I killing, when I cross'd you so?
(4.3.147–50)

Shakespeare is for once more reticent than the Athenian dramatists. There, women's deaths within the marriage chamber take place behind the *skene*, after which the corpse is wheeled out on the *ekkylema* and displayed.[2] Here, Portia's unexhibited body is evoked largely to create a frisson in a homosocial crisis.

The fictive chamber that encloses the character also inhibits the actor, for a death scene is not only something a character suffers; it is also something a player performs.[3] It is an ordeal, but also an opportunity, which in an offstage death belongs to the messenger. In *Julius Caesar*, the ordeal and the opportunity of Portia's death belong to the messenger Brutus—a Shakespearean way of killing a woman that denies the boy Portia his own art of dying.

Living and dying, Shakespeare's female characters are with few exceptions confined to the *locus*, the illusionistic space within which romantic and tragic actions are played. They rarely cross to the *platea*, where the clown's countervoice speaks "from outside the representative ideologies."[4] The Shakespearean clown, David Wiles remarks, playing *in propria persona*, is invariably an adult male (99). Neither he nor those heroes and villains like Hamlet and Richard III who also cross from the fiction of the *locus* into the unstructured space of the *platea* often speak from "outside the representative ideologies" of age and gender.

The *platea*, then, may have been for the boy actors less the site of bold subversions than the defended domain of the shareholders. Whatever powers and pleasures their masters found there, it did not encourage them to improvise, to find their youthful countervoice, to turn away from the misogynistic courses of ancient narratives. There are however places upon the Elizabethan stage far from the popular *platea* where the player's praxis may triumphantly transform a heroine's pathos. These places are created through the Senecanism that the elite tradition had contributed to the Shakespearean stage.

Seneca by Sunlight

Unlike Portia's death, Lavinia's takes place on stage and belongs to her role: "Die, die, Lavinia, and thy shame with thee, / And with thy shame thy father's sorrow die" [*He kills her*] (*Titus Andronicus*, 5.3.46–47, and stage direction). The character's ordeal is the player's opportunity. Yet the opportunity is fleeting. The frenetic action of the climactic scene hurries the playgoers' attention on to other murders:

Titus: [W]itness my knife's sharp point.
 He stabs the Empress.
Saturninus: Die, frantic wretch, for this accursed deed!
 [*Kills Titus.*]
Lucius: Can the son's eye behold his father bleed?

There's meed for meed, death for a deadly deed!
[*Kills Saturninus. A great tumult. Exeunt Lucius,*
Marcus, Aemilius, and others and enter above.]
                    (5.3.63–66, and stage direction)

Throughout this great tumult, the boy Lavinia is left to undertake
that most strenuous and disagreeable of a player's tasks: portraying
a corpse. Thus immobilized, he spends the last of the silence with
which the Elizabethan public playhouse, like the Athenian theater,
dowers a daughter for sacrifice.

   That silence, which proclaims the victim's ritual consent, is the
keynote of Lavinia's role and marks its sacrificial trajectory from
the opening scene. Immediately after Titus has betrothed Lavinia to
the newly elected emperor Saturninus, his brother Bassianus abducts
her: "Lord Titus, by your leave, this maid is mine" (1.1.276). Some
hundred lines later, he returns with Lavinia to answer the emperor's
charge:

Saturninus: Traitor, if Rome have law or we have power,
Thou and thy faction shall repent this rape.
Basianus: Rape call you it, my lord, to seize my own,
My true betrothed love, and now my wife?
But let the laws of Rome determine all,
Mean while am I possess'd of that is mine.
                                        (1.1.403–8).

This trial scene evokes the marriage strategy known in Roman law
as *raptus*, or bride theft. In the Theodosian code that criminalizes it,
raptus is the abduction of an unmarried woman by a man who hopes,
without a formal betrothal, "to force her parents' consent to what is
essentially a *de facto* marriage" (Evans-Grubbs, 61).

   The scene also registers conflicts in English law. While the medieval Westminster statutes, like the Theodosian code, are predicated
on distinguishing between lawful and unlawful exchanges of women,
sixteenth-century statutes begin to redefine rape as a violent crime
against a woman rather than a property crime against her guardians.[5]

Since the new laws acknowledge a woman's consent without validating her testimony, they escalate the violence of sexual crime. Injuries become the only admissible evidence of denial.

Titus Andronicus includes both the residual and the emerging ideas of rape in its story of the daughter's sacrifice. Throughout the trial of the *raptor* Bassianus and the *rapta* Lavinia, an archaic identification of rape and clandestine marriage implies that Lavinia's silence is consent. At the close of the rape and mutilation scene, an emerging recognition of endemic sexual violence demands that Lavinia be not only silent, but—notoriously—silenced: "Enter . . . Lavinia, her hands cut off, and tongue cut out, and ravish'd" (2.4, stage direction). Dismemberment provides the evidence required to distinguish rape from *raptus*.

Lavinia's irregular marriage has not permitted her safe passage from her father's house. Since she is still Titus's, her destruction repays the injuries he has inflicted: "fierce Andronicus would not relent: / Therefore away with her, and use her as you will" (2.3.165–66). And since she is still Titus's, she is, by precedent, lawfully vulnerable to his sword:

> [R]esolve me this:
> Was it well done of rash Virginius
> To slay his daughter with his own right hand,
> Because she was enforc'd, stain'd, and deflow'r'd?
> (5.3.35–38)

Twice exchanged, to Saturninus and to Bassianus, Lavinia's inauspicious rites of passage bear her in the two opposed directions that marriage is intended to evade. She passes beyond the verge of exogamy when she is raped by her father's enemies; she is then led back toward an incestuous *Liebestod*.

Lavinia's inexorable progress from *raptus* to rape to execution confines her within a dramatic fiction where a misogynistic narrative is enacted on her body. To this enactment, the popular theatrical tradition offers no resistance. Only Aaron, the Vice's direct descendant, benefits from the counterhegemonic *platea*, as he shares his motiveless malignity, restates the traditional blackness of the stage devil as racial difference, and affirms the equally traditional masculinism of the *platea*.[6] While Aaron retains the same chatty malevolence from his first entrance to his final exit, the scene of the boy Lavinia's greatest eloquence is paradoxically the scene in which his character is most brutally silenced.

This ill-famed scene in which Marcus grieves so voluably over the raped and mutilated Lavinia has often been called Senecan. Unlike other exuberant spectacles of carnage in the tragedy, it partly deserves the appellation.[7]

Senecan tragedy defines itself dramaturgically against the spectacles of the Roman stage and politically against the manias of the Neronian court. An adversarial discourse at once remote from public entertainment and wary of imperial power, it expends its energies on rhetorical, narrative, and poetic devices that deny the name of action in both theatrical and political arenas. It obsessively rehearses the errors and treacheries of an anarchic consciousness.

In the paludal atmosphere of *Thyestes*, where the Messenger's announcement of Atreus's cannibalistic banquet occupies fully half the text, this obsession erodes theatrical energy, slowly channeling the rhetoric of violence into a politics of despair. In *Titus Andronicus*, the public revelation that ends the banquet initiates the tumult of the final massacre. The rhetoric of violence points outward to theatrical spectacle, pressing language into enactment. The unyielding causality and emphatic closure of such scenes do not reproduce the malevolent convolutions of Seneca's universe.

Yet the notoriously Senecan amble of Marcus's epilogue to Lavinia's rape does run the certain risks and reap the uncertain rewards of adapting the Senecan disposition of dramatic time and space to the Elizabethan stage:[8]

> Who is this? my niece, that flies away so fast?
> . . . .
>   Why dost not speak to me?
> Alas, a crimson river of warm blood,
> Like to a bubbling fountain stirr'd with wind,

Doth rise and fall between thy rosed lips,
Coming and going with thy honey breath.

. . . .

Ah, now thou turn'st away thy face for shame!
And notwithstanding all this loss of blood,
As from a conduit with three issuing spouts,
Yet do thy cheeks look red as Titan's face
Blushing to be encount'red with a cloud.

. . . .

Come, let us go, and make thy father blind,
For such a sight will blind a father's eye.

. . . .

Do not draw back, for we will mourn with thee.
O, could our mourning ease thy misery!

(2.4.11–57)

Whatever crude and carnivalesque vigor animated the Rose production of *Titus Andronicus*, this harrowing scene is the legacy of Seneca's
prodigal textuality. In enlarging the contradictory motives of interpretation and denial, mourning and mythopoesis, the *dilatio* that
swells Marcus's speech slows the usually hectic action to an almost
Senecan torpor.[9]

Almost, but not quite. In Seneca's *Hippolytus*, Phaedra stabs herself at line 1200, while Theseus is reassembling the fragmented body
of his son. Engrossed in his grim task, Theseus does not acknowledge Phaedra's action or her corpse until line 1280. *Titus Andronicus*
does not replicate such radical isolation, for Marcus and Lavinia do
share a clearly delineated physical space. But Marcus's blazon of the
tortured body is a similarly otiose detour from the theatrically direct
route through the plot.

This detour sanctions Lavinia's theatrical intervention, for the
speech includes stage directions that pause to probe the meaning of
the *mise en scène*. As Marcus speaks, he conveys authorial stage directions to his partner: fly away, bleed, turn away, blush, draw back. The
technical and imaginative exigencies of these directions call the boy
player to the practice of his craft. Tension between the aestheticiza-

tion of the victim and the agency of the actor invites the boy to bleed and to blush, and so to turn Marcus's text into a gloss of Lavinia's eloquent silence.

Certainly twentieth-century productions have exploited this Senecan clash of verbal and visual cues to create a theater of cruelty in which, as Artaud recommends, the articulation of the body eludes "the customary language of words" (111). The scene, which then becomes Lavinia's, can also unite Artaudian somatics with Brechtian estrangement, creating what Rainer Nagele calls "Brecht's Theatre of Cruelty" (111–34).[10] Perhaps the Elizabethan apprentice too stole the scene from the shareholder or journeyman Marcus, creating some such Brechtian theater of cruelty, crossing the threshold of the narrative *locus*, not onto the clown's comic *platea*, but onto a tragic *platea* where a boy (or a woman) may act.

Like the *platea* of the popular tradition, this tragic *platea* of my imagination also estranges the scene, undermining dramatic illusion. Not through a plebeian countervoice, however. Rather it celebrates the histrionic excess of the player whose unbroken body blushes and bleeds at his own command. The tragic *platea* of *Titus Andronicus* is not conventional but occasional. It comes into being when Shakespearean Senecanism exposes an ancient narrative of sacrifice to the theatrical opportunism of the boy or woman who plays Lavinia.

The Joy o' th' Worm

There is a more subtle Senecanism in a later exploration of marriage and death, *Antony and Cleopatra*. Unlike Lavinia's execution, Cleopatra's suicide is an achieved rite of passage through eroticism into marriage:

> Methinks I hear
> Antony call; I see him rouse himself
> To praise my noble act. I hear him mock
> The luck of Caesar, which the gods give men

To excuse their after wrath. Husband, I come!
Now to that name my courage prove my title!
                              (5.2.283–88)

Cleopatra follows this claim to marital dignity with a maternal image:
"Peace, peace. / Dost thou not see my baby at my breast, / That sucks
the nurse asleep?" (5.2.308–10). This image, Ania Loomba suggests,
"tames" Cleopatra's "own earlier identification with the serpent, re-
placing the deadly Eastern inscrutability with a comprehensible version of the Madonna" (129–30). Cleopatra's suicide, then, would reiterate the classical protocols for a death in which a hero dwindles
into a wife.

    Yet the staging of Cleopatra's suicide partly eludes this domes-
tication of death. The serpent of old Nile maintains her histrionic
luster through the *coup de théâtre* that initiates the scene:

    The quick comedians
    Extemporally will stage us, and present
    Our Alexandrian revels: Antony
    Shall be brought drunken forth, and I shall see
    Some squeaking Cleopatra boy my greatness
    I' th' posture of a whore.
                              (5.2.218–21)

The celebrated bravura of Cleopatra's nonce verb subordinates the
dramatic fiction to the theatrical occasion: "The treatment Cleopatra
anticipates at the hands of the Roman comedians," writes Phyllis
Rackin, "is perilously close to the treatment she in fact received
in Shakespeare's theatre, where the word boy had an immediate
and obvious application to the actor who spoke it" ("Boy Cleopatra," 201).

    Since the boy Cleopatra alludes not only to his masculinity but
to his puerility, he jostles not only his own fiction of femininity but
also the structures of playhouse authority. The adult actors dominate

the crowded stage on which Lavinia is murdered, but the boy Cleopatra performs his death scene in a fatherless, masterless place:

> So, have you done?
> Come then, and take the last warmth of my lips.
> Farewell, kind Charmian, Iras, long farewell.
>   (5.2.290–92)

The boy Cleopatra kisses the boys Charmian and Iras and becomes
"fire and air" (5.2.289). The scene is Cleopatra's, yet it binds all three
apprentices into an ensemble reinforced by the shared line on which
Cleopatra dies:

Cleopatra: What should I stay—   *Dies.*
Charmian: In this [vild] world? So fare thee well.
                                    (5.2.313–14)

The originality of this tragic climax that takes place without father,
master, husband, hero, shareholder or journeyman, is, to be sure,
framed by the conventions of the popular playhouse. First, the
countervoice of the Clown who brings the asp disrupts the tragic dignity of the ensemble: "These same whoreson devils do the gods great
harm in their women; for in every ten that they make, the devils mar
five" (5.2.275–77). Later, Caesar rearranges the apprentices' tableau
to suit the conventions of the open-air stage for exhibiting corpses:
"Take up her bed, / And bear her women from the monument; / She
shall be buried by her Antony" (5.2.356–58). Yet neither the Clown's
jovial misogyny nor Caesar's chill authority deny the boy players
deaths of their own.

For the players, there is much joy of this worm, a jubilance
and exultation in their craft. Cleopatra's brave death has also con-
ferred another, posthumous reward on the boy player. The scene
still echoes, as Juliet Dusinberre remarks, in the imaginations of
twentieth-century actors and directors, who "manifest awareness of
the boy behind the woman which never occurs in their discussions
of other tragic heroines" (53). For this afterlife, the boy Cleopatra is

indebted to another strand of elite Senecanism: the metatheatricality of the children's companies.[11]

When the children's companies reopened at the turn of the century, they produced several neo-classical tragedies on the themes of female sacrifice and suicide, among them Marston's *The Wonder of Women, or the Tragedy of Sophonisba*, performed by the Children of the Revels at Blackfriars a year or two before *Antony and Cleopatra*. Like Shakespeare's tragedy, Marston's emerged from the Jacobean theatrical culture in which players, playwrights, spectators, censors, scripts, props, costumes, gestures, phrases, and inflections circulated among the playhouses in all the triumphant or disastrous permutations that collaboration, competition, and collusion might variously suggest. Such a culture both encourages and delimits experimentation within and across institutional structures, as the dramaturgical practices of one playhouse encounter the more or less resistant material circumstances of another.

In *Sophonisba*, Marston has diversified the allusiveness of his earlier *Antonio* plays. He has also modified their explicit theatricality, which exhibit the boy players mooting the demands of their roles: "I a voice to play a lady! I shall nere do it" (II *Antonio and Mellida*, Induction, 80–81). *Sophonisba* redirects this metatheatricality through the play's relentless exploitation of Senecan rhetorical and poetic devices. The abrupt ruptures of stichomythia, the digressive meanderings of ecpharsis, and the specious resolutions of *sententiae* contort the plot of *Sophonisba* much in the manner of Senecan tragedy, transforming the classical motifs of sacrifice and suicide into a lurid representation of sexual violence.

In act 1, scene 1, Sophonisba, the daughter of the Carthaginian general Asdrubal, becomes the bride of his ally Massinissa, but when war interrupts her wedding night, Asdrubal barters her to the malevolent king Syphax in exchange for further military aid against Rome. Like Lavinia, Sophonisba is twice exchanged. She too confronts the extremes of exogamy and endogamy, navigating a passage through rape to sacrifice. Throughout the play, she exploits increasingly ingenious variants on the bed trick to evade Syphax's increasingly feral attempts to rape her. When at last Sophonisba, like

Cleopatra, chooses suicide rather than live imprisoned in Rome, her death negotiates between the honorific suicide of the wife and the sacrifice of another daughter who failed to make her way from her father's house. Sophonisba is a "virgin wife" (5.3.103) whose anomolous status, like that of Shakespeare's riggish Madonna, only death can regulate.

Like some other plays of the children's companies, *Sophonisba* exploits the grandiose villainies of Senecan tragedy for an unsavory experiment in child pornography. Yet such metatheatrical grume enabled Shakespeare to design the sublimity of Cleopatra's suicide explicitly for the boy actors. Their debt (and that of their heirs, contemporary actresses) to the children's companies becomes conspicuous when absent, as in Thomas Heywood's *The Rape of Lucrece*, performed at the Red Bull in 1607. This is an adamantly popular play, unsullied, despite its classical theme, by the seductions of elitism.

The Rape of Lucrece is a very different kind of Roman tragedy. Though the playwright's *Apology for Actors* insists on the sober orthodoxy of the public playhouses, *Lucrece* enlists on the side of political turbulence from the usurpation of the first scene to the armed rebellion of the last. At the same time, Heywood's treatment of the rape itself involves misogynistic mockery that offers little scope for the art of the boy actor.

The railing of Junius Brutus, whose assumed madness gives him liberty to purge the infected body of Rome, and the songs of the patrician Valerius, who clownishly sings out the time during which Tarquin and Tullia have rendered his kind politically impotent, are expressions of the countervoice that validates revolt. The pretext for that revolt, the rape of Lucrece, is also subjected to the perspective of the clown. Played first as a tragedy derived from Livy and Shakespeare, the rape that roused the Roman patriciate to expel the Tarquins is immediately repeated as farce. This farce takes dramatic form in the bawdy song that follows the offstage rape:

> *Valerius, Horatius, and the Clown*
> *their Catch*
> *Valerius:* Did he take faire Lucrece by the toe man?
> *Horatius:* Toe man.

Valerius: Aye man.
Clown: Ha ha ha ha ha man.
Horatius: And further did he strive to go man?
Clown: Go man.
Horatius: Aye man.
Clown: Ha ha ha ha man, fa derry derry downe
                ha fa derry dino.

(2294–2304)

Thus sings the countervoice of the *platea*, rhyming its way past heel, shin, knee, and thigh, to reduce the matter of Rome to a salacious blazon. In violating the decorum of tragedy, the song undermines the chivalric ideology that makes the aristocratic female body a boundary marker and its unlawful penetration a pretext for civil wars. But Heywood's strategy for subversion authorizes a randy trio of goons to mock the victim of sexual violence. Since Valerius, played by the renowned comedian Robert Browne, is not graced with Touchstone's mordant wisdom or Feste's erotic melancholy, he more readily reveals the masculinism of the countervoice as he busks through his musical version of the rape of Lucrece.[12]

Like A and B, the clownish commentators of Medwall's *Fulgens and Lucrece*, Heywood's clowns display the misogyny that often characterizes popular strategies for eluding aristocratic hegemony. They direct the theatrical energies of the public playhouse toward a plebeian but androcentric perspective; they challenge hierarchies of rank and class while affirming sexual and domestic oppressions. The public playhouse reproduces those oppressions theatrically when it casts masters and apprentices to represent husbands and wives, fathers and daughters. It replicates them socially and economically when it denies the apprentices the fame that it grants heroes such as Alleyn and Burbage and clowns such as Tarlton, Kemp, Armin, and Browne.

The *mise en scènes* of the children's companies create no such masters, heroes, or clowns. Where almost every player is necessarily cast against type, discrepancies between actor and role grant the entire ensemble a countervoice. Young boys, costumed as warriors, witches, and royal virgins, frolic or flounder through imperial tragedies, mocking the symbolic order of age and authority. They shape the traditions of elite theatricality into extravagant parodies of hierarchy in the adults' workaday world.

They pay dearly for the privilege of mocking their elders. Legally defined as chattels, the choristers were kept more closely and trained more rigorously than the apprentices in the public playhouses.[13] Subordinated to the dubious privileges of their position, their franchise extends only as far as the stage where they encounter no journeyman Chiron or Demetrius to commit rape, no Valerius to annotate their sorrows with a clownish catch, no shareholding Titus to enforce a master's rights over an apprentice's body.[14]

Few Jacobean plays of the elite tradition are, at this distance of time and taste, stageworthy. Yet their innovations inflected Renaissance theatrical culture with a paradoxically democratizing extension of what Michael Goldman has called "the actor's freedom." Absorbed into Shakespeare's dramaturgy, not only Lyly's charm but Marston's sensationalism can be liberatory. If the boy actors cannot often leave the *locus* where narrative prevails, they may at least explore the theatrical energy on its borders. When Lavinia enters the territory that Marcus's *otium* creates, and when Cleopatra, Iras, and Charmian find themselves on a masterless stage, they more freely pursue the infinite variety of their characters and their craft.

Such Shakespearean ways of killing a woman do not merely reiterate the ancient myths of silence and consent. Refracting the fatal masquerades of femininity through the exquisite travesties of youth, Lavinia and Cleopatra animate the paradox that boys then (as women now) create their theatrical roles from materials at once strange and familiar to their social selves. Implicit in this paradox there is another: despite the technical demands of Lavinia's interminable pathos and Cleopatra's vertiginous multiplicity, performing these roles can be rather like child's play.

Agnosco Veteris Vestigia Flammae

In 1992, after a twenty-year hiatus, I took an acting class and worked once again on the role of Portia. Again I made discoveries that seemed self-evident once they had taken place. In my twenties, I had found Portia's courage through her vulnerability; in my forties, I learned how her erotic energy drives the orchard scene.

Portia is proud to be the daughter of dour Cato, proud to be Brutus's wife rather than his harlot, proud that, "being so father'd and so husbanded," she is "stronger than [her] sex" (2.1.296–97). Yet she is also a sexual creature struggling against an obscure threat to the fulfillment she once enjoyed:

> [U]pon my knees,
> I charm you, by my once commended beauty,
> By all your vows of love, and that great vow
> Which did incorporate and make us one,
> That you unfold to me, yourself, your half,
> Why you are heavy.
>
> (2.1.270–75)

What could I have known of Portia's "once commended beauty" when I first played her in my twenties? Only in these last few years have I learned that one speaks of "once commended beauty" only in the moments before commendation ceases.

Portia's sensuality is the role's alter ego, what Jacques Lecoq calls the countermask. The countermask, in Lecoq's gestural theater, replaces naturalism's psychological subtext. It is the mask within the mask, with an expression quite contrary to the one initially visible on the leather or papier-mâché. Revealed only through the posture and gesture of the actor who wears it, it is the cowardice of the domineering bully, the shyness of the gregarious bon vivant, or the sensuality of a severe Roman matron. Like Cleopatra's suicide, Portia's countermask is a tribute to the skill of the boy actor.

Like other scholars of Renaissance drama, I have sought knowledge of the boy actors in order to examine Shakespeare's representation of gender. Now that I am, once again, also an actor, these walking shadows no longer seem a curious relic of early modern sexual politics. They are instead my own distant ancestors. Seeking traces of the boy whose roles I had inherited, I found the laurels were always awarded elsewhere, to the clown Armin, the hero Burbage, or to

Field who outgrew women's roles. Even the boy Cleopatra, whose greatness grants him a posthumous influence on twentieth-century performance, remains anonymous. At last I had to create him, along with a reference work to chronicle his life. Here, from my imaginary archive, is *The Dictionary of Invented Biography* entry for the lad who created the roles of Shakespeare's women:

FARRANT, MICHAEL (1577?–1639), player in several London companies, including Shakespeare's; subsequently leader of a touring troupe on the continent. Born in Devonshire, about 1577, Farrant was the eldest child of a cobbler and a schoolmaster's daughter. From his father, locally celebrated as a storyteller, he heard of Alison Gross and Robin Hood. His mother, whose father had educated her, told him tales out of Ovid, Livy, and Vergil. He came to London in 1592 and by 1595 had joined the Lord Chamberlain's Men. He began his career playing Hermia and Celia. He went on to play Portia, Cressida, and eventually Cleopatra. Although specially celebrated for female roles, he occasionally played such epicene male roles as Osric and Lear's Fool.

He did not marry while resident in London, and indeed, there were rumors that he was in fact a woman. Contemporary witnesses report that his cheek remained smooth and his voice as supple as a soprano's, even when he was playing Cleopatra at the age of thirty. Perhaps these rumors were part of the reason he left London and began to tour central Europe. In Warsaw, Prague, and Budapest, he played Cleopatra, Lady Macbeth, and Lady Capulet. His younger brother CHRISTOPHER FARRANT accompanied him, playing Ophelia, Juliet, and Lady Macduff. Farrant never returned to England, but settled in Prague until 1618. Soon after the Thirty Years' War began, he went to Danzig (modern Gdansk), where he spent several years. He sometimes joined touring companies of English actors who played at the *Fechtschule*, a large outdoor amphitheater built along the lines of the Fortune Playhouse in London. There he played Hamlet for the first time. He had begun traveling again by 1624, eventually settling in Brussels, where he died in 1639.

Several of his letters survive, written to the costumer Elizabeth Cornish, sister of the player Giles Cornish. These letters describe Far-

rant's European performances in venues ranging from village fairs to
the courts of princes, at one of which he was given a sapphire ring
and brooch following a performance of *Antony and Cleopatra*. He reports playing to audiences who knew little or no English, describing
the way he was nonetheless able to communicate: "As our understanding comes from our hearts," he wrote on July 12, 1614, "so the
meaning of the words passes into our voices and bodies and the playgoers understand."

After his death, his Brussels landlady sent Farrant's belongings
to Elizabeth Cornish, including miniatures of a boy and a girl, inscribed on the verso as "Charles" and "Maria." They are dressed in
the style of circa 1620 and are thought to have been his children. Who
their mother was (or, were the rumors of Farrant's sex true, who their
father was) is unknown. It is thought that Charles and Maria were
members of the Farranti, a commedia dell'arte troupe touring France
and Italy during the 1650s. The Farranti were renowned for innovation; their *Mask of Columbine* is the only surviving *commedia* scenario
in which a female character plays masked.

Several memorials of Michael Farrant were published in London, including the "Epitaph for the Player Michael Farrant," thought
to have been written by Elizabeth Cornish:

> Egyptian queen, romane wife,
> And Troyan slave: He gave these life
> While he did live, and with his death
> They all must moulder i' th' earth,
> Which, cover him til Time has made
> Of all his Parts a single shade.[15]

Ethnicke Lamentations

There our murdered brother lies
Wake him not with women's cries
Mourn the way that manhood ought—
Sit in silent trance of thought.
　—William Drennan, *The Wake of William Orr*

AMONG THE SPEECHES Ian McKellen performed in his solo show, *Acting Shakespeare*, was Mistress Quickly's description of Falstaff's death. He comforted his imaginary Falstaff, biding him " 'a should not think of God." He put his hand into the bed and felt Falstaff's feet, "as cold as any stone." Then he felt "up'ard and up'ard, and all was as cold as any stone." McKellen's performance was, if not as cold, as polished as any stone. He squeezed and squinched and screaked himself into a falsetto femininity that was perhaps close to the original spirit of Shakespeare's character. Closer, surely, than Judi Dench's womanly Mistress Quickly in Kenneth Branagh's film of *Henry V*. In Dench's corporeal characterization, Mistress Quickly was literally inspired, breath animating each gesture and inflection. With breath came grief, and with grief a poignant dignity.

Dench's performance was more moving, but McKellen's was revelatory. Arch and provocative, it created (however inadvertently) the only truly successful Brechtian alienation effect I have ever seen in the theater: it revealed the space between the player and his part, through which I first glimpsed the cultural traditions that have made lamentation women's work. Not only McKellen's performance, but that of Shakespeare's original Mistress Quickly began to seem like theft—as though a Titan had stolen not fire from the gods, but tears from mortal women.

Multa Gemens

In early modern England, as in other cultures, to perform the rites of death is almost invariably women's work: "It is surely no accident," Maurice Bloch observes, "that in nearly all the cultures we know, it is principally women who are expected to weep, whether this be the organised weeping that we find in such places as Iran, or the disorganized individual weeping of Britain or France" (224). Nor is it accidental that the representation of lament—the male performance of female grief—pervades the world of Shakespeare's histories. Although military maneuvers and diplomatic strategems drive them forward, again and again these plays pause over atavistic images of the pollution—and the power—that clings to women who weep.

Players and critics who agree on little else agree that the dearth of women's roles in Shakespeare grows to something of great constancy in the histories. Yet when an actress is past playing Juliet and Viola she will find more roles in the histories than in any other Shakespearean genre. The mothers, widows, and women of sorrow who are so often absent from the comedies, tragedies, and romances are paradoxically present in this masculinist genre. Of the Shakespearean characters explicitly presented as mothers, half appear in the histories. And half the widows as well.[1]

Most of the roles, certainly, are not large. Women cast in the histories must spend long hours in the rehearsal room, waiting to play their few scenes. Still, the comic, tragic, and romance plots in which dying mothers leave their infant Rosalinds, Cordelias, and Marinas to fathers and to fate, have little power over the *dramatis personae* of the histories. For these plays that trace the bloodlines through which sovereignty flows must acknowledge the bartered princesses and bereaved queens on whom their genealogical enterprise depends: "Never present in patriarchal history, women could only be represented," observes Phyllis Rackin, "and what they represented was the material physical life that patriarchal discourse could never completely capture or control" (*Stages of History*, 193).

What "patriarchal discourse could never completely capture or control," theatrical representation can sometimes poignantly reanimate. Lament is a fragment of the physical life of historical women preserved in Shakespearean amber. It is at once savage and sophisticated, a feral cry that intrudes upon civil ceremonies and also an exacting art elaborated over many generations. As the playwright's rhetoric translates ritual into theater, the player's dream of passion both evokes and effaces the stylized violence and eldritch bawdry of lament.[2]

Elegy and Lament

Throughout the first three plays of the Lancastrian tetralogy, mourning seems rather men's than women's work. *Henry VI* Part 1 opens with the heraldic funeral of Henry V, performed exclusively by the play's male *dramatis personae*:

> Hung be the heavens with black, yield day to night!
> Comets, importing change of times and states,
> Brandish your crystal tresses in the sky,
> And with them scourge the bad revolting stars
> That have consented unto Henry's death.
>
> (1.1.1–5)

Bedford's request that the heavens be hung with black refers, as editors note, to a canopy that projected over the stage, traditionally draped in black when a tragedy was presented. The stage draperies mimic those that decorated churches during heraldic funerals, whose quality and quantity displayed the exact rank of the deceased. The heralds themselves, whose presence Bedford acknowledges in line 45, wore long mourning robes and over them, elaborately embroidered tabards, symbolizing the authority that the crown delegated to them for ordering the ceremony.[3]

In this *mise en scène* where death is interpreted visually, the silent heralds are more than supernumeraries. They give the scene its cultural resonance as well as its theatrical effect. The heraldic funeral originated in the late Middle Ages, an innovation that asserted the special status of the armigerous in despite of Death the Leveler.

Where the traditional rites for ordinary people enabled a community of mourners to maintain spiritual relations between the living and the dead, the heraldic funeral was individualistic, its raison d'être, the extravagant display of status. It was at the same time authoritarian, since that status could be ratified only by decree of the College of Arms.[4]

During Elizabeth's reign, the heraldic funeral came increasingly under state control through the offices of the College of Arms. Its costly furnishings were regularly imposed from above upon an increasingly truculent aristocracy. But imposed it was, for the heraldic funeral served the crown's purposes. In presenting the arms and achievements of the deceased to his legitimate heir, the heralds affirmed stratification and stability.[5]

Henry V's funeral fails to ensure stability. Even as the rite is performed, the eulogies that Bedford, Gloucester, Exeter, and the bishop of Winchester speak in Henry's praise degenerate into contention:

> Cease, cease these jars and rest your minds in peace.
> Let's to the altar. Heralds, wait on us.
> In stead of gold, we'll offer up our arms,
> Since arms avail not now that Henry's dead.
> Posterity, await for wretched years,
> When at their mothers' moist'ned eyes babes shall suck,
> Our isle be made a nourish of salt tears,
> And none but women left to wail the dead.
>
> (*1 Henry VI*, 1.1.44–51)

Bedford's prophecy will come to pass, although not much before Henry VI gives way to Richard III. For much of *Henry VI*, there are men enough to wail the dead. Above all, throughout Part 1 there is Talbot, who commemorates Salisbury at Orleans, and then Bedford at Rouen. Finally, at Bordeaux, he speaks his own elegy and his son's.

Talbot's mourning takes a form that Robert C. Jones calls "heroic renewal," in which the spirit of "the valiant dead" inspires the mourner to action. The eulogy for Salisbury exemplifies the process:

Accursed tower! accursed fatal hand
That hath contriv'd this woeful tragedy.
In thirteen battles Salisbury o'ercame;
Henry the Fift he first train'd to the wars;
Whilst any trump did sound, or drum struck up,
His sword did ne'er leave striking in the field.
. . . .
He beckons with his hand and smiles on me
As who should say, "When I am dead and gone,
Remember to avenge me on the French."
Plantagenet, I will . . .
. . . .
Frenchmen, I'll be a Salisbury to you.
Pucelle or puzzel, Dolphin or dogfish,
Your hearts I'll stamp out with my horse's heels,
And make a quagmire of your mingled brains.

                                        (1.4.76–109)

Like the heraldic funeral of the opening scene, Talbot's elegy is both individualistic and authoritarian. Talbot serves Salisbury's memory, which in turn serves Talbot's desire to succeed him.

As the heraldic funeral, with its sober provisions for patrilineal succession, extrudes individual acquisitiveness, the elegy, from its beginnings in Theocritus, Bion, and Moschus, serves both to mourn the dead and aggrandize their heirs. For what the heraldic funeral is to communal rites of mourning, the elegy is to traditional lament. Elegy is a lament, observes Peter Levi, that has "strayed" from its ritual origins in women's mourning for the dead. In this wandering it gathers "boasting and praises and usually some talk of vengeance" (9, 11).[6]

When Talbot's vengeance is achieved, with "at least five Frenchmen" dead "for every drop of [Salisbury's] blood," (2.2.8–9), he vows to erect

A tomb, wherein his corpse shall be interr'd;
Upon the which, that every one may read,

Shall be engrav'd the sack of Orleance,
The treacherous manner of his mournful death,
And what a terror he had been to France.

(2.2.13–17)

Talbot's boasting, praising, and talk of vengeance demand the continuity of the social order for which Salisbury died. If his threats seem
to out-Herod Herod, yet he restricts his vengeance to a world arrayed
in armies, courts, and families, where Salisbury's inscribed monument may remain legible to unborn generations. Literacy snatches
hierarchy from the jaws of death. So too after the battle of Agincourt
in *Henry V*, the French herald Montjoy will crave Henry's leave "To
book our dead, and then to bury them; / To sort our nobles from our
common men" (4.7.73–74).

The last elegy of the tetralogy is Henry's grisaille pastoral for
the father who has killed his son and the son who has killed his father
(3 *Henry VI* 2.5). After that, Bedford's dire prediction is fulfilled:
England becomes "a nourish of salt tears" where there are few but
women left to wail the dead.

Scenes of Rude Impatience

From the first scene of *Richard III*, the labor of last things becomes almost exclusively women's work, as the strangely solitary
Lady Anne follows Henry VI to the grave. A woman is by default
and against the regulations of the heralds, a deposed king's chief—
and only—mourner. The meager burial of this "poor key-cold figure
of a holy king," Jones observes, suits the opening of *Richard III*,
as Henry V's heraldic funeral suited the opening of *1 Henry VI*, for
"dead victims rather than dead heros live in memory here, and they
haunt the present rather than inspiring it" (32).

The contrast between the funerals of Henry V and Henry VI
is not simply between public pomp and private sorrow, nor does
Richard III merely exchange the triumphant emulation of heroes for
the horrible apparition of victims. Certainly, for the women who

weep in Shakespeare's histories, the dead are not testators who bequeath their courage, lands, and titles to the living. They are husbands, fathers, sons, and brothers who leave behind them only grief and dread. Yet women's lamentation is not sequestered behind a domestic cordon sanitaire. There is less boasting and praising among the women of the histories than the men, but there is much talk of vengeance:

> Lo, in these windows that let forth thy life
> I pour the helpless balm of my poor eyes.
> O, cursed be the hand that made these holes!
> Cursed the heart that had the heart to do it!
> Cursed the blood that let this blood from hence!
>
> (1.2.12–16)

Although she speaks of harvest when the corn is green, Anne's tears are not helpless. Nor are they medicinal, for they are shed within a world where women transform mourning into mayhem.

This transformation takes place through a rhetoric unashamed of its rancor. When Elizabeth enters from Edward's deathbed, the Duchess of York asks her, "What means this scene of rude impatience?" "To make an act of tragic violence," she responds (2.2.38–39). Elizabeth's vengeance strives against the natural world, engulfing cosmos in chaos:

> All springs reduce their currents to mine eyes,
> That I, being govern'd by the watery moon,
> May send forth plenteous tears to drown the world!
>
> (2.2.68–70)

The microcosmic sacrifice of tears does not renew but rather destroys the macrocosm that exacts it. In this cataclysm, lamentation so distends and disfigures that those who weep seem almost as much transformed as the corpses they lament.

The She-Wolf of France

It is Margaret whom grief transforms most fully. In the course of her journey from *1 Henry VI* to *Richard III*, Margaret loses all but grief, rage, and a certain pride, as lamentation at last becomes a craft in which incessant practice makes her perfect. Excluding Henry VI, who appears as corpse and then ghost in *Richard III*, Margaret is the only character to appear in each of the Lancastrian plays. She becomes something like a tragic protagonist when the entire tetralogy is produced. (So, on the crowded stage of Adrian Noble's *The Plantagenets*, Penny Downie's Margaret was the one enduring presence, the one character whose story continued to unfold.)[7]

She first enters, at the close of *1 Henry VI*, in the aftermath of battle. She is, as commentators have observed, the third of the play's dangerous Frenchwomen, the avatar of Joan of Arc, who will be led off to execution in the following scene.[8] The prize that the earl of Suffolk gathers from among the dead and dying, she begins the tetralogy as a figure of fatal lust.

Her intimacy with death increases after Suffolk's assassination in Part 2, when she enters cradling his bloody head:

> Oft have I heard that grief softens the mind,
> And makes it fearful and degenerate;
> Think therefore on revenge and cease to weep.
> But who can cease to weep and look on this?
> Here may his head lie on my throbbing breast;
> But where's the body that I should embrace?
>   (4.4.1–6)

Amidst *Henry VI*'s scenes of heraldic ceremony, martial *laudatio*, and pastoral elegy, Margaret's erotic energy ripens into a savage lamentation that evokes the severed heads and bleeding hearts of folktales and border ballads.

Her journey into savagery continues in Part 3, where she ruthlessly presides over the torture and battlefield execution of her enemy:

Come make him stand upon this molehill here

.   .   .   .

Look, York, I stain'd this napkin with the blood
That valiant Clifford with his rapier's point
Made issue from the bosom of [your] boy;
And if thine eyes can water for his death,
I give thee this to dry thy cheeks withal.

.   .   .   .

I prithee grieve, to make me merry, York.

.   .   .   .

Why art thou patient, man? Thou should'st be mad;
And I, to make thee mad, do mock thee thus.
Stamp, rave, and fret, that I may sing and dance.
                                        (1.4.67–91)

Maddened and athwart chivalric codes of elegiac restraint, Margaret finally unsettles the purposes of her allies as well as her enemies. Her political and military presence casts its dark shadow on matrilineal Lancaster, as the queen wages war to enforce her son's succession to the throne.[9]

On a stage whose heavens are hung with black, to dramatize the relations between mother and son is, sooner or later, to represent lamentation. Edward's death at Tewkesbury brings forth the first of Margaret's maledictions:

But if you ever chance to have a child,
Look in his youth to have him so cut off
As, deathsmen, you have rid this sweet young prince!
                                        (5.5.65–67)

With Edward's death, Margaret's natural life too seems to end. Henceforth she will perform a work of death sanctioned only by things that are themselves unhallowed.

When she reappears in *Richard III*, she is something like a revenant whose mortal dross of adultery and ambition have been consumed in purgatorial fires. She hovers, cunning and vulturine, on the margins of Richard's morbid kingdom:

> So now prosperity begins to mellow
> And drop into the rotten mouth of death.
> Here in these confines slily have I lurk'd,
> To watch the waning of mine enemies.
> A dire induction am I witness to,
> And will to France, hoping the consequence
> Will prove as bitter, black, and tragical.
>
> (4.4.1–7)

With Anne's curses and Elizabeth's complaints, Margaret's choral commentaries augur the lamentation of act 4, when Lancastrian Margaret and the women of York unite to curse those who caused their bereavement.

Like a hired mourner, Margaret laments her own dead at others' funerals. Consummate skill gives her curses a dire efficacy to which Elizabeth can only aspire: "O, thou didst prophesy the time would come / That I should wish for thee to help me curse / That bottled spider, that foul bunch-back'd toad" (4.4.79–81). And so Margaret tutors Elizabeth in imprecation:

> Forbear to sleep the [nights], and fast the [days];
> Compare dead happiness with living woe;
> Think that thy babes were sweeter than they were,
> And he that slew them fouler than he is.
> Bett'ring thy loss makes the bad causer worse;
> Revolving this will teach thee how to curse.
>
> (4.4.118–23)

In their grief, the women of York and Lancaster create a sororal heterocosm. Their ritualistic lament is mantic and magical, a spondaic liturgy for the bringing-in of retributive violence: "Dead life, blind sight, poor mortal-living ghost, / Woe's scene, world's shame,

grave's due by life usurp'd" (4.4.26–27), "Earth gapes, hell burns,
fiends roar, saints pray / To have him suddenly conveyed from hence"
(4.4.75–76). Unlike elegy, such lamentation leaves behind no inscribed monuments. Women's words of grief are only

> Windy attorneys to their client's woes,
> Aery succeeders of [intestate] joys,
> Poor breathing orators of miseries,
> Let them have scope! though what they will impart
> Help nothing else, yet they do ease the heart.
>
> (4.4.127–31)

These "breathing orators of miseries" do more than "ease the heart."
They also, at times, threaten the state. Audible at the crossroads
where religion and politics meet, women's lamentation is, in one culture after another, at one epoch after another, subject to restrictive
legislation.

Hinc Illae Lachrimae

The lamentation scenes of *Richard III*, Harold Brooks observes, recall the ritual mourning of the classical *Troades*: Anne evokes the
sacrificial victim Polyxena and Elizabeth the paragon of marital and
maternal virtue Andromache. Like Hecuba, the Duchess of York has
given birth to the firebrand that consumes her country; Lancastrian
Margaret dwells among the Yorkists as Spartan Helen dwelt in Troy
(Brooks, 725). Whether or not these parallels demonstrate a literary transmission of Euripidean odes and Senecan soliloquies, they
suggest an anthropology of performance through which women's
mourning rituals entered both classical and Elizabethan play texts.
Attic tragedy and the Shakespearean chronicle each originated during a moment of Western history in which the institutionalization
of theater participated in the formation of a state. Each incorporates
women's mourning rites into men's theatrical representations, transforming them into the materials of political identity.[10]

In archaic (as indeed in modern) Greece, women in mourning expressed grief viscerally and vociferously, channeling it into ritual laments that included demands for blood vengeance, bitter complaints against gods and men, ecstasies of deathward longings that abjure life and hope. Such songs for the dead can be sung only by those who are immersed in and inspired by *ponos*. To be in *ponos* is to be in pain, yet *ponos* is the active antonym of tragic *pathos*. *Ponos* is grief and exertion, toil and trouble. In the Hippocratic tradition, it is the distressed body's attempt to restore its equilibrium. In the context of lament, it is a method for achieving depth and authenticity in performance. For lamentation is an art, and, as the focus of funerary rites, grants a skillful creator and performer religious, social, and domestic powers that could at times disrupt the sexual politics of Greek culture.[11]

Fifth-century Athens, as Margaret Alexiou and Gail Holst-Warhaft demonstrate, submitted these powers to restrictive legislation. Solon, Plutarch reports, had abolished many traditional rites: the practice of lacerating the flesh at funerals, of reciting set dirges, and of bewailing one person at the funeral ceremonies of another (21.4–5). In the "Letter to Apollonius," Plutarch justifies the prohibitions: mourning is "feminine, and weak, and ignoble, since women are more given to it than men, and barbarians more than Greeks, and inferior men more than better" (113a).

The lament was replaced by the *epitaphios logos*, an encomium for a patriot fallen in the service of the democratic *polis*. The *epitaphios logos* allowed the city to take precedence over the family, as men's patriotic praise of military and civic virtue displaced women's laments for husband, mother, father, brother, sister, daughter, or son. Still, lament remains audible; *ponos* becomes a subtext of tragic *pathos*, as scenes of rude impatience are inscribed within the tragic odes of Aeschylus, Sophocles, and Euripides.

The *Oresteia* records the transformation of ritual lament into civic tragedy. From this perspective, the entire action of the *Agamemnon*, the story of Clytemnestra's revenge, is her lament for Iphigenia (an action eloquently foreshadowed in the play of rage and grief on the face of Irene Papas's Clytemnestra in the final lingering frame of Michael Cacoyannis's film, *Iphigenia*). *The Libation Bearers* also represents the forbidden lament: taking the occasion of Electra's rites for Agamemnon to mourn their own dead, the chorus of enslaved Trojan women spurs Electra to vengeance through a lament that violates each of Solon's prohibitions. They lacerate their flesh: "My cheek shows bright, ripped in the bloody furrows / of nails gashing the skin" (24–25). They prophesy vengeance: "under earth / dead men [hold] a grudge still / and smoulder . . . at their murderers" (39–41). And they secretly lament their own dead: "under veils I weep / the vanities that have killed / my lord: and freeze with sorrow in the secret heart" (82–84). Finally, *The Eumenides* offers the celebrated binding song of the Furies, which, like the forbidden lament, is the articulate magic of crones, witches, professional mourners:

> Over the beast doomed to the fire
> this is the chant, scatter of wits,
> frenzy and fear, hurting the heart,
> song of the Furies
> binding brain and blighting blood
> in its stringless melody.
>   (341–46)

To free Orestes from the blood guilt of matricide in the closing trial scene, Athena must subdue this ancient, magical lament to the new power of the *polis*, coaxing the Furies out of their shrill-voiced *ponos*, transforming them into the Kindly Ones.[12]

Sine Teste Doleant

As the female characters of Greek tragedy elude Solon's restrictions, those of the Shakespearean histories exceed the recommendations of English priests and preachers. For like the *epitaphios logos*, the English funeral sermon of the sixteenth and seventeenth centuries took the moderation of ostentatious grief as an ideological task. In early modern England, however, moderation represents a further stage in the centuries-long process that Frederick Paxton calls "Christianizing death." Christianizing death demanded dispelling pagan (and Jewish) dread of the ritual pollution that follows contact with death.[13]

"Christianizing death" also demanded inculcating restraint. 1 Thessalonians commands that the congregation "sorrow not, even as others which have no hope" (4.13). Writing of his mother's death in his *Confessions*, Augustine elaborates: "We did not think it [fitting] to solemnise that funeral with lamentations, tears, and howlings: for this is the fashion whereby those that die miserably, or be utterly perished as it were, use to be lamented" (9.12). Citing Paul's command, Saint John Chrysostom is among the first but not the last to recommend excommunication for those who hire women to incite lament (374).

Yet pagans, Roman as well as Greek, had long endeavored to moderate the expression of grief. The Twelve Tables, following Solon's legislation, provided that "Women shall not during a funeral lacerate their faces, or tear their cheeks with their nails; nor shall they utter loud cries bewailing the dead" (10.8); "When a corpse is prepared for burial at home, no more than three women, their heads covered with mourning veils, shall be permitted to perform this service" (10.7). Yet women and lamentation remained so intertwined in Rome that, while the substantive derived from the past participle of *praeficio*, *praefectus*, refers generally to an overseer or superintendent, the noun *praefica* refers to a woman who is chief mourner at a funeral.

Lamentation was a women's ritual that neither Athens, nor Rome, nor Christendom could annul. Centuries later, the humanists of the Italian Renaissance renewed demands that public grieving be restrained and restricted to men. "Order that wailing women should not be permitted to step outside their own homes," wrote Petrarch to Francesco da Carrara in 1373; "if some lamentation is necessary to the grieved, let them do it at home and do not let them disturb the public thoroughfares" (78).[14] The public thoroughfares of early modern Europe were to be occupied only by processions of "priests, monks, candlebearers, and paupers, stiff and solemn supernumeraries" who would create events of "religious dignity in which the singing of psalms replaced the traditional cries and gestures of mourning" (Ariès, 168).

In the north, too, similar caveats suggest analogous anxieties. In England, these anxieties were exacerbated though not initiated by the religious conflicts of the Reformation. Catholic ceremonies were condemned, as James Pilkington's *Exposition upon Nehemiah* (1585) put it, for the "great cost and sumptuousness" of their "shrines, tombs, tapers, torches, candles, mourning coats, feastings etc. which do no good to the dead and are too chargeable and unprofitable to their friends" (317). *Mr. Boltons Last and Learned Worke of the Foure Last Things* (1635) argues "that we should show ourselves Christians, and by the sacred rules of religion ever prevent that unseasonableness and excess, which many times with a fruitless torture doth tyrannize over the hopeless hearts of mere natural men."[15] In *The Rule and Exercise of Holy Dying* (1651), Jeremy Taylor advocates banishing from the deathbed "the pomps of death, the disguises and solemn bugbears, the tinsel, and the actings by candlelight, and proper and phantastic ceremonies, the minstrels and the noisemakers, the women and the weepers, the swoonings and the shreikings, the nurses and the physicians, the kindred and the watchers" (103).

Both Anglicans and Puritans proscribed the pagan superstitions they thought had engulfed the Catholic church. Once the primitive and the decadent were thus identified, antiquarian inquiries into the customs of ancient Greece and Rome began to fuse with a queasy ethnographic exploration of Catholicism in the country against which England was waging its first imperial war.

Ethnicke Lamentations

The significance of Elizabeth's Irish Wars for Shakespeare's histories, and especially *Henry V*, has often been placed in the context of Essex's 1599 expedition. Jonathan Dollimore and Alan Sinfield argue that the presence of Jamy the Scotsman, Fluellen the Welshman, and Macmorris the Irishman, fighting alongside English Gower in Henry's army at the battle of Agincourt, by dramatizing "an ideal subservience of margin to centre," provides a "displaced, imaginary resolution" to the intractable contemporary problem of Ireland (217,

224).[16] Commentaries on topical events, however, do not exhaust the ways that Elizabethan culture deploys Gaelic difference to establish its political realm, nor does *Henry V*'s quartet of captains exhaust the histories' fascination with the Celtic fringe. As the ritual laments of ancient Greece turn the mythic materials of Athens's civic tragedy into performance, so the keening of Celtic Ireland lends the Shake-spearean chronicle an elemental theatricality that the annals of Hall and Holinshed could not have imparted.

Among the barbarous customs that English and Anglo-Irish commentators attributed to the Gaelic Irish were the incest and cannibalism that would later serve to demonize the inhabitants of America. There were also more circumstantial reports of alien mari-tal, childbearing, child-rearing, and funeral customs. Of these, the behavior of women at deathbed and grave site was especially horri-fying, as the reiterated descriptions of Edmund Campion, Edmund Spenser, Barnaby Rich, William Camden, and Fynes Morrison re-veal.[17] In Ireland, writes Camden in *Britannia*,

When one lieth ready to die, before he is quite gone, certain women hired of purpose to lament, standing in the meeting of cross highways, and hold-ing their hands all abroad, call unto him, with certain outcries fitted for the nonce, and go about to stay his soul as it laboureth to get forth of the body, by reckoning up the commodities that he enjoyeth of worldly goods, of wives, of beauty, fame, kinsfolk, friends, and horses. . . . At length they piteously make moan and say, that the soul is now ready to leave the body, is going away to these kind of haggish women that appear by night and in darkness. But after it is departed once out of the body, they keep a mourn-ing and clapping of their hands together. Now they follow the corpse when it goes to burial, with such a peal of outcries, that a man would think the quick as well as the dead past all recovery. (147)

In Ireland, as in Scotland and the north of England, women played a far more prominent part in funeral rites than they did in the politi-cally central south and east. They served as bearers or token bearers of coffins; they led the funeral from the house; they sang the lyke-wake dirge and keened over the body of the dead.[18]

The women who performed these tasks were not only the moth-ers, wives, sisters, and daughters of the dead, but, like the mourners of the ancient Mediterranean, paid professionals. The antiquarian John Weever, describing the "ethnicke lamentations" of the Greeks and Romans, remarks that

They had, at these burials, suborned counterfeit hired mourners, which were women of the loudest voices, who betimes in the morning did meet at appointed places, and then cried out mainly, beating of their breasts, tearing their hair, their faces, and garments, joining therewith the prayers of the defunct . . . still keeping time with the melancholic music. This is a custom observed at this day in some parts of Ireland. (15)

The women of Ireland may not only go about to stay the departing soul, they may disrupt its Christian interment after it has gone. In *De rebus in Hibernia gestis* (1584), the Anglo-Irish commentator Richard Stanyhurst too shudders at the excesses of women's lamentation:

As soon as a leading member of their community expires, many women may be seen running hither and thither through field and village, piercing the ears of all with wolfish and shrieking cries. I cannot easily describe the great wail with which they fill the church where the funeral rites take place. They shout dolefully through swollen cheeks, they cast off their necklaces, they bare their heads, they tear their hair, they beat their brows, they excite emotion on all sides, they spread their palms, they raise their hands to the heavens, they shake the coffin, tear open the shroud, embrace and kiss the corpse and scarcely allow the burial to take place. (156)

In obstructing the performance of official rites, these acts reassert traditional roles that religious authorities were still striving to eradicate centuries later. From the synod of Tuam in 1631 through the pastoral letter of the archbishop of Cashel in about 1800, the church repeatedly forbade the keening of hired mourners. So tenacious was the custom that in 1748 the Diocese of Leighlin made "those who will or do make it their trade to cry or rhyme at burials" liable to excommunication for a second offense.[19]

    In the context of the English invasion, traditional lament could represent not only religious recalcitrance but political resistance. So it does for Spenser in *A View of the Present State of Ireland*. Like Weever, Spenser compares contemporary Irish to ancient mourning customs. He draws on classical historiography that identified the

Celts and the Scythians to make the sixteenth-century Irish, like the
ancient Scythians, the barbarous enemies of empire:[20]

There be other sorts of cries alls used amongs the Irish which savor greatly of
the Scythyan barbarism as their lamentations at their burials with despairful
outcries and ymoderate wailings . . . [Some] think this custom to come from
the Spaniards for that they do so inmeasurably likewise bewail their dea[d].
But the same is not proper Spanish but altogether heathenish, brought in
first thither either by the Sycthians or by the Moors which were Africans but
long possessed that country, for it is the manner of all pagans and infidels to
be intemperate in their wailings of their dead. (105)

Unlike Stanyhurst and other writers, Spenser does not discourse
upon the "hideous howlings" and "wolfish cries" of Irishwomen's
customary rites, but he does record an incident in which those rites
have become embroiled in political as well as religious conflict:

At the execution of a notable traitor at Limerick called Murrough O'Brien
I saw an old woman which was his foster mother take up his head whilst he
was quartered and sucked up all the blood running thereaout saying that the
earth was not worthy to drink it and therewith also [steeped] her face, and
breast and torn [hair] crying and shreiking out most terrible. (112)

Like Shakespeare's image of the French Queen Margaret cradling
Suffolk's bloody head, Spenser's harrowing anecdote of the Irish
peasant preserves a primeval, almost necromantic expression of alien
grief.[21] Thus the rites of death that clerics such as Taylor and Bolton
sought to exile from the emergent Protestant nation return via the
"ethnicke lamentations" of narrative and drama.

The Vild Prison of Afflicted Breath

Even after Margaret's departure from Shakespeare's stage, women's
lamentation infuses the rhetoric of the chronicles with an uneasy
magic. Constance's journey through *King John* in some measure re-
peats Margaret's through *3 Henry VI* and *Richard III*, for Constance too moves from political ambition to a frenzy of lament. Until
Arthur's capture in Act 3, she struggles to intervene in the course

of military and diplomatic events, chastising France and Austria for making peace with John:

> You have beguil'd me with a counterfeit
> Resembling majesty, which being touch'd and tried,
> Proves valueless. You are forsworn, forsworn!
> You came in arms to spill mine enemies' blood,
> But now in arms you strengthen it with yours.
> The grappling vigor and rough frown of war
> Is cold in amity and painted peace,
> And our oppression hath made up this league.
>
> (3.1.99–106)

And here, expressing maternal ambition through political machination, Constance remains in *The Troublesome Reign*, for she does not return to lament Arthur's capture. In Shakespeare's version, however, Constance reappears. Her body has become, in King Philip's description, "a grave unto a soul / Holding th' eternal spirit, against her will, / In the vild prison of afflicted breath" (3.4.17–19). She turns from her perjured allies to apostrophize death:

> O, amiable, lovely death!
> Thou odoriferous stench! sound rottenness!
> Arise forth from the couch of lasting night,
> Thou hate and terror to prosperity,
> And I will kiss thy detestable bones,
> And put my eyeballs in thy vaulty brows,
> And ring these fingers with thy household worms,
> And stop this gap of breath with fulsome dust,
> And be a carrion monster like thyself.
>
> (3.4.25–33)

Constance's rasping oxymorons, like those of Elizabeth, Margaret, and the Duchess of York, exquisitely express the morbid vitality of lament. They enable Constance to ally herself with forces that erode political prudence and religious faith. She exits spuring the representatives of the church and state that cannot help her lament: "Fare you well! Had you such a loss as I, / I could give better comfort than you do" (3.4.99–100).

Funeral Games

Women continue to mediate between the living and the dead in the second tetralogy. Some, like Margaret, strive to perpetuate the retributive violence of internecine war: "Thou dost consent," the Duchess of Gloucester warns Gaunt,

> In some large measure to thy father's death,
> In that thou seest thy wretched brother die,
> Who was the model of thy father's life.
> Call it not patience, Gaunt, it is despair.
> In suff'ring thus thy brother to be slaught'red
> Thou showest the naked pathway to thy life,
> Teaching stern murder how to butcher thee.
> That which in meaner men we entitle patience
> Is pale cold cowardice in noble breasts.
> What shall I say? To safeguard thine own life
> The best way is to venge my Gloucester's death.
>   (*Richard II*, 1.2.25–36)

Inextricably entwined in feudal violence, women's lament again concludes and then recommences the work of *homo necans*. For Graham Holderness, this minatory speech reveals that the duchess has allied herself to patriarchy, first in espousing "masculine values and feelings that repress the female," and second in accepting the need for a male champion to defend her honor, which is anyway defined as the honor of her menfolk (174–75). Certainly, the duchess has not got clean hands. But her theatrical energy does not obey the law of the father. The Duchess of Gloucester, like the Erinys, speaks for the ata-

vistic obligations of kinship against the emerging claims of the *polis*.
She sings a version of the ancient binding song, calling for a blood
vengeance that the state can ill afford.

Women's work of mourning is not always so bloodthirsty in the
second tetralogy. In the taverns and brothels of the *Henriad*, those
"meaner" characters whose status enforces patience only watch and
wait, listening for death and recognizing it by touch:

Now I, to comfort him, bid him 'a should not think of God; I
hop'd there was no need to trouble himself with any such thoughts
yet. So 'a bade me lay more clothes on his feet. I put my hand into
the bed and felt them, and they were as cold as any stone; then I felt
to his knees, and so up'ard and up'ard, and all was as cold as
any stone.

                                                      (*Henry V*, 2.3.19–26)

Weeping in earnest for the man who had once died in jest, Mistress
Quickly's exuberant idiolect recalls the scene in *1 Henry IV* during
which Falstaff's counterfeit corpse rises to dispute Hal's plans for his
burial:

Prince: Embowell'd will I see thee by and by,
Till then in blood by noble Percy lie.
                          Exit. Falstaff riseth up.
Falstaff: Embowell'd! if thou embowel me to-day,
I'll give you leave to powder me and eat me too
tomorrow.

                                                      (5.4.109–13)

Hal's offer is as generous as it is inappropriate. "Embowelling," that
is, disemboweling, readies the corpse for the costly heraldic funeral.[22]
Falstaff relinquishes the status that Hal would confer upon his corpse
to retain a protean fluidity that is "the true and perfect image of life
indeed" (5.4.119).

This "image of life" is for many commentators the spirit of the
carnivalesque. Falstaff is the Lord of Misrule, the grotesque body

of the people or a "literary fat lady" of irresolvable paradoxes and
unquenchable comedy.²³ Indeed, Falstaff's shape-shifting continues
even after he has come to dust, for Mistress Quickly's report does
not mortify the meaning of the corpse:

Nym: They say he cried out of sack.
Hostess: Ay, that 'a did.
Bardolph: And of women.
Hostess: Nay, that 'a did not.
Boy: Yes, that 'a did, and said they were dev'ls incarnate.
Hostess: 'A could never abide carnation—'twas a color he
never liked.
Boy: 'A said once, the dev'l would have him about women.
Hostess: 'A did in some sort, indeed, handle women; but then he was
rheumatic, and talk'd of the whore of Babylon.

(Henry V, 2.3.27–39)

Falstaff's dubiously penitential gestures do not immediately bring in
the Lenten deprivation that should follow carnivalesque indulgence.
Rather, his repentance evokes residual traditions of funereal festivity.
In "Remaines of Gentilisme and Judaisme," John Aubrey describes
the card-playing, ale-drinking, smoking, games, and masquerades
that were still to be found at Yorkshire wakes in the late seventeenth
century:

To this day, they continue the custom of watching and sitting-up all night
till the body is interred. In the interim, some kneel down and pray by the
corpse, some play cards, some drink and take tobacco; they have also mimi-
cal plays and sports [for instance] they choose a simple young fellow to be a
judge, then the suppliants (having first blacked their hands by rubbing under
the bottom of the pot), beseech his Lordship: and smut all his face. They
play likewise at hot cockles. (173)

Ecclesiastical authorities fulminated against these customs, and especially against masquerades of role reversal and erotic games of hot
cockles, but they endured even into the Restoration.²⁴

The ludic requires the ergic; the wake cannot be held until the corpse has been laid out. In assigning the description of Falstaff's death to Mistress Quickly, Shakespeare seems also to charge her with the task of preparing Falstaff's corpse for burial. For it is not only women who weep but women who must risk the pollution of death: "It is they who must wash the corpse and then wash themselves. . . . Again and again women are *given* death while the social order is re-affirmed elsewhere" (Bloch, 215; 224). So it is in early modern England. Christianity had denied the ritual pollution of death, yet the whirligig of time was bringing in a change that would renew ancient terrors of decay and dissolution. During the late sixteenth century, the dead came to inspire a new dread and to require a new breed of exorcist who would transform cadavers into commodities.

The Funerals of Unqueened Katherine

In Shakespeare's last English history play, the collaborative *Henry VIII*, women are quite explicitly "given death while the social order is reaffirmed elsewhere." In act 4, the dying Katherine bids her friends farewell and turns to her gentlewoman Patience:

> Remember me
> In all humility unto his Highness.
> Say his long trouble now is passing
> Out of this world; tell him in death I blest him
> (For so I will.) Mine eyes grow dim. Farewell,
> My lord. Griffith, farewell. Nay, Patience,
> You must not leave me yet. I must to bed.
> Call in more women.
>
> (4.2.160–67)

This scene is immediately preceded by the coronation of Anne in 4.1. It is followed by the announcement of Elizabeth's birth in 5.1. The dramatic structure quarantines the women who do the work of death. Katherine's gentlewomen are "given" their lady's death while "elsewhere" the birth of Elizabeth reaffirms the continuity of the Tudor dynasty.

Like the histories of the 1590s, *Henry VIII* registers contemporary conflicts over death and mourning. But by the time of its 1613 performances, this conflict had entered a new phase. Like the rites of birth, which were passing from the control of midwives into that of obstetricians, the rites of death were passing from communities of women to organizations of men.[25] As obstetricians supplanted midwives, so barber-surgeons and undertakers supplanted the women who traditionally laid out corpses. Furnishing funerals came to provide more and more business for workers in lead such as Abraham Greene, joiners such as Clement Chapman, and drapers such as Henry Machyn. By the end of the seventeenth century, such men would be incorporated into a new guild. They would do a deed without a name, becoming euphemistically known as undertakers.[26] They would by then have commodified funerals for the middle class. During the early decades of the century, however, the College of Arms still struggled to control a market that depended on the surgical embalming of aristocratic corpses.

The expense of the heraldic funeral stirred discontent. The women of the aristocracy had other objections. Citing their unwillingness to submit their bodies to the male embalmer's knife, noblewomen demanded speedy night burials to circumvent the regulations of the College of Arms. In 1572, Mary, countess of Northumberland, left instructions "not in any wise to let me be opened after I am dead. I have not loved to be very bold afore women, much more would I be loath to come into the hands of any living man, be he physician or surgeon." In the following decades, numerous other women including Lucy Lady Latimer, Katherine Lady Cavendish, and Helena, marchioness of Northampton, left similar instructions in their wills. Frances, duchess of Richmond and Lennox, refusing the services of the surgeons, asked that her women prepare her body for burial, "for so my sweet Lord out of his tender love commanded me that I should not be opened." Instead, she would "be presently put up in bran, and in lead before I am fully cold." Queen Elizabeth herself, who had always insisted that her courtiers endure the expense of the heraldic funerals, left instructions that she not be disemboweled; court gossip reported both that her wishes were and were not respected.[27]

By the 1630s, the nobility had more or less freed themselves from

state-controlled funerals. "Almost all the ceremonial rites of obse-
quies heretofore used are altogether laid aside," remarks Weever; the
nobility and gentry are now "silently buried in the night time, with
a torch, a two-penny link, and a lantern; or parsimoniously interred
in the day time by the help of some ignorant country-painter, without the attendance of any one of the officers of arms" (17–18). The
heralds continued to protest, but by midcentury, only royal funerals remained unquestionably within the jurisdiction of the College
of Arms, and only royal corpses were compelled to endure the embalmer's knife.

The distinction between the night burials of the rebellious aristocracy and the heraldic state funeral was not fully articulated until
well after Shakespeare's time. Nevertheless, the Elizabethan testa-
trices' resistance to the heraldic funeral illuminates Katherine's requests to Patience:

> When I am dead, good wench,
> Let me be us'd with honor; strew me over
> With maiden flowers, that all the world may know
> I was a chaste wife to my grave. Embalm me,
> Then lay me forth. Although unqueen'd, yet like
> A queen, and daughter to a king, inter me.
>
> (4.2.167–72)

While the historical Katherine was buried in 1536 as the "late weife
of Prince Arthur,"²⁸ Shakespeare's Katherine orders a funeral that
would resolve "the King's Great Matter" in her favor. She requests an
evisceration that at once preserves the physical body and reinstates
its significance in patrilinear history.

Katherine's testament is a fictive palimpsest over the historical
record of the revolt that the duchess of Richmond, the marchioness
of Northampton, and other noblewomen were waging against embalming. Where they left plain instructions, hers are as contradictory
as Mistress Quickly's malapropisms: Katherine requests winding as
well as embalming. Winding, the traditional laying-out performed by
women who wind the corpse in a sheet with herbs and flowers, ritu-

ally expresses the biological cycles that the linear processions of the heraldic funeral deny. Katherine further specifies "maiden flowers" for this winding, which, like Ophelia's "virgin crants," were the funeral gear of the unmarried. "It is a custom still at the funeral of young virgins," Aubrey observes, "to have a garland of flowers carried on the corpse" (174).[29] "Maiden flowers" evoke Katherine's unconsummated nuptials with Arthur, obscuring her marriage to Henry. Katherine's women can wind the corpse of Prince Arthur's virgin widow, but they cannot embalm Henry's queen—an operation for which, several years before *Henry VIII* was performed, the barber-surgeons had secured a monopoly.[30] Katherine's body cannot be wound with "maiden flowers" and yet embalmed as a queen consort.

Katherine, like Anne, Elizabeth, Margaret, Constance, and Mistress Quickly, reinterprets the tradition of lament on the Shakespearean stage. Women's mortuary labor was at once given and taken away, as their cultural performance of the rites of death was incorporated into the theatrical representation of a transvestite stage. Playing the grieving women of the histories, male actors subdued the female folk genres of lamentation, translating women's customary rituals and political protests into the language of their theatrical craft. They exploited the traditional association of women and mourning for a new commercial enterprise conducted entirely by men.

Thus the hired mourner became a professional player, transformed, like Woolf's Orlando, into the same person of a different sex. As in ancient Athens, ritual once again evolved into theater. Again the raging Erinys became the benevolent Eumenides; again they bequeathed to the player their ancient art of lamentation; again they taught him how to weep for Hecuba.[31]

Verum Factum

This history of lament is my last scholarly essay; like the story of my own scholarship, it has a theatrical epilogue. This epilogue is for me also a new prologue, for it represents a way of transforming historical knowledge into theatrical practice. The contradiction between winding and embalming in Katherine's dying speech, discovered through historical research, can be resolved via a player's process.

Reading this speech silently makes Katherine's demands seem simultaneous and hence contradictory. Hearing and *a fortiori* speaking the words makes them sequential, restoring the process through which Katherine arrives at her decision. "Strew me over / With maiden flowers, that all the world may know / I was a chaste wife to my grave. Embalm me." During the caesura that precedes her request for embalming, Katherine takes a breath and changes her mind. For in the pause, audible if not legible, between the reflection "I was a chaste wife to my grave" and the demand "Embalm me," Katherine rescinds her initial request. Unqueened Katherine forgoes her maiden flowers, willing to endure the mortuary insult that will confer regal dignity on her corpse. Historical inquiry revealed a textual paradox; now theatrical process resolves it: breathing when Katherine breathes, I learn what she knows.

Epilogue

Well, go thy ways, thou bundle of straw. I'll give
thee this gift: thou shalt be a clown while thou
liv'st.
> —Thomas Nashe,
> *Summer's Last Will and Testament*

KATHERINE'S CHOICE BETWEEN winding and embalming is, alas,
my only example of interconnection between theatrical and historical interpretation. More often, the knowledge of the study, however
hard won, seems specious and superficial on stage. It becomes obfus-
cation and evasion, its meticulous methodologies merely dishonorable stratagems for keeping one's hands clean and one's withers un-
wrung. Like sandbags strapped to a dancer's ankles, it hinders me at
every step.

This is my own ancient dilemma of forum and hall, practice and
theory, performance and scholarship, which I have never resolved.
While trying, I submitted to the judgments of many committees.
From them I learned that I was too radical and too conservative, too
subtly theoretical and too crudely empiricist, too flamboyantly theatrical and too mustily learned, too devoted to arcane scholarship
and too engaged in pedagogical experiments. Though I would like to
think I was a free and inquiring spirit whom Bounderby's rules could
not shackle, some would say I was an unclubbable character with a
nervous disposition, unstable convictions, and an arrogant aversion
to the workaday world.

At last I learned I was too old. In the spring of 1992, I left academic life. With some relief, much chagrin, and not a little terror, I

found myself, in my late forties, in almost exactly the position that I'd fled from at the unemployment office in my late twenties.

Since then, I have worked to retrieve the art I relinquished. I discovered that the restrictions of academic discourse had taken their toll on me physically. The scholarly spinal column deteriorates unnoticed, until one day breath is fetched so shallowly that verse becomes unspeakable. The voice that "interrogates" and "problematizes" grows cranky, phlegmatic, and lusterless. After half a lifetime spent learning Shakespeare's plays, I found the lines came to me only in unscannable fragments, jangled, out of tune, and harsh. While I was studying the material culture of Shakespeare's England, I had lost the actor's corporeal knowledge. While I was reading essays about the erasure of women's voices, I had quite literally lost my own. My voice, once trained to sing and to speak Shakespeare's verse, had to be trained all over again. The quiddities and quodlibets of academic life had very nearly done to my throat what the sacrificial knife did to Iphigenia's.

Now, in 1997, having served yet another apprenticeship, I am performing once more. When I recall my academic years, I am grateful that, like Winters's Gawain, I have been allowed to leave with what I know. What I know never really answered my questions about the public and private playhouses of Elizabethan England, but it has given me some stories to tell about them. And all this while, the ancient dilemma has remained a habit of thought, a collection of penumbral categories, not only in this book of stories for scholars but also in my theatrical stories for popular audiences.

In *Shakespeare by Heart*, an actress, speaking directly to the audience, recalls Shakespearean roles she has played. As she enters the playing space, the draped furniture, trunks and boxes, costume rack, and various props—an hourglass, wine goblets, a mortar and pestle, a skull, a crown, a knife—evoke her memories. Moving in and out of her characters, she performs parts of the plays, and as she does, she discovers how these roles have shaped her experience.

With Cressida, she realizes the dangers of playing Shakespeare's "dark ladies"; with Helena, the "Doctor She" of *All's Well that Ends Well*, she reflects on the time she lost the courage to practice her art.

As Emilia, who tried too late to challenge a world in which men murder their wives, she recalls the cruelty of her own early marriage. She finds the lucidity of Margaret's wild lamentation in the course of mourning her mother's death, and in the three father-daughter relationships of *King Lear* she traces her changing relationship to her father as he, and she, age. At last, she discovers the Shakespearean role she most needs to play: the clown. As the piece ends, she transforms herself once more to sing Feste's epilogue, "When I was a little tiny boy," from *Twelfth Night*.

When I began working on *Shakespeare by Heart*, this actress was my alter ego, the one who didn't leave the unemployment office so discouraged that she became an English major. As I revised and rehearsed, she and I became more alike. I have given her more of my memories; she has shared her courage and confidence, and some of her skill. With her help, I begin anew. I play Shakespeare once more.

The Ancient Dilemma Again

In the audience are people who think Cressida is a kind of Toyota. They have had a high school or college course in Shakespeare and don't much like what they learned. Others have seen Olivier's or Branagh's films, and the productions of the local Shakespeare festival, popularized with a postmodern panache. None of them fret over historicism and essentialism or ask whether Shakespeare's characters are people. Some have come because it's Shakespeare; some have come although it's Shakespeare. Some have come because it's theater and there's a chance, however slight, that they will discover something to help them live their lives. It's a very slight chance. For it is only I on stage, with all my imperfections on my head. Nevertheless, that is my charge.

I neither fulfill the playwright's intention nor resist the strategies of the text. These are critical fantasies that only enfeeble a response that must be reckless, visceral, inevitable. I gather each character into myself or perhaps flow outward to meet her. Eventually, I feel her coiled in my spine waiting for impulses of memory and imagination. These impulses arise from Shakespeare's words or my life, from Shakespeare's knowledge or my own experience, in some stratum where such distinctions lack difference.

Yet there are differences I don't want to lose. I have seen too many performances in which the torque of American method acting glozes over the mysteries of Shakespeare's alien polis, smoothing the rough spots, turning verse into prose, treating the characters like next-door neighbors who have had too much to drink. This is weary, stale, flat, and unprofitable. But they know already, my unlearned audience, that Shakespeare is not their contemporary. They know the difference between the fancied creatures of an early modern mind and this body that, as they watch, will travel an hour toward its grave. What I have to tell them is that despite all this, Shakespeare is my contemporary, as I am theirs. There's life in it yet.

Notes

Prologue

1. So "personal criticism" is now another weapon, no sooner wielded than blunted, in the debate about critical theory and political practice. Examples of autobiographical criticism include Freedman et al.; Greene and Kahn; Kaplan; Miller; and the essays in Veeser. For discussions, see Gorra's judicious essay and the more severe strictures of Simpson.

2. I have remarked on the distinction between theater and theatricality in "Acts of Resistance," 107–8, and will return to the more recent term "performativity" below. See the introductions to Veeser's *Confessions of the Critics* and to Parker and Sedgwick's *Permormativity and Performance*.

3. Studies of rhetoric and English Renaissance drama include Sr. Miriam Joseph; Doran; Altman; Eden; and more recently, Desmet. On rhetoric and the Elizabethan actor, see B. L. Joseph; Burns; and Roach. I am especially indebted to Altman's study of the relation between rhetorical structure and drama as a method of inquiry.

Seneca by Candlelight

1. For a summary of references to this paradigm, see Bruce R. Smith, 4–7.

2. The scholarly division of native and neoclassical elements in Renaissance drama is thus part of the larger story of the ascendance of English literature over classics. On "the rise of English," see Williams, *Writing in Society*, 177–91; Eagleton, *Literary Theory*, 17–53; and Jardine's feminist critique of these histories in "Girl Talk." For the United States, see Wallace Douglas and the bibliographical essay in Graff and Warner.

3. These paragraphs do not, of course, pretend to trace the rise and fall of critical attention to Renaissance neoclassicism. They simply introduce some analytic terms and categories that I inherited from earlier scholarship, which I take up in subsequent sections and chapters. For recent discussions of the classics and English Renaissance drama, see Braden; Martindale and Martindale; Miola; and Bruce Smith.

4. While there are various monographs on individual companies like Gair's *The Children of Paul's* and Eccles's *The Rose Theatre*, many influential studies, such as Cohen's *Drama of a Nation*, Bristol's *Carnival and Theater*, Helgerson's *Forms of Nationhood*, and Howard's *The Stage and Social Struggle in Early Modern England* focus more or less exclusively on the public playhouses. Others, such as Dollimore's *Radical Tragedy*, discuss texts from the public and private playhouses and even closet drama independently of their venues.

5. Cf. Peter Burke: "To understand any item of culture, we need to place it in context, which includes its physical context or social setting, public or private, indoor or outdoor, for this physical space helps to structure the events which take place in it" (108). For a useful summary of differences between indoor and outdoor venues for contemporary performers, see Mason, 87–88. Royal Shakespeare Company productions at the Swan in Stratford, which have enabled reappraisals of numerous Elizabethan and Jacobean plays, offer Shakespeare scholars presumptive evidence for the significance of venue in creating the historical as well as modern meanings of Renaissance drama. On the building of the Swan and its operations from the opening in 1986 through 1988, see Mulrayne and Shrewring.

6. Andrew Gurr's 1987 *Playgoing in Shakespeare's London* sifts the evidence thoroughly. He casts doubt on the view that the elite withdrew from the public playhouses much before 1630 (76–77), but ultimately confirms "the broad assumption that from 1599 on the composition of audiences at different playhouses did diverge quite markedly," citing the admission price as the strongest material basis for the assumption (72, 75).

7. Quoted in Gair, 137.

8. Harbage summarizes the issues of the original debate in "Elizabethan Acting." In its contemporary variant, the debate can be represented by Jardine, who argues for the visibility (and hence homoeroticism) of the boy actor, and McLuskie, who argues for a conventionality that renders the actor's gender largely invisible. There are, of course, theater historians who have devoted essays and monographs to the children's companies, several of which are cited below.

9. Orgel, who does distinguish carefully between choristers and apprentices, also brings out new information on the "clumsy use of the apprentice system" in the adult companies, by which the boys were apprenticed not as actors, who had no guild, but as goldsmiths, drapers, and so on, according to the guild memberships of many of the players (*Impersonations* 64–68). Since, despite this curious split between their de jure and de facto status, they were apprentices by both criteria, I continue to refer to them as such.

10. Quoted in Gurr, "Who Strutted and Bellowed," 97.

11. Nungezer's 1929 *Dictionary of Actors* remains the most comprehensive catalog of biographical information, but for further discussion of Alleyn,

Burbage, and the incipient star system in the public playhouses, see William Armstrong. On Kemp and Armin, see Wiles. Field is the subject of a monograph by Brinkley.

12. On the playing style (or styles) of the children's companies, see Shapiro; Foakes. Hunter's comment in *John Lyly* is also helpful: the children could not "impose the illusion of living their parts and express powerful adult emotions over a coherent range of adult life." They were, however, able "to speak clearly and move becomingly in a group, with a total effect of grace and fluency" (99). After the revivals in 1599 and 1600, all but some dozen of the extant plays are satirical comedies. The tabulation is based on Appendix B, "The Repertories," 343–50, in Harbage, *Rival Traditions*. For a full discussion of the generic differences between public and private playhouse repertories, see Reibetanz.

13. On the legal histories of the children's companies, see Hillebrand. On the legal status of the child actors, see also Bradbrook, 220, 238, and passim; and Gurr, *Shakespearean Stage* 93–97.

14. This so-called war, some historians argue, originated in personal animosities among the dramatists. Others suggest a publicity stunt designed to increase theater attendance, an artistic experiment with new dramatic forms, or an ideological conflict between the plebeian public playhouse and the elite private theater. Then again, it may all have been the invention of nineteenth-century scholars rather than seventeenth-century playwrights. Still, the texts associated with this otherwise nebulous skirmish, which include plays by Jonson, Marston, and Dekker, as well as the Cambridge *Parnassus* plays, are valuable sources of contemporary comment on theatrical practice. For a full discussion of the Elizabethan evidence for a Poetomachia and of its elaboration among nineteenth- and twentieth-century critics, see Omans. On Jonson's role in it, see Kay.

15. Since the Wood edition of Marston's *Histriomastix* is unlineated, I have cited it by page, act, and scene numbers.

16. Cunningham contrasts this "moral" style with what he calls the "sweet" style, offering these terms to replace C. S. Lewis's prejudicial "drab" and "golden" styles.

17. My discussion of the relevant Greek and Roman texts draws throughout on Trimpi, to whose guidance through the complexities of the rhetorical tradition I am deeply indebted.

18. An analogous shift characterizes the history of Attic comedy. The spectacular theatricality, obscure diction, and formidable invective of Aristophanes' political fantasies make his style a comic parallel to Aeschylean grandeur. But New Comedy, like Euripidean tragedy, made the old forms seem primitive to the cultivated critics of later times. In his *paragone* of Aristophanes and Menander, Plutarch condemns the earlier playwright for much the same reasons that Aristophanes' Euripides had condemned Aeschylus.

He is a poet for the uneducated, careless, full of noise and bombast, mixing "tragic, comic, pompous, and prosaic elements, obscurity, vagueness, dignity, and elevation, loquacity, and sickening nonsense" (*Moralia* 10:853d). Menander's diction, on the other hand, is "so polished and its ingredients mingled into so consistent a whole that [it] appears as one." Plutarch's praise reinforces the association between elitism and *akribeia*: "for what reason, in fact, is it truly worthwhile for an educated man to go to the theatre, except to enjoy Menander?" Menander invites philosophers and men of learning, "to a meadow flowery, shady, and full of breezes" (853e–854c).

19. For further discussion of the classical reputations of Plautus and Terence, see Chalmers, Duckworth, Rinconi, and Wright.

20. The vexed question of the original auspices for Senecan tragedy, with its assumptions about and implications for performance, is adjudicated by Fantham (48–49). Echoes of declamation in Senecan tragedy, Bonner observes, include "the cast of the speeches, the development of *loci communes*, especially in the Choruses, the superabundance of *sententiae*, the nature of the descriptions, and even the characterization and subject-matter of the Tragedies themselves" (160).

21. These phrases are taken, respectively, from Wilson, Ludham (quoted in Howell, 111), Hoskyns, and Webbe, but the categories are omnipresent throughout the Renaissance. They emerge, for example, in forensic rhetorics (Hoskyns, Elyot); sermons (Hooker, Ludham); Terentian commentaries (from Donatus and Evanthius through Heinsius); and poetics (Puttenham, Webbe, Sidney). There are also, of course, tremendous changes in the uses to which the categories are put. While religious rhetoric retains some of the characteristics of ancient deliberative oratory, political rhetoric, directed to Renaissance monarchs, takes on aspects of epideixis. (See Fumeroli, "Rhetoric, Politics, and Society.") Lawyers you have always with you, and so forensic rhetoric passed through antiquity to the Renaissance most its old self. I do not know of a full study of rhetorical education at the Inns of Court, but there are essays by Schoeck and by Bland. In his introduction to the second volume of *The Reports of Sir John Spelman*, Baker observes that "some of the [moot] cases had cryptic names, such as *Jacob and Esau*, *Le Verge*, *Rosa inter spinas*, *Lesperver*, *Parva rosa*, and so on. This suggests that they constituted a familiar cycle, passed down from one generation to the next" (133). It also seems to suggest a fictional element reminiscent of the Roman declamations. On Italian Renaissance Terence commentaries, see Weinberg and Herrick; on sixteenth-century preaching treatises, see O'Malley.

22. The Latin text is as follows: "Sciendum quod his qui tragoedias in theatris recitabant, actus pugantium gestibus populo repraesantabant. Sic tragicus noster pugnam Christi populo christian in theatro ecclesiae gestibus suis repraesentat, eique victoriam redemptionis suae inculcat." *Gemma*

Animae, lib. 1, cap. 73, "De Tragoediis." Quoted in Bevington, *Medieval Drama*, 9.

23. On "the close study that the theorists made of their audiences," see Caplan, 130–31, and Murphy, 279. For a full discussion of the development of the *sermo ad clerum*, see Chenu.

24. See, for example, "De modo compenendi sermones," by the fourteenth-century English Dominican Thomas Walys. On sermon *exempla*, see Jacques de Vitry. For discussions of the preaching revival, see Owst and Smalley. The quotation is from *Cilium Oculi Sacerdotis*, quoted in Owst, *Preaching in Medieval England*, p. 196.

25. Quoted in Oesterly, 100. On the empathetic relation between doctrine and drama, see Prosser, 43–64; Jeffrey; and Wickham, *Early English Stages*, 3:127–30. For a recent and wide-ranging inquiry, see Knapp: "[D]espite a resurgence of Marxist criticism, and our increasing awareness of the dialogic character of all texts, I would not want to claim that the plays embody a dialectical tension between official teaching and popular expression or entertainment. The difficulty, rather, is the absence of such a contradiction, and of any other obvious opposition in these texts between earnest and game, high and low, sentence and integument" (45). For a recent full-length study of medieval drama and rhetoric, see Enders.

26. *The Chester Mystery Cycle*, quoted in Mills, p. 73.

27. The Corpus Christi plays do not of course owe their theatrical devices to Attic tragedy, but V. A. Kolve calls attention to two documents in which medieval writers explicitly take up the dilemma with which Greek philosophers, rhetoricians, and dramatists had also wrestled. The first, the fifteenth-century *Dives et Pauper*, states the ancient dilemma in terms strikingly similar to those of Flavius Philostratus. In Philostratus's *The Life of Apollonius of Tyana*, the Greek Apollonius argues that true reverence imagines the gods in the noblest forms, such as Phidias's colossal statues of Zeus and Athena. The Egyptian Thespesion counters that high and holy mysteries can only be evoked through lowly animal forms of secret, symbolic significance (Philostratus, 6.19). While Apollonius brightly hopes that mimesis can transcend human ignorance, Thespesion, despairing of metaphor and similitude, strives for startling unlikeness. Similarly, *Dives et Pauper* asks, "Why ben aungelles peynted in liknes of young men sith they be spirites & haf no bodies?" and answers, like Philostratus's Greek, that "There may noo peyntoure peynte a spirit in his kind. And therfore the bettre representacion they be peynted in the lyknesse of a man / Which in soule is mooste according to aungellys kynde." Like Philostratus's Egyptian, Kolve's second text, a post-Reformation version of the banns for the Chester plays, doubts the power of mimesis to represent divinity. It announces that God will be only a voiceover in that day's pageant, "for no man can 'proportion' to the

godhead." The new technique encodes a new aesthetic criterion. Whatever resemblance humanity may bear to its gods now seems inadequate to dramatize the divine; whatever art cannot reproduce in illusionistic proportion can no longer be represented at all. See Kolve, 30–31. On Philostratus's *Life of Apollonius*, see Trimpi, *Muses* 103–4. For remarks on the banns as evidence of post-Reformation attitudes toward images, see Woolf, 313–14.

28. For contemporary descriptions of the effects of candlelit performances at Oxford and Cambridge, see Boas, 100; and at Blackfriars, see Chambers 2:46–47.

29. Cope and Gibbons both discuss *Dido*'s humor as a function of its theatrical context.

30. On this and other declamations as sources for other plays, see Waith, "*Controversia*," "*Pericles*," "Fletcher," and *Pattern of Tragicomedy*, 87–98. See also Altman, 28–34 and passim.

31. Mary Beard devoted much of her 1946 study, *Woman as Force in History*, to demonstrating that when English common law is compared either to equity courts or to Roman law, its bias against women becomes evident (87–155; 181–214). Milsom suggests that the origins of English equity lie in testators' desires to bequeath property to brotherless daughters who could not inherit under common law (87). Although there is, as far as I know, no full discussion in recent feminist scholarship, Jordan also raises the question of gender and the equity courts, 5 and 291–92.

32. In *Arguments for a Theatre*, Barker, one of a group of playwrights whose somber explorations of eros and politics have earned them the name "the new Jacobeans," sets forth his relation to seventeenth-century theater, and especially to Middleton, whose *Women Beware Women* he has rewritten.

33. The contemporary performance artist for whom mice are disposable props is Joe Coleman. See Carr, 154–58.

34. For a discussion of the contrast between polemical and commercial drama, see Yachnin. On the radical effects of Greville's *Mustapha*, see Dollimore, 120–33. Hall discusses what may have been Anne's most startling theatrical experiment, *The Masque of Blackness*.

Iphigenia in Durham

1. The historical method I was seeking was, I suppose, a cross between what Elaine Showalter calls gynocritics (131–32), a problematic method for earlier periods, and "the new philology" of medieval studies, which stresses the cultural setting of literary texts. On "the new philology," see Stephen Nichols's special issue of *Speculum*.

2. Analogies and homologies between death and marriage remain a

persistent motif throughout the Western literary tradition, especially in viri-local cultures where the bride must leave her native home. Henry Goodyere's 1613 epithalamion on the wedding of Elizabeth of Bohemia is a striking example from early modern English literature:

> Lift up thy modest head,
> Great and fair bride; and as a well-taught soul
> Calls not for Death, nor doth control
> Death when he comes, come you unto this bed.
> Do not pursue nor fly.
> Enter, for when these sheets
> Open, the book of fate thee meets.

3. For Foley, drawing on René Girard's theory of violence and the sacred, the king's daughter is the victim needed to resolve the community's crisis. The sacrifice originally disguised as marriage becomes, through Iphigenia's consent, a martyrdom which redresses Helen's violation of marriage (84–92). Thus the sacrifice of Iphigenia is justified, its violence a cultural imperative. But if Vernant is correct, Iphigenia's consent cannot make her death lawful. An attempt like Girard's to endue sacrificial violence with cultural creativity then comes to seem an example of sacrificial ideology, as Jay argues, rather than a theory of it (131). For another perceptive feminist critique of Girard, see Joplin, "Voice of the Shuttle."

4. In addition to the works discussed in my text, Lumley appears in Hogrefe, Reynolds, and several recent bibliographies of women's writings, such as Cotton and Hageman. She is mentioned dismissively in Lucas's study of the early modern reputation of Euripides and not at all in Conley's or Lathrop's studies of Tudor translation. More surprisingly, her *Iphigenia* was not included in Cerasano and Wynne-Davies' recent volume of Renaissance women's dramatic texts.

5. Lumley's death date, like that of more celebrated Renaissance writers, is better documented than her birth. Her husband's elegy in *Funeral Processions, 1557–1603* (British Library, Add. MS 35324) states that she was forty-two when she died in 1577 (N.S.). If then she was born in 1535, rather than 1537, as Nichols and Child surmise, she was at least fifteen at the time of her marriage and hence of the translation. She may have been older, if Child has incorrectly assumed that the translation must have been completed in the early days of her marriage.

6. Barnstone suggests that shame still taints the translator's task, mitigated only when the translator is an Erasmus, Dryden, or Pound with his own independent fame (9–10).

7. On the marginality of Greek studies on the continent, see Grafton

and Jardine, 119; and in England, Bolgar, "Classical Reading in Renaissance Schools." Oxford undergraduates did not unanimously welcome an addition to the curriculum that promised no reward but intellectual distinction: when the study of Greek was first established at Corpus Christi College in 1516, a group of students, calling themselves Trojans, rebelled. The episode is documented in letters of More and of Erasmus, though not in the university's official records. See Sandys, 2:230; McConica, 67; and, for a different interpretation, Bolgar, *The Classical Heritage*, 313. Spencer suggests that the Renaissance, viewing Greek culture through Latin intermediaries, found it suspect; hence, the distasteful Greeklings of *Timon of Athens* and *Troilus and Cressida*. Even in the late eighteenth century, when the study of Greek was fully established in England, it was something of a luxury: "Greek is like lace," comments Johnson, "every man gets as much as he can" (Hill 4:27).

8. See also the discussion of this passage in Lamb, 115–16; and for a discussion of "gender and the metaphorics of translation," Lori Chamberlain.

9. On *metaphora* and *translatio* as violence or transgression, see Norton, 191–92 and passim; and Parker, 36–53.

10. *Reflections on Ancient and Modern Learning* [1697], quoted in Reynolds, 22. Wotton's notion of classical learning as a Tudor charm school finds some recent support. Some women, or rather their families, Warnicke speculates, may have indeed thought Greek and Latin enriched their marriage prospects, at least in Henrician times: "it is likely that [the female dependents of Somerset, Suffolk, Norfolk, and Arundel] were educated as humanists to help further their family's position at court through advantageous marriages" (100). On learned women outside England, see the essays in Labalme.

11. On women's illiteracy, see Cressy, *Literacy*, 128–29 and 144–49.

12. On Salter, see Holm. This passage is also quoted in Kelso, 36.

13. This version is from Percy's collection; Sypherd lists many but not all the medieval and early modern treatments of the theme. For a discussion of the endogamous subtext of the daughter's sacrifice in Judges, see Bal.

14. The Latin is as follows: "Ego autem non sum saturata thalamo meo / nec repleta sum coronis nuptiarum mearum." For the text, translation, and a discussion of the relevant sections of Philo, see Alexiou and Dronke, 819–25.

15. The translation is mine. For a discussion of Abelard's *planctus*, see Alexiou and Dronke, 851–59.

16. For a full discussion of Christopherson's *Jephthah*, see Boas, 43–62.

17. The Latin is as follows:

cum staret aras ante tristes victima
iam destinata virgo, purpureum decus
per alba fudit ora virgineus pudor,
coetus viriles intuerier insolens,

ut si quis Indum purpura violet ebur,
rosasve niveis misceat cum liliis.

(1372–77)

References to Buchanan's Latin text are to line numbers; references to the
English prose translation are to page numbers.

18. The Latin is as follows:

fletu sacerdos obrutus vix solvere
animae meatus potuit; et maestro diu
taciturna turba torpuit silentio.
ut vocis autem pervium patuit iter,
non ille gemitus, esse nec qualis solet
fremitus doloris atque lamentatio.

(1432–37)

19. The Latin is as follows:

Solamen ipso luctuosius malo
quod leniendo exasperat malum vetus,
luctusque acerbi memoriam semper novans
reducta cogit vulnera recrudescere.
quo fortiore nata tulit animo necem,
hoc angit animum tristior meum dolor.

(1445–50)

20. For a different interpretation of this scene, see Shuger, *Renaissance
Bible*, chapter 4.

21. The Latin is as follows:

Eheu, recenti corda palpitant metu,
mens horret, haeret vox in ipsis faucibus,
nec ora verbis pervium praebent iter.

(73–75)

22. These saints' lives are taken from Caxton. For modern references,
see Farmer.

23. There is a particularly caustic appraisal in Eustace, 117.

24. For the history of the Lumley Library, see Jayne and Johnson, 1–26.

25. On John Lumley's art collections, see Strong, 45–46 and passim;
Jackson-Stops, 61. On the inventory of 1590, see Piper; of 1609, Hervey; and
on both, Cust.

26. Her name is mentioned in the sale of lands in Gloucestershire for

£40 needed to pay her father's debts, and again when she and John conveyed the manor of Buckland, which Arundel settled on Jane after her marriage, to Herbert Pelham and Roger Dallender. See Milner, 63; and Malden, 174.

27. This unidentified manuscript, no. 990e in Jayne and Johnson, is described as "The true copie under Mr Doctor Halles owne hande, of his epistle sent to Francantianus and Bellicatus doctors of physick in Padwaie, touchinge the diseased bodies of John lorde Lumley and the ladie Jane his wife daughter to the earle of Arundell, with their answers returned from Padua under their hands."

28. This unidentified manuscript is no. 1448 in Jayne and Johnson. On John Lumley's genealogical and antiquarian pursuits, see Mervyn James, 109–10; and Jackson-Stops, 96–97 and passim.

29. On the Cooke sisters, see Lamb.

30. See for example Plowden, 127, and Chapman, 56. For an argument that Grey was and was seen as a religious and political dissident, see Levin.

31. White makes the point that Lady Jane Grey, alone of Foxe's martyrs, maintains the tradition of the beautiful wellborn lady martyred for her faith (149).

32. There is another, broken alliance in the convoluted history of the Grey and Fitzalan families, for Jane Grey's father, Henry Grey, had been contracted to marry Henry Fitzalan's sister, another Catherine. The match was broken off so that he could marry Frances Brandon, a rupture for which his mother paid a fine of four thousand marks (Wood [Green], 2:346–49).

33. The Greek text is as follows:

> O potnia potnia mater, hos dakrua ge soi
> dosomen ametera
> par hierois gar ou prepei.
>
> (489–91)

Erasmus's Latin is as follows:

> O veneranda,
> Veneranda parens,
> Quomodo tibi debitas
> Impertiemus lachrumas?
> Nam nefas neque convenit
> Miscere sacra fletu.
>
> (2132–37)

34. Since it was through his marriage to Jane that Lumley eventually acquired Nonsuch and most of the Arundel fortune, this strange portrait of

the living and the dead would seem to have functioned as a document of lineage and inheritance. On other paintings that combine living and dead members of a family, see Goldberg, 89–112.

35. My reference is to the page number, as the Hazlitt edition of Webster lacks act, scene, and line numbers.

36. For an argument that the twentieth century is only now painfully acknowledging its inheritance of incest from early modern Europe, see Boehrer.

The Saint in the Brothel

1. On the social and literary history of Roman declamation, see Bonner; Caplan, 160–95; and Trimpi, *Muses* 306–27. For discussions of declamation as a literary source for Renaissance drama, see above, "Seneca by Candlelight," note 30. On the influence of declamation on the representation of rape in Renaissance drama, see Gossett.

2. On "the paradoxes that govern the laws of rape" when they are based on rules of morality, see Ferguson.

3. For discussions of the virgin martyr, see Anson and Schulenburg. For more general discussions of the complicated history linking "valor and virginity," see Huston; McNamara; and Warner, 68–78. Gradval discusses the representation of rape in medieval French hagiography (21–41 and passim) and Jardine discusses "the saving stereotypes of female heroism" in Elizabethan drama in *Still Harping*, 169–98.

4. On the deployment of marriage and death as homologous narrative resolutions from preclassical Greece to modern novels, see, for example, Foley, 84–92; and Higonnet, 74. See also above, "Iphigenia in Durham," note 2.

5. In one romance, however, Xenophon of Ephesus's *Ephesiaca*, the imprisoned heroine Anthia does kill a guard who tries to rape her. See Heiserman, 51–52, and Hägg, 31–32. For another perspective on Shakespeare's response to the economic subtexts of ancient romance, see Mullaney, 137–42, and, on "the peculiar sensibility that made [Greek romance] available to Shakespeare," Comito.

6. Studies of the sixteenth-century syphilis epidemic include Dennie; Morton; Pusey; and most recently, Quetel. Evans notes the effect of the epidemic on prostitution: "From this time on, the problem of the prostitute could never be dissociated from that of disease; henceforward she represented a sanitary as well as a moral problem" (64). See also Burford, 113–15 and passim; and Karras. Welsh notes *Pericles*'s emphasis on venereal disease, 103–5.

7. On the motif of "the nun and the judge" in other Shakespearean plays, see Salinger, 298–325.

8. I quote the English translation of Ciotti's *A Booke of Strange and Curious Inventions* from a microfilm copy in the Huntington Library. On the "elevated class associations" and the femininizing functions of embroidery as a component of sixteenth- and seventeenth-century women's educations, see Rosika Parker. Schneider also describes some of the economic foundations and symbolic associations of women's needlework.

9. In Jonson's *Poetaster*, Captain Tucca, having had Histrio audition his pages, refuses to let them join the acting company, saying, "I will not part from 'hem: you'll sell 'hem for enghles you" (3.4.275–76). See Bray for a discussion of homosexual prostitution in the London theatrical milieu (54–56). On the status of apprentices at the public theaters, see Bentley, 113–41. Mullaney notes analogies between bawdyhouse and playhouse and between prostitutes and actors, but without distinguishing the status of adult males from either boy actors or female prostitutes (143–47).

10. On Isabella's performance choices, see Paola Dionisotti's and Juliet Stevenson's remarks on the 1978 and 1983 Royal Shakespeare Company's productions in Rutter, 26–52. On the ways productions of other plays have used "Shakespeare's open silences," see McGuire.

11. On the residual orality of Renaissance culture and on the differences between oral and literate cultures generally, see Ong. In a recent study of rhetorical *memoria*, however, Carruthers demonstrates that this distinction has often been too sharply drawn. For an argument on "the modernist return to rhetoric," see Bender and Wellbery.

12. I have here drawn on my review of Burns.

13. For examples of the mutual incomprehension with which radical critics and liberal directors greet each other's work, see the essays and interviews in Holderness, *The Shakespeare Myth*. In this collection, the scholars predictably win every round. For a director's riposte, see Bogdanov and Pennington, and, for an unusually impartial assessment, Isobel Armstrong.

14. Cavell's *faux-naïf* insistence that characters on a stage *are* people, but people who occupy a different space than the audience (327–39), is one of several arguments that remain unanswered in the historicist discussions of Shakespearean character.

15. In the 1990 pedagogy issue of *Shakespeare Quarterly*, Ann Thompson remarks that the contributors to the pedagogy issue of 1984, who recommend classroom performance with "a remarkable degree of unanimity," seem for the most part "untouched" by cultural materialism, feminism, deconstruction, and new historicism: "They are equally silent on the fact that teaching Shakespeare is a political issue" (139).

16. When I discussed this soliloquy in "Acts of Resistance" (120–21),

I was more pessimistic about its feminist interpretation. For my new optimism, I am indebted to Ron Leeson, whose work in corporeal mime has enlarged my sense of theatrical options. For essays on corporeal mime and other alternatives to American method acting, see Zarilli.

17. I am indebted to Kalpana Guttman for this observation.

18. Greenblatt makes a similar point about the "public character" of Hamlet's "innermost thoughts" (87). For a lucid discussion of the impersonal rhetoric of Hamlet's monologues, see Williams, *Writing in Society*, 31–64.

Voluntary Wounds

1. For discussions of the endogamous subtext of the exchange of women as it appears in Greek, Hebrew, and Shakespearean texts, see references to Bal, Boose, and Loraux above in "Iphigenia in Durham." Cf. Clément's catalog of women's death in nineteenth-century opera: "Nine by knife, two of them suicides; three by fire; two who jump; two consumptives; three who drown; three poisoned; two of fright; and a few unclassifiable, thank god for them, dying without anyone knowing why or how" (47). These deaths too are the old tragic ways of killing a woman. In opera as in tragedy, "one must know how to keep the right distance according to the laws of exogamy. Too close and it is incest; too distant and it is war. Too close, it is Jocasta, or Isolde: death. Too distant, it is Othello: death again" (122). Over and over, the exchange of women is symbolically enacted upon the body of the performer—the masked and buskined *hypokritēs*, Shakespeare's boy actors, or that consummate female impersonator, the prima donna "dressed up as a woman" (29).

2. For recent general studies of the performance conditions of Greek tragedy, see Taplin and Walton. On the sexual politics of those conditions, see Zeitlin.

3. Cf. Goldman: "A character, in a play, is something an actor *does*" (149).

4. Weimann, 157–59 (see also above, "Seneca by Candlelight"). Rosalind's epilogue in *As You Like It*, an exception to this rule, calls attention to its own singularity: "It is not the fashion to see the lady the epilogue." I have discussed other exceptions in "Acts of Resistance," 112–30.

5. On medieval and early modern rape laws, see Bashar; Post; and Pollack and Maitland, 2:490–91. Gossett also summarizes the legal materials in her analysis of rape in Jacobean drama.

6. For a discussion of Aaron as the descendant of the Vice, see Spivack, 379–86. See also Green: "Aaron, the racial Other, is still speaking at

the end of the play, even after the women, good and bad, have been killed—silenced and finally fixed" (326).

7. Hunter usefully restores a sense of popular staging practices that literary-critical investigations of Senecanism have neglected (*Dramatic Identities*, 159–213). I shall, however, also argue for the special theatrical effects of those uncommon scenes that do deploy Senecan dramaturgy on the popular stage. See also Braden's study of the continuities between Roman Stoicism and Renaissance constructions of subjectivity, which addresses some of Hunter's arguments against Renaissance Senecanism.

8. Several critics, including Hunter (*Dramatic Identities*, 165–66), Waith "Metamorphosis," and Barkan (243–47), emphasize the Ovidian resonances of the speech. Again, I would argue for a specifically Senecan dramaturgy as well as a more diffuse incorporation of Silver Age rhetoric (Ovidian and Senecan), here adapted for the apparently recalcitrant setting of the London playhouse.

9. For an analysis of this gender-inflected rhetorical term, see Patricia Parker, 8–35.

10. For several reviewers, Deborah Warner's 1987 production for the Royal Shakespeare Company had this dissonant effect. See Dessen, 51–69; and MacDonald. Other responses to the scene's clash of text and image include Green, 324 n. 20 and Hulse, 110–11.

11. In "Boying Her Greatness," Shapiro anticipates my argument that Cleopatra's metatheatrical gesture reflects the practices of the private playhouses, although he focuses on the motif of the "pathetic heroine," while I am interested in the way the player exploits pathos in the practice of his craft. See also Foakes, who argues, on other grounds, that the tragedies of the children's companies influenced public theater plays at the turn of the century (51).

12. For a discussion of Robert Browne's career and his probable influence on *The Rape of Lucrece*, see Holladay. On the ideology of rape in the Lucrece theme, see Donaldson; Jed; Joplin; Kahn; Maus; and Stimpson.

13. See "Seneca by Candlelight" above, notes 9 and 13.

14. William Cornish, the master of Paul's Boys, who played Calchas in his troupe's production of *Troilus and Criseyde*, is an exception from the earlier period of the children's companies (Bradbrook, 219–20).

15. I must accept responsibility for inventing *The Dictionary of Invented Biography*, but the continental turn of Michael Farrant's career owes something to Zdeněk Stříbrný's inspiring lecture on Shakespearean productions in Prague during the early 1980s, which first introduced me to the riches of the Czech theatrical tradition. The history of English troupes touring central Europe is told in Limon.

Ethnicke Lamentations

1. One answer, then, to Mary Beth Rose's question "Where Are the Mothers in Shakespeare?" is that they are playing supporting roles in the histories. On "the absent mother," see also Kahn, "The Absent Mother," Orgel "Prospero's Wife," and Dubrow.

2. David Bevington also notes that women "take the initiative in ceremonial mourning . . . on Shakespeare's stage as they do in many traditional societies" (*Action is Eloquence*, 84). Whereas he asserts that this initiative is represented ironically to reveal female impotence, I find that in performance, the laments of Margaret, Elizabeth, the Duchess of York, and Constance possess considerable power.

3. On the heraldic funeral, see Gittings, chapter 8 and passim; Rifkin, 102–40; Stone, 572–81; and M. E. James. On royal funerals, see Huntington and Metcalf, 159–65; Blank; Litten, 173–94; and Fritz. For a full discussion of funeral pageantry on the Elizabethan stage, see Neill.

4. Gittings, 37 and passim. On differences between pre- and post-Reformation English funerals, see Rifkin, 1–6, and Thomas, 602–6.

5. The presentation of arms to the heir lends significance to Laertes' rebellion when Claudius buries Polonius "in hugger-mugger":

> That drop of blood that's calm proclaims me bastard,
> Cries cuckold to my father, brands the harlot
> Even here between the chaste unsmirched brow
> Of my true mother.
>   (*Hamlet*, 4.5.118–21)

6. For a full discussion of the English elegy "from Spenser to Yeats," see Sacks. For a feminist critique of the genre, see Schenck. On the rhetorical genres of the eulogy in the histories, see Riggs.

7. In this spectacular production, which compressed the tetralogy into a trilogy offered to playgoers as a theater marathon, doubling made Margaret's endurance prominent. As Oliver Cotton's earl of Suffolk metamorphosed into Jack Cade and then the duke of Buckingham and Richard Bremmer's duke of Anjou became a lawyer, a murderer, the earl of Oxford, a clerk of Chatham, and at last Sir Richard Ratcliffe, Downie's Margaret remained on stage from morning on through the night. See also Downie's essay on the role.

8. Rackin notes this intersection of xenophobia and misogyny in *Stages of History*, 152.

9. On this distinction between patrilineal York and matrilineal Lancaster, see Hodgdon, 69–70.

10. For full discussions of lament in Greek tragedy, see Alexiou; Holst-Warhaft; and Loraux, *The Invention of Athens*, on which I have largely drawn. I am especially indebted to Holst-Warhaft's work. See also Caraveli's discussion of lament in twentieth-century rural Greece, which reveals the often uncanny continuity of the tradition.

11. *Ponos*, the state in which lament is performed, is induced through methods that, *mutatis mutandis*, are oddly reminiscent of the emotional memory of the early Stanislavskian system.

12. See Holst-Warhaft's fine discussion of lament in the *Oresteia*, *Dangerous Voices*, 127–70. Loraux interprets Euripides' *The Suppliant Women* as another dramatization of the transformation of lament into tragedy (*Invention*, 48–49).

13. Biblical references to the ritual pollution incurred by those who come into contact with a corpse include Numbers 19.11–22 and Leviticus 21.1–12. On the Christian rejection of death pollution, see Paxton, 19–27, and Brown, 4–5.

14. On women and mourning in the Italian Renaissance, see Strocchia. Schiesari offers a psychoanalytic interpretation of "the gendering of melancholia," focusing primarily on Italian texts.

15. Quoted in Stannard, 103. On Puritan funeral sermons, see also Rifkin, 20–28.

16. See also Cairns and Richards, 9–11; and Leerssen, 93–95. For general discussions of English drama and national identity, see Helgerson, 193–245; and Philip Edwards, 66–109 and passim.

17. In my remarks on Tudor Ireland, I have relied mostly on Quinn; Laurence; and Muldoon. See also Canny; Ellis; and Dudley Edwards on the English invasion. On the status of women, see the essays in MacCurtain and O'Dowd; MacCurtain and Ó Córrain; and Ni Chuilleanain. For other discussions of the Elizabethan commentaries, see Leerssen, 33–84, and Jones and Stallybrass.

18. On keening, see O Suilleabhain, 130–45, and Angela Partridge; on the relation between keening women and the supernatural wailing of the banshee, see Lysaght; and for a musicological analysis of Irish lament, see Ó Madagáin.

19. On the clerical battle against keening, see O Suilleabhain, 138–43.

20. On ancient parallels and intersections between Celtic and classical cultures, see Rankin; Momigliano, 50–73; and Leerssen, 3–39. Grafton and Jardine note that Latin texts in the Greek historiographical tradition referred to "all barbarous opponents of the Empire, whether Avars, Goths, Huns, Arabs, or Turks, as 'Scyths'" (100). Macintosh discusses the continuing relation of Greek and Irish attitudes to death and mourning as they have influenced twentieth-century Irish drama.

21. On the Gaelic cult of the severed head, see Rankin, 262–63. On drinking blood as a traditional part of lament, see Angela Partridge, 31–32.

22. Litten discusses the history of embalming in Tudor England (32–56). On its later historical relations with scientific dissection, see Richardson, 169–71. I am indebted to Scott McMillin for observing the relevance of this scene to my discussion of Katherine below.

23. See, for example Bristol, 182–83. On Falstaff as "literary fat lady," see Parker, 20–22; and for a psychoanalytic approach, see Traub. I am also indebted to a fine paper of Lewis A. Celluci.

24. For a fuller discussion of these customs, see Gittings, 105–7. On the games, contests, and storytelling of the far more tenacious Irish wake, see O Suilleabhain.

25. See Chamberlain and Richardson; Clark, 265–85; and Smith.

26. Although women still washed corpses and prepared them for burial, they were more often employed by male undertakers and less often in charge of the procedure as a whole. On the development of the professional undertaker, see Fritz, 76; Rifkin, 86–87; Gittings, 94; and Litten, chapter 1. *The Diary of Henry Machyn* suggests the process through which one merchant-tailor came to rely on furnishing funerals for an increasing portion of his business.

27. For the wills of Mary, Lucy, Katherine, and Helena, see Stone, 579; Frances's will is quoted in Rifkin, 76. On Elizabeth, see Blank, 26–27. According to Manningham, "It is certain the Queen was not embowelled, but wrapped in cere cloth, and that very ill too, through the covetousness of them that defrauded her of the allowance of cloth was given them for the purpose" (223). But Elizabeth Southwell, who was then present in court, reports that Cecil ordered it performed despite her wishes (Blank, 27).

28. Quoted in Cunnington and Lucas, 216.

29. On the special burial rites for virgins, see Gittings, 117–18.

30. On the Barber-Surgeons' monopoly, see Rifkin, 75.

31. This evocation of Hecuba, along with note 5, on Laertes, must serve in lieu of a discussion of mourning and melancholia in *Hamlet*. I concentrate on the histories not only because my topic is the intersection of lament, theater, historiography, and national identity but also because so much criticism, including feminist criticism, has interpreted the histories as a merely masculinist enterprise, thereby ignoring the fact that these plays have the most rewarding roles for middle-aged and old women.

Works Cited

Abelard, Peter [Abelardo, Pietro]. *I "Planctus."* Ed. Guiseppe Vecchi. Instituto di Romanza della Universita di Roma 35. Modena: Societa Tipografica Modenese, 1951.

Aers, David. "Reflections on Current Histories of the Subject." *Literature and History* 2 (1991): 20–34.

Aeschylus. *The Oresteia*. Trans. Richmond Lattimore. In Vol. 1 of *The Complete Greek Tragedies*, 7 vols. Chicago: University of Chicago Press, 1942.

Alexiou, Margaret. *The Ritual Lament in Greek Tradition*. Cambridge: Cambridge University Press, 1974.

Alexiou, Margaret, and Peter Dronke. "The Lament of Jephtha's Daughter: Themes, Traditions, Originality." *Studi medievali* 12 (1971): 819–63.

Altman, Joel B. *The Tudor Play of Mind: Rhetorical Inquiry and the Development of Elizabethan Drama*. Berkeley: University of California Press, 1978.

Anson, John. "The Female Transvestite in Early Monasticism: The Origin and Development of a Motif." *Viator* 5 (1974): 1–32.

Ariès, Philippe. *The Hour of Our Death*. Trans. Helen Weaver. New York: Vintage, 1981.

Aristophanes. *The Frogs*. Trans. Benjamin Bickley Rogers. Loeb Classical Library. Cambridge, MA: Harvard University Press, 1924.

Aristotle. *Rhetoric*. Trans. John Henry Freese. Loeb Classical Library. Cambridge, MA: Harvard University Press, 1926.

Armstrong, Isobel. "Thatcher's Shakespeare?" *Textual Practice* 3 (1989): 1–14.

Armstrong, William. "Shakespeare and the Acting of Edward Alleyn." *Shakespeare Survey* 7 (1954): 82–89.

Artaud, Antonin. *The Theatre and Its Double*. Trans. Mary Caroline Richards. New York: Grove Press, 1958.

Ascham, Roger. *The Schoolmaster*. 1570. Ed. Lawrence V. Ryan. Charlottesville: University of Virginia Press, 1967.

Aubrey, John. "Remaines of Gentilisme and Judaisme." In *Three Prose Works*, ed. John Buchanan-Brown. Carbondale: Southern Illinois University Press, 1972.

Augustine. *The City of God*. Vol. 2. Trans. G. E. McCracken. Loeb Classical Library. Cambridge, MA: Harvard University Press, 1957.

———. *Confessions*. Vol. 2. Trans. William Watts. Loeb Classical Library. Cambridge, MA: Harvard University Press, 1957.

———. *On Christian Doctrine*. Trans. D. W. Robertson Jr. Library of Liberal Arts. Indianapolis: Bobbs-Merrill, 1958.

Bacon, Nicholas. *Sir Nicholas Bacon's Great House Sententiae* [ca. 1575]. Ed. Elizabeth McCutcheon. *English Literary Renaissance Supplements* 3 (1977).

Baker, J. H. Introduction to *The Reports of Sir John Spelman*. London: Seldon Society, 1978.

Bal, Mieke. *Death and Dissymmetry: The Politics of Coherence in the Book of Judges*. Chicago: University of Chicago Press, 1988.

Ballard, George. *Memoirs of Several Ladies of Great Britain*. 1752. Ed. Ruth Perry. Detroit: Wayne State University Press, 1985.

Barish, Jonas. *The Anti-theatrical Prejudice*. Berkeley: University of California Press, 1981.

Barkan, Leonard. *The Gods Made Flesh: Metamorphosis and the Pursuit of Paganism*. New Haven, CT: Yale University Press, 1986.

Barker, Francis. *The Tremulous Private Body*. London: Methuen, 1984.

Barker, Howard. *Arguments for a Theatre*. London: John Calder, 1989.

Barnstone, Willis. *The Poetics of Translation: History, Theory, Practice*. New Haven, CT: Yale University Press, 1993.

Bashar, Nazife. "Rape in England between 1550 and 1700." In *The Sexual Dynamics of History*, London Feminist History Group, 28–42. London: Pluto Press, 1983.

Beauvoir, Simone de. *The Second Sex*. Trans. H. M. Parshley. New York: Knopf, 1953.

Beard, Mary R. *Woman as Force in History: A Study in Traditions and Realities*. 1946. Reprint, New York: Farrar, Straus, and Giroux, 1976.

Beckerman, Bernard. *Shakespeare at the Globe, 1599–1609*. New York: Macmillan, 1962.

Beilin, Elaine V. *Redeeming Eve: Women Writers of the English Renaissance*. Princeton, NJ: Princeton University Press, 1987.

Belsey, Catherine. *The Subject of Tragedy: Identity and Difference in Renaissance Drama*. London: Methuen, 1985.

Bender, John, and David E. Wellbery. "Rhetoricality: On the Modernist Return to Rhetoric." In *The Ends of Rhetoric: History, Theory, Practice*, ed. John Bender and David Wellbery. Stanford, CA: Stanford University Press, 1990.

Benjamin, Walter. *Illuminations*. Ed. Hannah Arendt. Trans. Harry Zohn. New York: Schocken Books, 1969.

Bentley, Gerald Eades. *The Profession of Player in Shakespeare's Time, 1590–1642*. Princeton, NJ: Princeton University Press, 1986.

Bevington, David. *Action Is Eloquence: Shakespeare's Language of Gesture*. Cambridge, MA: Harvard University Press, 1984.

———. *From Mankind to Marlowe*. Cambridge, MA: Harvard University Press, 1962.

———, ed. *Medieval Drama*. Boston: Houghton Mifflin, 1975.

Bland, D. S. "Rhetoric and the Law Student in Sixteenth-Century England." *Studies in Philology* 54 (1957): 498–508.

Blank, Olivia. *The Royal Way of Death*. London: Constable, 1986.

Bloch, Maurice. "Death, Women, and Power." In *Death and the Regeneration of Life*, ed. Maurice Bloch and Jonathan Parry, 211–30. Cambridge: Cambridge University Press, 1982.

Boal, Augusto. *Games for Actors and Non-Actors*. Trans. Adrian Jackson. London: Routledge, 1992.

Boas, Frederick S. *University Drama in the Tudor Age*. Oxford: Clarendon Press, 1914.

Boehrer, Bruce Thomas. *Monarchy and Incest in Renaissance England*. Philadelphia: University of Pennsylvania Press, 1992.

Bogdanov, Michael, and Michael Pennington. *The English Shakespeare Company: The Story of "The Wars of the Roses," 1986–1989*. London: Nick Hern Books, 1990.

Bolgar, R. R. *The Classical Heritage and Its Beneficiaries*. Cambridge: Cambridge University Press, 1954.

———. "Classical Reading in Renaissance Schools." *Durham Research Review* 2 (1955): 18–26.

Bolton, Robert. *Mr. Boltons Last and Learned Worke of the Foure Last Things*. London, 1635.

Bonner, S. F. *Roman Declamation in the Late Republic and Early Empire*. Liverpool: University Press of Liverpool, 1949.

Boose, Lynda E. "The Father's House and the Daughter in It." In *Daughters and Fathers*, ed. Lynda E. Boose and Betty S. Flowers, 19–74. Baltimore: Johns Hopkins University Press, 1989.

Bradbrook, Muriel. *The Rise of the Common Player*. Cambridge, MA: Harvard University Press, 1964.

Braden, Gorden. *Renaissance Tragedy and the Senecan Tradition: Anger's Privilege*. New Haven, CT: Yale University Press, 1985.

Bray, Alan. *Homosexuality in Renaissance England*. London: Gay Men's Press, 1982.

Brinkley, Roberta Florence. *Nathan Field, the Actor-Playwright*. 1924. Reprint, Hamden, CT: Archon Books, 1973.

Bristol, Michael D. *Carnival and Theater*. New York: Routledge, 1985.

Brooks, Harold. "*Richard III*, Unhistorical Amplifications: The Women's Scenes and Seneca." *Modern Language Review* 75 (1980): 721–37.

Brown, Peter. *The Cult of the Saints*. Chicago: University of Chicago Press, 1981.

Buchanan, George. *Tragedies*. Ed. P. Sharratt and P. G. Walsh. Edinburgh: Scottish Academic Press, 1983.

Bullough, Geoffrey, ed. *Narrative and Dramatic Sources of Shakespeare*. 8 vols. London: Routledge, 1966.

Burford, E. J. *Bawds and Lodgings: A History of the London Bankside Brothels c. 100–1675*. London: Peter Owen, 1976.

Burke, Peter. *Popular Culture in Early Modern Europe*. New York: Harper and Row, 1978.

Burns, Edward. *Character: Acting and Being on the Pre-Modern Stage*. London: St. Martin's Press, 1990.

Butler, Martin. *Theatre and Crisis, 1632–1642*. Cambridge: Cambridge University Press, 1984.

Cairns, David, and Shaun Richards. *Writing Ireland: Colonialism, Nationalism, and Culture*. Manchester: Manchester University Press, 1988.

Camden, William. *Britannia*. 1607. Trans. Philemon Holland. London, 1610.

Campion, Edmund. *Two Bokes of the Histories of Ireland*. Ed. A. F. Vossen. Assen: Van Gorcum, 1963.

Canny, Nicholas P. *The Elizabethan Conquest of Ireland: A Pattern Established, 1565–76*. New York: Barnes and Noble, 1976.

Caplan, Harry. *Of Eloquence: Studies in Ancient and Medieval Rhetoric*. Ed. Anne King and Helen North. Ithaca, NY: Cornell University Press, 1970.

Caraveli, Anna. "The Bitter Wounding: The Lament as Social Protest in Rural Greece." In *Gender and Power in Rural Greece*, ed. Jill Dubisch, 169–94. Princeton, NJ: Princeton University Press, 1986.

Carr, C[ynthia]. *On Edge: Performance at the End of the Twentieth Century*. Hanover, NH: University Press of New England, 1993.

Carruthers, Mary J. *The Book of Memory: A Study of Memory in Medieval Culture*. Cambridge: Cambridge University Press, 1990.

Carter, Angela. *Wise Children*. New York: Farrar, Straus, Giroux, 1991.

Cavell, Stanley. "The Avoidance of Love: A Reading of *King Lear*." In *Must We Mean What We Say?* 267–353. New York: Charles Scribner's Sons, 1969.

Caxton, William. *The Golden Legend, or Lives of the Saints as Englished by William Caxton*. 7 vols. London: J. M. Dent, 1900.

Cazelles, Brigitte. Introduction to *Images of Sainthood in Medieval Europe*, ed. Renate Blumenfeld-Kosinski and Timea Snell, 1–17. Ithaca, NY: Cornell University Press, 1991.

Celluci, Lewis A. " 'Nothing Confutes Me but Eyes': History, the Sacred, and Performance." Paper presented to the Ohio Shakespeare Conference, Ohio University, February 25–27, 1987.

Cerasano, S. P., and Marion Wynne-Davies, eds. *Renaissance Drama by Women: Texts and Documents*. London: Routledge, 1996.

Chalmers, Walter R. "Plautus and His Audience." In *Roman Drama*, ed. T. A. Dorey and Donald R. Dudley, 21–50. New York: Basic Books, 1965.

Chamberlain, Lori. "Gender and the Metaphorics of Translation." *Signs* 13 (1988): 454–72.

Chamberlain, Mary, and Ruth Richardson. "Life and Death." *Journal of the Oral History Society* 11–12 (1983–84): 31–43.

Chambers, E. K. *The Elizabethan Stage*. 4 vols. Oxford: Clarendon Press, 1923.

Chapman, Hester. *Lady Jane Grey*. London: Jonathan Cape, 1962.

Chenu, M.-D. Introduction to *Artes praedicandi: Contribution à l'histoire de la rhétorique au moyen âge*, ed. Th.-M. Charland. *Publications de l'institut d'études médiévales d'Ottawa* 7 (1936): 1–13.

Christopherson, John. *Jephthah*. Ed. and trans. Francis Howard Forbes. Newark: University of Delaware Press, 1928.

Chrysostom, Saint John. *In Mattilaeum Homil*. In *Patrologiae cursus completus, series graeca*, ed. Jacques-Paul Migne, 57:374–76. Paris: 1857–1912.

Cicero, Marcus Tullius. *De inventione*. Trans. H. M. Hubbell. Loeb Classical Library. Cambridge, MA: Harvard University Press, 1949.

———. *De optimo genere oratorum*. Trans. H. M. Hubbell. Loeb Classical Library. Cambridge, MA: Harvard University Press, 1960.

———. *De oratore*. 2 vols. Trans. E. W. Sutton and H. Rackham. Loeb Classical Library. Cambridge, MA: Harvard University Press, 1942.

———. *Orator, Brutus*. Trans. H. M. Hubbell and G. L. Hendrickson. Loeb Classical Library. Cambridge, MA: Harvard University Press, 1971.

Ciotti, Giovanni Battista. *The First Part of Needleworks: Or, A Booke of Curious and Strange Inventions*. Printed for William Barley. London, 1596.

Clark, Alice. *Working Life of Women in the Seventeenth Century*. 1919. Reprint, London: Routledge, 1982.

Clément, Catherine. *Opera, or the Undoing of Women*. Trans. Betsy Wing. Minneapolis: University of Minnesota Press, 1988.

Clowes, William. *A Short and Profitable Treatise Touching the Cure of the Morbus Gallicus by Unctions*. 1579. Reprint, New York: Scholars' Facsimile, 1945.

Cohen, Walter. *Drama of a Nation: Public Theatre in Renaissance England and Spain*. Ithaca, NY: Cornell University Press, 1985.

Comito, Terry. "Exile and Return in the Greek Romances." *Arion* n.s. 2 (1975): 58–80.

Conley, C. H. *The First English Translators of the Classics* 1927. Reprint, Port Washington, NY: Kennikat Press, 1967.

Cook, Ann Jennalie. *The Privileged Playgoers of Shakespeare's London, 1576–1642*. Princeton, NJ: Princeton University Press, 1981.

Cooper, Thomas. *Thesaurus Linguae*. London, 1578.

Cope, Jackson. "Marlowe's *Dido* and the Titillating Children." *English Literary Renaissance* 4 (1974): 315–25.

Cotton, Nancy. *Women Playwrights in England c. 1363–1750*. Lewisburg, PA: Bucknell University Press, 1980.

Crane, Frank. "Euripides, Erasmus, and Lady Lumley." *Classical Journal* 39 (1944): 223–28.

Cressy, David. "Death and the Social Order: The Funerary Preferences of Elizabethan Gentlemen." *Continuity and Change* 5 (1989): 99–119.

———. *Literacy and the Social Order: Reading and Writing in Tudor and Stuart England*. Cambridge: Cambridge University Press, 1980.

Crewe, Jonathan. *Trials of Authorship: Anterior Forms and Poetic Reconstruction from Wyatt to Shakespeare*. Berkeley: University of California Press, 1990.

Cunningham, J. V. "Lyric Style in the 1590s." In *The Collected Essays of J. V. Cunningham*, 311–24. Chicago: Swallow Press, 1976.

Cunnington, Phyllis, and Catherine Lucas. *Costume for Births, Marriages, and Deaths*. London: Adam and Charles Black, 1972.

Curtius, Ernst. *European Literature and the Latin Middle Ages*. Princeton, NJ: Princeton University Press, 1973.

Cust, Lionel. "The Lumley Inventories." In *The Sixth Volume of the Walpole Society, 1917–1918*, 15–35. Oxford: Oxford University Press, 1918.

Davies, Sir John. *The Complete Poems*. Ed. Alexander B. Grosart. London: Chatto and Windus, 1876.

Dekker, Thomas. *The Dramatic Works of Thomas Dekker*. Vol. 1. Ed. Fredson Bowers. Cambridge: Cambridge University Press, 1953–61.

———. *The Gull's Hornbook*. In *The Seventeenth Century Stage*, ed. Gerald Eades Bentley. Chicago: University of Chicago Press, 1968.

Dench, Judi. Mistress Quickly, *Henry V*, dir. Kenneth Branagh. Samuel Goldwyn, 1989.

Dennie, Charles. *A History of Syphilis*. Springfield, IL: Charles Thomas, 1962.

Desmet, Christy. *Reading Shakespeare's Characters: Rhetoric, Ethics, and Identity*. Amherst: University of Massachusetts Press, 1992.

Dessen, Alan C. *Titus Andronicus. Shakespeare in Performance* series. Manchester: Manchester University Press, 1989.

Dollimore, Jonathan. *Radical Tragedy: Religion, Ideology, and Power in the Drama of Shakespeare and His Contemporaries*. Chicago: University of Chicago Press, 1984.

Dollimore, Jonathan, and Alan Sinfield. "History and Ideology: The Instance of *Henry V.*" In *Alternative Shakespeares*, ed. John Drakakis, 206–27. London: Methuen, 1985.

Donaldson, Ian. *The Rapes of Lucretia: A Myth and Its Transformations.* Oxford: Clarendon Press, 1982.

Doran, Madeleine. *The Endeavors of Art.* Madison: University of Wisconsin Press, 1954.

Douglas, Mary. *Purity and Danger: An Analysis of the Concepts of Pollution and Taboo.* London: Routledge, 1966.

Douglas, Wallace. "Accidental Institution: On the Origin of Modern Language Study." In *Criticism in the University*, ed. Gerald Graff and Reginald Gibbons, 35–61. *Triquarterly Series on Criticism and Culture* 1. Chicago: Northwestern University Press, 1985.

Downie, Penny. "Queen Margaret." In *Players of Shakespeare 3*, ed. Russell Jackson and Robert Smallwood, 114–39. Cambridge: Cambridge University Press, 1993.

———. Queen Margaret, *The Plantagenets*, dir. Adrian Noble. Royal Shakespeare Company. Barbican Theatre, London, July 1, 1989.

Duckworth, George E. *The Nature of Roman Comedy: A Study in Popular Entertainment.* Princeton, NJ: Princeton University Press, 1952.

Dubrow, Heather. "A Death in the Family: Reinterpreting Absent Mothers and Fathers." Paper presented for *Attending to Women in Early Modern England*, University of Maryland, College Park, November 8–10, 1990.

Dusinberre, Juliet. "Squeaking Cleopatras: Gender and Performance in *Antony and Cleopatra*." In *Shakespeare, Theory, and Performance*, ed. James C. Bulman. London: Routledge, 1996.

Eagleton, Terry. *Literary Theory: An Introduction.* Oxford: Basil Blackwell, 1983.

Eccles, Christine. *The Rose Theatre.* New York: Routledge, 1990.

Eden, Kathy. *Poetic and Legal Fictions in the Aristotelian Tradition.* Princeton, NJ: Princeton University Press, 1986.

Edwards, Philip. *Threshold of a Nation: A Study in English and Irish Drama.* Cambridge: Cambridge University Press, 1979.

Edwards, R. Dudley. *Ireland in the Age of the Tudors: The Destruction of Hiberno-Norman Civilization.* London: Croom Helm, 1977.

Ellis, Steven G. *Tudor Ireland: Crown, Community and the Conflict of Cultures, 1470–1603.* London: Longman, 1985.

Elyot, Sir Thomas. *The Book Named The Governor.* 1531. Ed. S. E. Lehmberg. London: Dent, 1962.

Enders, Jody. *Rhetoric and the Origins of Medieval Drama.* Ithaca, NY: Cornell University Press, 1992.

Erasmus. *Euripidis Hecuba [et] Iphgenia, tragediae graece.* Louvain, 1520. Lumley Library, catalog no. 1736a.

———. *Opera Omnia*. The Hague: M. Nyhoff, 1969– .

Estienne, Robert. *Dicionarii sivi Latinae Linguae Thesauri*. 2 vols. Paris, 1536.

Euripides. *Iphigeneia at Aulis*. Trans. A. S. Way. Loeb Classical Library. Cambridge, MA: Harvard University Press, 1912.

———. *Iphigenia Aulidensis*. In Vol. 3 of *Fabulae*. 3 vols. Ed. Gilbert Murray. Oxford: Clarendon Press, 1913.

Eustace, G. W. *Arundel Borough and Castle*. London: Robert Scott, 1922.

Evans, Hilary. *Harlots, Whores, and Hookers: A History of Prostitution*. New York: Taplinger, 1977.

Evans-Grubbs, Judith. "Abduction Marriage in Antiquity: A Law of Constantine (*CTh*.9.24.1) and Its Social Contexts." *Journal of Roman Studies* 79 (1989): 59–83.

Fantham, Elaine. Introduction to *Seneca's Troades*, 3–124. Princeton, NJ: Princeton University Press, 1982.

Farmer, David Hugh. *The Oxford Dictionary of Saints*. 2d ed. Oxford: Oxford University Press, 1987.

Farnham, Willard. *The Medieval Heritage of Elizabethan Tragedy*. Berkeley: University of California Press, 1936.

Ferguson, Frances. "Rape and the Rise of the Novel." In *Misogyny, Misandry, and Misanthropy*, ed. R. Howard Bloch and Frances Ferguson, 88–113. Berkeley: University of California Press, 1989.

Fischer-Licht, Erika. "Theatre and the Civilizing Process: An Approach to the History of Acting." In *Interpreting the Theatrical Past: Essays in the Historiography of Performance*, ed. Thomas Postlewait and Bruce A. McConachie, 19–36. Iowa City: University of Iowa Press, 1989.

Florio, John. Dedicatory epistle to Michel de Montaigne, *The Essays*. 1603. Trans. John Florio. Reprint, Menston, England: Scolar Press, 1969.

Foakes, R. A. "Tragedy of the Children's Theatres after 1600: A Challenge to the Adult Stage." In *The Elizabethan Theatre II*, ed. David Galloway, 37–59. London: Macmillan, 1970.

Foley, Helene P. *Ritual Irony: Poetry and Sacrifice in Euripides*. Ithaca, NY: Cornell University Press, 1985.

Foxe, John. *Acts and Monuments*. 1563. Vol. 6. Ed. Josiah Pratt. Rev. George Townsend. London: George Seeley, 1870.

Freedman, Diane P., Olivia Frey, and Frances Murphy Zauhar. *The Intimate Critique: Autobiographical Literary Criticism*. Durham, NC: Duke University Press, 1993.

Fritz, Paul S. "From 'Public' to 'Private': The Royal Funerals in England, 1500–1830." In *Mirrors of Mortality: Studies in the Social History of Death*, ed. Joachim Whaley, 61–79. New York: St. Martin's Press, 1981.

Fumeroli, Marc. *L'âge de l'éloquence: Rhétorique et «res literaria» de la Renaissance au seuil de l'époque classique*. Geneva: Librarie Droz, 1980.

———. "Rhetoric, Politics, and Society: From Italian Ciceronianism to French Classicism." Trans. Ruth B. York. In *Renaissance Eloquence: Studies in the Theory and Practice of Renaissance Rhetoric*, ed. James J. Murphy, 253–73. Berkeley: University of California Press, 1983.

Funeral Processions, 1557–1603. British Library Add. MS 35324.

Gair, Reavley. *The Children of Paul's: The Story of a Company, 1553–1608*. Cambridge: Cambridge University Press, 1983.

Gallop, Jane. *The Daughter's Seduction: Feminism and Psychoanalysis*. Ithaca, NY: Cornell University Press, 1982.

Gibbons, Brian. "Unstable Proteus: Marlowe's *The Tragedy of Dido Queen of Carthage*." In *Christopher Marlowe*, ed. B. Morris. Mermaid Critical Commentaries. London: Benn, 1968.

Girard, René. *Violence and the Sacred*. Trans. Patrick Gregory. Baltimore: Johns Hopkins University Press, 1979.

Gittings, Clare. *Death, Burial, and the Individual in Early Modern England*. London: Croom Helm, 1984.

Goldberg, Jonathan. *James I and the Politics of Literature*. Baltimore: Johns Hopkins University Press, 1983.

Goldman, Michael. *Acting and Action in Shakespearean Tragedy*. Princeton, NJ: Princeton University Press, 1985.

Goodyere, Sir Henry. "Epithalamion of the Princess' Marriage." 1613. In *English Epithalamies*, ed. Robert H. Case, 51–53. Bodley Head Anthologies. London: John Lane, 1896.

Gorra, Michael. "The Autobiographical Turn." *Transition* 68 (1995): 143–53.

Gossett, Suzanne. " 'Best Men Are Molded out of Faults': Marrying the Rapist in Jacobean Drama." *English Literary Renaissance* 14 (1984): 305–27.

Gosson, Stephen. *Plays Confuted in Five Actions*. 1582. In *The English Drama and Stage*, ed. William Hazlitt. London: Roxburghe Library, 1869.

Gower, John. *The Complete Works of John Gower: The English Works*. Ed. G. C. Macauley. Oxford: Clarendon Press, 1901.

Gradval, Kathryn. *Ravishing Maidens: Writing Rape in Medieval French Literature and Law*. Philadelphia: University of Pennsylvania Press, 1991.

Graff, Gerald, and Michael Warner, eds. "Bibliographical Note." In *The Origins of Literary Study in America: A Documentary Anthology*, 194–98. New York: Routledge, 1985.

Grafton, Anthony, and Lisa Jardine. *From Humanism to the Humanities: Education and the Liberal Arts in Fifteenth- and Sixteenth-Century Europe*. Cambridge, MA: Harvard University Press, 1986.

Green, Douglas E. "Interpreting 'Her Martyr'd Signs': Gender and Tragedy in *Titus Andronicus*." *Shakespeare Quarterly* 40 (1989): 317–26.

Greenblatt, Stephen. *Renaissance Self-Fashioning*. Chicago: University of Chicago Press, 1980.

Greene, David. "Lady Lumley and Greek Tragedy." *Classical Journal* 36 (1941): 537–47.

Greene, Gayle, and Coppelia Kahn, eds. *Changing Subjects: The Making of Feminist Literary Criticism*. London: Routledge, 1993.

Gurr, Andrew. *Playgoing in Shakespeare's London*. Cambridge: Cambridge University Press, 1987.

———. *The Shakespearean Stage, 1574–1642*. 2d ed. Cambridge: Cambridge University Press, 1980.

———. "Who Strutted and Bellowed?" *Shakespeare Survey* 16 (1963): 95–102.

Haag, Thomas. *The Novel in Antiquity*. Oxford: Basil Blackwell, 1983.

Hageman, Elizabeth H. "Recent Studies on Women Writers of Tudor England." *English Literary Renaissance* 14 (1984): 409–25.

Hall, Joseph. *Collected Poems*. Ed. A. Davenport. Liverpool: University Press, 1924.

Hall, Kim F. "Sexual Politics and Cultural Identity in *The Masque of Blackness*." In *The Performance of Power*, ed. Sue-Ellen Case and Janelle Reinelt, 3–18. *Studies in Theatre History and Culture*. Iowa City: University of Iowa Press, 1991.

Halley, Janet E. "Textual Intercourse: Anne Donne, John Donne, and the Sexual Poetics of Textual Exchange." In *Seeking the Woman in Late Medieval and Renaissance Writings: Essays in Feminist Contextual Criticism*, ed. Sheila Fisher and Janet E. Halley, 187–206. Knoxville: University of Tennessee Press, 1989.

Harbage, Alfred. *Annals of English Drama, 975–1700*. Rev. S. Schoenbaum. London: Methuen, 1964.

———. "Elizabethan Acting." *PMLA* 54 (1939): 685–708.

———. *Shakespeare and the Rival Traditions*. Bloomington: University of Indiana Press, 1952.

———. *Shakespeare's Audience*. New York: Columbia University Press, 1941.

Harleian Ms. 2342. British Library.

H. D. [Hilda Dolittle], trans. *Choruses from the Iphigeneia in Aulis and the Hippolytus of Euripides*. London: The Egoist, 1919.

Heinsius, Daniel. "Dissertatio de Plauto et Terentio Judicium." In *Publii Terenti Afri Comodiae*, ed. N. E. Lemaire, 1:94–120. Paris: Nicolaus Eligius Lemaire, 1827.

Heiserman, Arthur. *The Novel before the Novel*. Chicago: University of Chicago Press, 1977.

Helgerson, Richard. *Forms of Nationhood*. Chicago: University of Chicago Press, 1992.

Helms, Lorraine. "Acts of Resistance: The Feminist Player." In Dympna

Callaghan, Lorraine Helms, and Jyotsna Singh, *The Weyward Sisters: Shakespeare and Feminist Politics*. Oxford: Basil Blackwell, 1994.

———. Rev. of Edward Burns, *Character: Acting and Being on the Pre-Modern Stage*. New York: St. Martin's Press, 1990.

———. "Roaring Girls and Silent Women: The Politics of Androgyny on the Jacobean Stage." In *Women in Theatre*, ed. James Redmond, 59–73. Cambridge: Cambridge University Press, 1989.

Herington, C. J. "Senecan Tragedy." *Arion* 5 (1966): 422–71.

Herrick, Marvin T. *Comic Theory in the Sixteenth Century*. Urbana: University of Illinois Press, 1964.

Hervey, Mary F. S. "A Lumley Inventory of 1609." *The Sixth Volume of the Walpole Society, 1917–1918*, 36–50. Oxford: Oxford University Press, 1918.

Heywood, Thomas. *An Apology for Actors*. 1612. Reprint, London: Shakespeare Society, 1841.

———. *The Rape of Lucrece*. Ed. Allan Holaday. Urbana: University of Illinois Press, 1950.

Higonnet, Margaret. "Speaking Silences: Women's Suicide." In *The Female Body in Western Culture: Contemporary Perspectives*, ed. Susan Rubin Suleiman, 68–83. Cambridge, MA: Harvard University Press, 1986.

Hill, George Birkbeck. *Boswell's Life of Johnson*. Vol. 4. New York: Bigelow Brown, n.d.

Hillebrand, Harold. *The Child Actors*. 1926. Reprint, New York: Russell and Russell, 1964.

Hodgdon, Barbara. *The End Crowns All: Closure and Contradiction in Shakespeare's History*. Princeton, NJ: Princeton University Press, 1991.

Hogrefe, Pearl. *Tudor Women: Commoners and Queens*. Ames: Iowa State University Press, 1975.

Holderness, Graham. "'A Women's War': A Feminist Reading of *Richard II*." In *Shakespeare Left and Right*, ed. Ivo Kamps, 167–83. London: Routledge, 1991.

———, ed. *The Shakespeare Myth*. Manchester: University of Manchester Press, 1988.

Holinshed, Raphael. *Chronicles of England*. 1586. Vol. 4. Ed. Henry Ellis. London: J. Johnson et al., 1808.

Holm, Janis Butler. "The Myth of a Feminist Humanism: Thomas Salter's *The Mirrhor of Modestie*." In *Ambiguous Realities: Women in the Middle Ages and the Renaissance*, ed. Carole Levin and Jeanie Watson, 197–218. Detroit: Wayne State University Press, 1987.

Holst-Warhaft, Gail. *Dangerous Voices: Women's Lament in Greece*. London: Routledge, 1992.

———. "Dangerous Voices: Women's Lament in Greece." George Sefaris Lecture, Harvard University, March 2, 1989.

Hoskyns, John. *Direccons for Speech and Style* [ca. 1599]. Ed. Louise Brown Osborn. Yale Studies in English 87 (1937). Reprint, Hamden, CT: Archon Books, 1973.

Houlbrooke, Ralph. "Death, Church, and Family in England between the Late Fifteenth and Early Eighteenth Centuries." In *Death, Ritual, and Bereavement*, ed. Ralph Houlbrooke, 25–42. London: Routledge, 1989.

Howard, Henry Graville, ed. *The Lives of Philip Howard, Earl of Arundel and of Anne Dacres His Wife.* 1630. London: Hurst and Blackett, 1857.

Howard, Jean E. *The Stage and Social Struggle in Early Modern England.* New York: Routledge, 1994.

Howell, Wilbur S. *Logic and Rhetoric in England, 1500–1700.* Princeton, NJ: Princeton University Press, 1956.

Hulse, S. Clark. "Wresting the Alphabet: Oratory and Action in *Titus Andronicus.*" *Criticism* 21 (1979): 106–18.

Humbert of Romans. "De eruditione praedicatorum." In *Maxima Bibliotheca Veterum Patrum*, ed. M. De La Bigne, 25:426–567. Lyons, 1677.

———. "Treatise on Preaching." Trans. Dominican Students, Province of St. Joseph. Ed. W. M. Conlon. Westminster, MD, 1951.

Hunter, G. K. *Dramatic Identities and Cultural Traditions: Studies in Shakespeare and His Contemporaries.* Liverpool: Liverpool University Press, 1978.

———. *John Lyly: The Humanist as Courtier.* London: Routledge and Kegan Paul, 1962.

Huntington, Richard, and Peter Metcalf. *Celebrations of Death: The Anthropology of Mortuary Ritual.* Cambridge: Cambridge University Press, 1979.

Huston, Nancy. "The Matrix of War: Mothers and Heroes." In *The Female Body in Western Culture: Contemporary Perspectives*, ed. Susan Rubin Suleiman, 119–36. Cambridge, MA: Harvard University Press, 1986.

Jackson-Stops, Gervase. *The Treasure Houses of Britain: Five Hundred Years of Private Patronage and Art Collecting.* Catalog of the exhibit at the National Gallery of Art, Washington. New Haven, CT: Yale University Press, 1985.

Jacques de Vitry. *The Exempla or Illustrative Stories from the Sermones Vulgares of Jacques de Vitry*, ed. Thomas F. Crane. *Publications of the Folklore Society* 26 (1890).

James, Mervyn. *Family, Lineage, and Civil Society: A Study of Society, Politics, and Mentality in the Durham Region, 1500–1640.* Oxford: Clarendon Press, 1974.

James, M[ervyn] E[vans]. "Two Tudor Funerals." *Transactions of the Cumberland and Westmoreland Antiquarian and Archaeological Society*, n.s., 66 (1966): 165–78.

Jardine, Lisa. " 'Girl Talk' (for Boys on the Left), or Marginalising Feminist Critical Praxis." *Oxford Literary Review* 8 (1986): 208–17.

———. *Still Harping on Daughters: Women and Drama in the Age of Shakespeare*. 1983. Reprint, New York: Columbia University Press, 1989.

Jay, Nancy. *Throughout Your Generations Forever: Sacrifice, Religion, and Paternity*. Chicago: University of Chicago Press, 1992.

Jayne, Sears, and Francis R. Johnson. *Catalogue of the Library of John Ld. Lumley*. London: British Museum Publications, 1955.

Jed, Stephanie. *Chaste Thinking: The Rape of Lucretia and the Birth of Humanism*. Bloomington: Indiana University Press, 1989.

Jeffrey, David L. "Franciscan Spirituality and the Rise of Early English Drama." *Mosaic* 8 (1975): 17–46.

Jones, Ann Rosalind, and Peter Stallybrass. "Dismantling Irena: The Sexualization of Early Modern Ireland." In *Nationalisms and Sexualities*, ed. Andrew Parker, Mary Russo, Doris Sommer, and Patricia Yaeger, 157–71. New York: Routledge, 1992.

Jones, Robert C. *These Valiant Dead: Renewing the Past in Shakespeare's Histories*. Iowa City: University of Iowa Press, 1991.

Jonson, Ben. *Ben Jonson*. 11 vols. Ed. C. H. Herford, Percy Simpson, and Evelyn Simpson. Oxford: Clarendon Press, 1925–52.

Joplin, Patricia Klindienst. "Ritual Work on Human Flesh: Livy's Lucrece and the Rape of the Body Politic." *Helios* 17 (1990): 51–70.

———. "The Voice of the Shuttle." *Stanford Literature Review* 1 (1984): 25–53.

Jordan, Constance. *Renaissance Feminism*. Ithaca, NY: Cornell University Press, 1990.

Joseph, B. L. *Elizabethan Acting*. 2d ed. Oxford: Oxford University Press, 1964.

Joseph, Sr. Miriam. *Shakespeare's Use of the Arts of Language*. New York: Hafner, 1966.

Justinian. *Corpus Juris Civilis*. Vol. 1. Trans. S. P. Scott. 1932. Reprint, New York: AMS, 1973.

Kahn, Coppélia. "The Absent Mother in *King Lear*." In *Rewriting the Renaissance: The Discourses of Sexual Difference in Early Modern Europe*, 33–49. Chicago: University of Chicago Press, 1986.

———. "The Rape in Shakespeare's 'Lucrece.'" *Shakespeare Studies* 9 (1976): 45–72.

Kaplan, Alice. *French Lessons: A Memoir*. Chicago: University of Chicago Press, 1993.

Karras, Ruth Mazo. "The Regulation of Brothels in Later Medieval England." *Signs* 14 (1989): 399–433.

Kay, David. "Ben Jonson, Horace, and the Poetomachia: The Development of an Elizabethan Playwright's Public Image." Diss., Princeton University, 1968.

Kelso, Ruth. *Doctrine for the Lady of the Renaissance*. 1956. Reprint, Urbana: University of Illinois Press, 1978.

Kolve, V. A. *The Play Called Corpus Christi*. Stanford, CA: Stanford University Press, 1966.

Knapp, Robert. *Shakespeare—The Theatre and the Book*. Princeton, NJ: Princeton University Press, 1989.

Kushner, Tony. *Angels in America*. New York: Theatre Communications Group, 1992.

Labalme, Patricia H., ed. *Beyond Their Sex: Learned Women of the European Past*. New York: New York University Press, 1984.

Lamb, Mary Ellen. "The Cooke Sisters: Attitudes toward Learned Women in the Renaissance." In *Silent But for the Word: Tudor Women as Patrons, Translators, and Writers of Religious Works*, ed. Margaret Patterson Hannay, 107–25. Kent, OH: Kent State University Press, 1985.

Lathrop, Henry Burrowes. *Translations from the Classics into English from Caxton to Chapman, 1477–1620. University of Wisconsin Studies in Language and Literature* 35 (1933).

Laurence, Anne. "The Cradle to the Grave: English Observation of Irish Social Customs in the Seventeenth Century." *Seventeenth Century* 3 (1988): 63–84.

Lecoq, Jacques. "Acting the Mask." Trans. Virginia Scott. *Commedia dell' Arte and the Comic Spirit*, program of the 1990 Classics in Context Festival, Actors' Theatre of Louisville.

Leerssen, Joseph Th. *Mere Irish & Fíor-Ghael*. Amsterdam: John Benjamins, 1986.

Levi, Peter. "The Lamentation of the Dead." Inaugural lecture, University of Oxford, October 25, 1984. London: Anvil Press Poetry, 1984.

Levin, Carole. "Lady Jane Grey: Protestant Queen and Martyr." In *Silent But for the Word: Tudor Women as Patrons, Translators, and Writers of Religious Works*, ed. Margaret Patterson Hannay, 92–106. Kent, OH: Kent State University Press, 1985.

Limon, Jerzy. *Gentlemen of a Company: English Players in Central and Eastern Europe, 1590–1660*. Cambridge: Cambridge University Press, 1985.

Litten, Julian. *The English Way of Death*. London: Robert Hale, 1991.

Loomba, Ania. *Gender, Race, Renaissance Drama*. Manchester: University of Manchester Press, 1989.

Loraux, Nicole. *The Invention of Athens: The Funeral Oration in the Classical City*. Trans. Alan Sheridan. Cambridge, MA: Harvard University Press, 1986.

———. *Tragic Ways of Killing a Woman*. Trans. Anthony Forster. Cambridge, MA: Harvard University Press, 1989.

Lucas, F. L. *Euripides and His Influence*. Boston: Marshall Jones, 1923.

Lumley, Jane, trans. *Iphigenia at Aulis*. Ed. Harold H. Child. London: Malone Society Reprints, 1909.

———. "Exercises and translations out of Greake into latin and otherwise of Marie duchesse of Suffolke, Jane ladie Lumley, & Sir John Ratclif when they were yoonge, of their owne hande wryting, bownde up together." Royal MSS 12.A.i–iv and 7.D.ix.

———. "Isocrates orations ad Nicolem & c., translated out of greeke into Latin by Jane ladie Lumley and dedicated to my lorde of Arundell hir father, Euripides tragedie called Iphygenia, translated likewise by hir out of greeke into English, and written with hir owne hande." Royal MS 15.A.ix.

Lyly, John. *The Collected Works of John Lyly*. 3 vols. Ed. R. W. Bond. Oxford: Clarendon Press, 1902.

Lysaght, Patricia. *The Banshee: The Irish Supernatural Death-Messenger*. Dublin: Glendale Press, 1986.

MacCurtain, Margaret, and Mary O'Dowd, eds. *Women in Early Modern Ireland*. Edinburgh: Edinburgh University Press, 1991.

MacCurtain, Margaret, and Donncha Ó Córrain, eds. *Women in Irish Society: The Historical Dimension*. Contributions in Women's Studies, no. 11. Westport, CT: Greenwood Press, 1979.

MacDonald, Joyce Green. "Women and Theatrical Authority: Deborah Warner's *Titus Andronicus*." In *Cross-Cultural Performances: Differences in Women's Re-Visions of Shakespeare*, ed. Marianne Novy, 185–205. Urbana: University of Illinois Press, 1993.

Machyn, Henry. *The Diary of Henry Machyn, Citizen and Merchant-Taylor of London, from A.D. 1550 to A.D. 1563*. Ed. John Gough Nichols. London: Camden Society, 1848.

Macintosh, Fiona. *Dying Acts: Death in Ancient Greek and Modern Irish Tragic Drama*. New York: St. Martin's Press, 1995.

Maitland, Frederic William. "The Meaning of Words." In *Frederic William Maitland, Historian: Selections from His Writings*, ed. Robert Livingston Schuyler, 81–105. Berkeley: University of California Press, 1960.

Malden, H. E., ed. *A History of Surrey*. In vol. 3 of *The Victoria History of the Counties of England*. London, 1911.

Mann, David. *The Elizabethan Player*. London: Routledge, 1991.

Manningham, John. *The Diary of John Manningham of the Middle Temple, 1602–1603*. Ed. Robert Parker Sorlien. Hanover, NH: University Press of New England, 1976.

Marlowe, Christopher. *Complete Works*. Vol. 1. Ed. Fredson Bowers. Cambridge: Cambridge University Press, 1973.

Marston, John. *1 & 2 Antonio and Mellida*. 1602. Ed. W. W. Greg. Malone Society Reprints, 1921.

———. *Histriomastix*. 1610. In vol. 3 of *The Plays of John Marston*, ed. H. Harvey Wood. Edinburgh: Oliver and Boyd, 1934–39.

———. *The Malcontent*. Ed. George K. Hunter. London: Methuen, 1975.

———. *The Wonder of Women, or The Tragedy of Sophonisba*. 1605. Ed. James William Kemp Jr. New York: Garland Press, 1979.

Martindale, Charles, and Michelle Martindale. *Shakespeare and the Uses of Antiquity*. London: Routledge, 1990.

Mason, Bim. *Street Theatre and Other Outdoor Performances*. London: Routledge, 1992.

Maus, Katherine Eisaman. "Taking Tropes Seriously: Language and Violence in Shakespeare's *Rape of Lucrece*." *Shakespeare Quarterly* 37 (1986): 66–82.

McConica, James. "The Rise of the Undergraduate College." In *The History of the University of Oxford*, ed. T. H. Aston, 3: 1–68. Oxford: Clarendon Press, 1984–94.

McGuire, Philip C. *Speechless Dialect: Shakespeare's Open Silences*. Berkeley: University of California Press, 1985.

McKellen, Ian. *Acting Shakespeare*. Westwood Playhouse, Los Angeles, May 17, 1987.

McLuskie, Kathleen. "The Act, the Role, and the Actor: Boy Actresses on the Elizabethan Stage." *New Theatre Quarterly* 3 (1987): 120–30.

McNamara, JoAnn. *A New Song: Celibate Women in the First Three Christian Centuries*. New York: Harrington Park, 1985.

Medwall, Henry. *Fulgens and Lucrece*. In *Five Pre-Shakespearean Comedies*, ed. Frederick S. Boas. London: Oxford University Press, 1934.

Miller, Nancy K. *Getting Personal: Feminist Occasions and Other Autobiographical Acts*. New York: Routledge, 1991.

Mills, David. "The Language of Medieval Drama." In *The Revels History of Drama in English*, 1: 69–78. London: Methuen, 1975–83.

Milner, Edith. *Records of the Lumleys of Lumley Castle*. London: George Bell, 1904.

Milsom, S. F. C. *Historical Foundations of the Common Law*. Toronto: Butterworth's, 1981.

Miola, Robert S. *Shakespeare and Classical Tragedy: The Influence of Seneca*. Oxford: Oxford University Press, 1992.

Momigliano, Arnaldo. *Alien Wisdom: The Limits of Hellenization*. Cambridge: Cambridge University Press, 1975.

Morrison, Fynes. *An Itinerary*. 1617. Reprinted in C. Litton Falkiner, *Illustrations of Irish History and Topography*. London: Longmans, 1904.

Morton, R. S. *Venereal Diseases*. Baltimore, MD: Penguin, 1966.

Muldoon, James. "The Indian as Irishman." *Essex Institute Historical Collections* 111 (1975): 267–89.

Mullaney, Steven. *The Place of the Stage: License, Play, and Power in Renaissance England*. Chicago: University of Chicago Press, 1988.

Mulrayne, Ronnie, and Margaret Shrewring. *This Golden Round: The Royal Shakespeare Company at the Swan*. Stratford-on-Avon: Mulrayne and Shrewing Ltd., 1989.

Murphy, James J. *Rhetoric in the Middle Ages*. Berkeley: University of California Press, 1974.

Nagele, Rainer. *Reading after Freud: Essays on Goethe, Holderlin, Habermas, Nietzsche, Brecht, Celan, and Freud*. New York: Columbia University Press, 1987.

Nashe, Thomas. Preface to Greene's *Menaphon*. 1589. In *Elizabethan Critical Essays*, ed. G. Gregory Smith, 1: 307–20. Oxford: Oxford University Press, 1904.

Neill, Michael. "Exeunt with a Dead March." In *Pageantry in the Shakespearean Theater*, ed. David Bergeron, 153–93. Athens: University of Georgia Press, 1985.

Nichols, J[ohn] G[ough], ed. *The Chronicles of Queen Jane and Queen Mary, Written by a Resident in the Tower of London*. London: Camden Society, 1850.

———, ed. "The Life of Henrye Fitzallen, Written by His Chaplin." *Gentlemen's Magazine*, vol. 103, part 2 (1833).

———, ed. *The Literary Remains of King Edward VI*. London: Roxburgh, 1857.

Nichols, Stephen G., ed. *The New Philology*. Special issue of *Speculum* 65 (1990).

Ni Chuilleanain, Eilean, ed. *Irish Women: Image and Achievement: Women in Irish Culture from Earliest Times*. Dublin: Arlen House, 1985.

Nicolas, Nicholas Harris, ed. *The Literary Remains of Lady Jane Grey*. London: Harding, Triphook, and Lepard, 1825.

Norton, Glyn P. *The Ideology and Language of Translation in Renaissance France and Their Humanist Antecedents*. Geneva: Librairie Droz, 1984.

Nungezer, Edwin. *A Dictionary of Actors*. New Haven, CT: Yale University Press, 1929.

O'Brian, Ellen J. "Inside Shakespeare: Using Performance Techniques to Achieve Traditional Goals." *Shakespeare Quarterly* 35 (1984): 621–31.

Oesterly, H., ed. *Shakespeare's Jest Book: A Hundred Merry Tales*. London, 1866.

Ó Madagáin, Breandán. "Irish Vocal Music of Lament and Syllabic Verse." In *The Celtic Consciousness*, ed. Robert O'Driscoll, 311–39. New York: George Braziller, 1982.

O'Malley, John W. "Content and Rhetorical Forms in Sixteenth-Century Treatises on Preaching." In *Renaissance Eloquence: Studies in the Theory and Practice of Renaissance Rhetoric*, ed. James Murphy. Berkeley: University of California Press, 1983.

Omans, Stuart E. "The War of the Theatres: An Approach to Its Origins, Development, and Meaning." Diss., Northwestern University, 1969.

Ong, Walter J. "Latin Language Study as a Renaissance Puberty Rite." *Studies in Philology* 56 (1959): 103–24.

———. *Orality and Literacy*. London: Methuen, 1982.

———. "Oral Residue in Tudor Prose Style." *PMLA* 80 (1965): 145–54.

———. *The Presence of the Word*. New Haven, CT: Yale University Press, 1967.

Orgel, Stephen. *Impersonations: The Performance of Gender in Shakespeare's England*. Cambridge: Cambridge University Press, 1996.

———. "Nobody's Perfect: Or Why Did the English Stage Take Boys for Women?" *Displacing Homophobia*. Special Issue of *South Atlantic Quarterly* 88 (1989): 7–28.

———. "Prospero's Wife." In *Rewriting the Renaissance: The Discourses of Sexual Difference in Early Modern Europe*, 50–64. Chicago: University of Chicago Press, 1986.

Ó Súilleabháin, Seán. *Irish Wake Amusements*. Dublin: Mercier Press, 1967.

Owst, G. R. *Literature and Pulpit in Medieval England*. 1926. Reprint, New York: Barnes and Noble, 1961.

———. *Preaching in Medieval England*. 1926. Reprint, New York: Russell and Russell, 1965.

Papas, Irene. Clytemnestra, *Iphigenia*, dir. Michael Cacoyannis. Greek Film Centre, 1978.

Parker, Andrew, and Eve Sedgwick eds. *Performativity and Performance*. Essays from the English Institute. New York: Routledge, 1995.

Parker, Patricia. *Literary Fat Ladies: Rhetoric, Gender, Property*. London: Methuen, 1987.

Parker, Rozsika. *The Subversive Stitch: Embroidery and the Making of the Feminine*. London: The Women's Press, 1986.

The Parnassus Plays. Published as *The Three Parnassus Plays*. Ed. J. B. Leishman. London: I. Nicholson and Watson, 1949.

Patridge, Angela. "Wild Men and Wailing Women." *Eigse* 18 (1980): 25–37.

Partridge, Edward. "Re-Presenting Shakespeare." In *Shakespeare: The Theatrical Dimension*, eds. Philip C. McGuire and David A. Samuelson, 1–10. New York: AMS Press, 1979.

Patterson, Lee. "On the Margin: Postmodernism, Ironic History, and Medieval Studies." *Speculum* 65 (1990): 87–108.

Paxton, Frederick S. *Christianizing Death: The Creation of a Ritual Process in Early Medieval Europe*. Ithaca, NY: Cornell University Press, 1990.

Percy, Thomas. *Reliques of Ancient Poetry*. Routledge's British Poets. London, n.d.

Petrarch, Francesco. "How a Ruler Ought to Govern His State." In *The Earthly Republic: Italian Humanists on Government and Society*, eds. Benjamin G. Kohl and Ronald G. Witt, 35–78. Philadelphia: University of Pennsylvania Press.

Philostratus. *The Life of Apollonius of Tyana*. Vol. 2. Loeb Classical Library. Trans. F. C. Conybeare. London: Heinemann, 1969.

Pilkington, James. "A Godlie Exposition upon Several Chapters in Nehemiah." 1585. In *The Works of James Pilkington*, ed. James Scholefield. Cambridge: Cambridge University Press, 1842.

Piper, David. "The 1590 Lumley Inventory: Hilliard, Segar, and the Earl of Essex." *Burlington Magazine* 90 (1957): 224–31.

Plato. *Collected Dialogues*. Ed. Edith Hamilton and Huntington Cairns. Bollingen Series 71. New York: Pantheon Books, 1963.

Pliny the Elder. *Natural History*. Vol. 9. Loeb Classical Library. Trans. H. Rackham. London: Heinemann, 1952.

Plowden, Alison. *Lady Jane Grey and the House of Suffolk*. London: Sedgwick and Jackson, 1985.

Plutarch. "Letter to Apollonius." In vol. 2 of *Plutarch's Moralia*. 15 vols. Trans. Frank Cole Babbitt. Loeb Classical Library. Cambridge, MA: Harvard University Press, 1928.

———. "Solon." In vol. 1 of *Plutarch's Lives*. 11 vols. Trans. Bernadotte Perrin. Loeb Classical Library. Cambridge, MA: Harvard University Press, 1914.

———. "Summary of a Comparison between Aristophanes and Menander." In vol. 10 of *Plutarch's Moralia*. 15 vols. Trans. Harold North Fowler. Loeb Classical Library. Cambridge, MA: Harvard University Press, 1936.

Pollack, Sir Frederick, and Frederick William Maitland. *The History of English Law*. 1895. Reprint, 2 vols., Cambridge: Cambridge University Press, 1968.

Post, J. B. "Ravishment of Women and the Statutes of Westminster." In *Legal Records and the Historian*, ed. J. H. Baker, 150–64. Cambridge: Cambridge University Press, 1978.

Prosser, Eleanor. *Drama and Religion in the English Mystery Plays*. Stanford, CA: Stanford University Press, 1961.

Pusey, William. *The History and Epidemiology of Syphilis*. Springfield, IL: Charles Thomas, 1933.

Puttenham, George. *The Arte of English Poesie*. 1589. Ed. Gladys Doidge Willcock and Alice Walker. Cambridge: Cambridge University Press, 1936.

Quétel, Claude. *History of Syphillis*. Trans. Judith Braddock and Brian Pike. Cambridge: Polity Press, 1990.

Quinn, David Beers. *The Elizabethans and the Irish*. Ithaca, NY: Cornell University Press, 1966.

Quintilian. *Institutio Oratoria*. 4 vols. Trans. H. E. Butler. Loeb Classical Library. London: Heinemann, 1921.

Rackin, Phyllis. "Shakespeare's Boy Cleopatra, the Decorum of Nature, and the Golden World of Poetry." *PMLA* 84 (1972): 201–12.

———. *Stages of History: Shakespeare's English Chronicles*. Ithaca, NY: Cornell University Press, 1990.

Rankin, H. D. *Celts and the Classical World*. London: Croom Helm, 1987.

Reibetanz, John H. "The Two Theatres: Dramatic Structure and Convention in English Public and Private Plays, 1599–1613." Diss., Princeton University, 1968.

Reynolds, Myra. *The Learned Lady in England, 1650–1760*. Boston: Houghton Mifflin, 1920.

Richardson, Ruth. *Death, Dissection, and the Destitute*. London: Penguin, 1988.

Rifkin, Myra Lee. "Burial, Funeral, and Mourning Customs in England, 1558–1662." Diss., Bryn Mawr, 1977.

Riggs, David. *Shakespeare's Heroical Histories*. Cambridge, MA: Harvard University Press, 1971.

Rinconi, Alessandro. "Sulla Fortuna di Plauto e di Terenzio nel Mondo Romano." *Maia* 22 (1970): 19–37.

Roach, Joseph R. *The Player's Passion: Studies in the Science of Acting*. Ann Arbor: University of Michigan Press, 1993.

Rose, Mary Beth. "Where Are the Mothers in Shakespeare?" *Shakespeare Quarterly* 42 (1991): 292–314.

Rutter, Carol. *Clamorous Voices: Shakespeare's Women Today*. London: Women's Press, 1988.

Sacks, Peter M. *The English Elegy: Studies in the Genre from Spenser to Yeats*. Baltimore: Johns Hopkins University Press, 1985.

St. Germain, Christopher. *Doctor and Student*. 1530. Ed. T. F. T. Plucknett and J. L. Barton. London: Seldon Society, 1974.

Salinger, Leo. *Shakespeare and the Traditions of Comedy*. Cambridge: Cambridge University Press, 1974.

Salter, Thomas. *The Mirrhor of Modestie* [1579?]. Ed. Janis Butler Holm. Renaissance Imagination 32. New York: Garland, 1987.

Sandys, John Edwin. *A History of Classical Scholarship*. Vol. 2. Cambridge: Cambridge University Press, 1908.

Schenck, Celeste Marguerite. *Mourning and Panegyric: The Poetics of Pastoral Ceremony*. State College: Pennsylvania State University Press, 1988.

Schiesari, Juliana. *The Gendering of Melancholia: Feminism, Psychoanalysis, and the Symbolics of Loss in Renaissance Literature*. Ithaca, NY: Cornell University Press, 1992.

Schneemelcher, Wilhelm, trans. *The Acts of Paul and Thecla*. In *The Other Bible*, ed. Willis Barnstone, 447–53. San Francisco: Harper and Row, 1984.

Schneider, Jane. "Trousseau as Treasure: Some Contradictions of Late Nineteenth-Century Change in Sicily." In *The Marriage Bargain: Women and Dowries in European History*, ed. Marion A. Kaplan, 81–119. New York: Harrington Park, 1985.

Schoeck, Richard. "Lawyers and Rhetoric in Sixteenth-Century England." In *Renaissance Eloquence: Studies in the Theory and Practice of Renaissance Rhetoric*, ed. James J. Murphy, 274–91. Berkeley: University of California Press, 1983.

———. "Rhetoric and Law in Sixteenth-Century England." *Studies in Philology* 50 (1953): 110–27.

Schulenburg, Jane Tibbetts. "The Heroics of Virginity: Brides of Christ and Sacrificial Mutilation." In *Women in the Middle Ages and the Renaissance*, ed. Mary Beth Rose, 29–72. Syracuse, NY: Syracuse University Press, 1986.

Scott, Joan. *Gender and the Politics of History*. New York: Columbia University Press, 1988.

Seneca the Elder. *Controversiae and Suasoriae*. 2 vols. Trans. Michael Winterbottom. Loeb Classical Library. London: Heinemann, 1974.

Seneca [the Younger]. *Tragedies*. 2 vols. Trans. Frank Justus Miller. Loeb Classical Library. Cambridge, MA: Harvard University Press, 1917.

Shakespeare, William. *The Riverside Shakespeare*. Boston: Houghton Mifflin, 1974.

Shapiro, Michael. *Children of the Revels: The Boy Companies of Shakespeare's Time and Their Plays*. New York: Columbia University Press, 1977.

———. "Boying Her Greatness: Shakespeare's Use of Coterie Drama in *Antony and Cleopatra*." *Modern Language Review* 77 (1982): 1–15.

Shepherd, Simon. "Acting against Bardom: Some Utopian Thoughts on Workshops." In *Shakespeare and the Changing Curriculum*, ed. Lesley Aers and Nigel Wheale. London: Routledge, 1991.

Shirley, James. *Dramatic Works and Poems*. Vol. 4. Ed. William Gifford and Alexander Dyce. 1833. Reprint, New York: Russell and Russell, 1966.

Showalter, Elaine. "Toward a Feminist Poetics." In *The New Feminist Criti-

cism: Essays on Women, Literature, and Theory, ed. Elaine Showalter. New York: Pantheon, 1985.

Shuger, Debora Kuller. *The Renaissance Bible: Scholarship, Sacrifice, and Subjectivity.* Berkeley: University of California Press, 1994.

———. "Subversive Fathers and Suffering Subjects: Shakespeare and Christianity." In *Religion, Literature, and Politics in Post-Reformation England, 1540–1688*, ed. Richard Strier and Donna Hamilton, 46–69. Cambridge: Cambridge University Press, 1996.

Sidney, Sir Philip. "An Apology for Poetry" [ca. 1583]. In *Elizabethan Critical Essays*, ed. G. Gregory Smith, 1: 148–207. Oxford: Oxford University Press, 1904.

Simpson, David. *The Academic Postmodern and the Rule of Literature.* Chicago: University of Chicago Press, 1995.

Smalley, Beryl. *English Friars and Antiquity in the XIV Century.* Oxford: Blackwell, 1960.

Smith, Bruce R. *Ancient Scripts and Modern Experience on the English Stage, 1500–1700.* Princeton, NJ: Princeton University Press, 1988.

Smith, Hilda. "Gynecology and Ideology in Seventeenth-Century England." In *Liberating Women's History*, ed. Berenice A. Carroll. Urbana: University of Illinois Press, 1976.

Spencer, T. J. B. "'Greeks' and 'Merrygreeks': A Background to *Timon of Athens* and *Troilus and Cressida*." In *Essays on Shakespearean and Elizabethan Drama in Honor of Hardin Craig*, ed. Richard Hosley, 223–33. Columbia: University of Missouri Press, 1962.

Spenser, Edmund. *A View of the Present State of Ireland.* In vol. 9 of *The Works of Edmund Spenser*, ed. Edwin Greenlaw, et al. Baltimore: Johns Hopkins University Press, 1932–49.

Spivack, Bernard. *Shakespeare and the Allegory of Evil.* New York: Columbia University Press, 1958.

Stallybrass, Peter. "Patriarchal Territories." In *Rewriting the Renaissance: The Discourses of Sexual Difference in Early Modern Europe*, ed. Margaret W. Ferguson, Maureen Quilligan, and Nancy J. Vickers, 123–42. Chicago: University of Chicago Press, 1986.

Stannard, David E. *The Puritan Way of Death.* New York: Oxford University Press, 1977.

Stanyhurst, Richard. *De rebus in Hibernia gestis.* Antwerp, 1584. Trans. in Colm Lennon, *Richard Stanihurst the Dubliner, 1547–1618.* Blackrock, Co. Dublin: Irish Academic Press, 1981.

Stimpson, Catherine R. "Shakespeare and the Soil of Rape." In *The Woman's Part*, ed. Carolyn Ruth Swift Lenz, Gayle Greene, and Carol Thomas Neely, 56–64. Urbana: University of Illinois, 1980.

Stone, Lawrence. *The Crisis of the Aristocracy, 1558–1641*. Oxford: Clarendon Press, 1965.

Stříbrný, Zdeněk. [Shakespearean Performance in Prague.] Paper presented at Stanford University, ca. October 1983.

Strocchia, Sharon T. "Funerals and the Politics of Gender in Early Renaissance Florence." In *Refiguring Woman: Perspectives on Gender and the Italian Renaissance*, ed. Marilyn Migiel and Juliana Schiesari, 155–68. Ithaca, NY: Cornell University Press, 1991.

Strong, Roy. *The English Icon: Elizabethan and Jacobean Portraiture*. Paul Mellon Foundation for British Art. London: Routledge, and New Haven, CT: Yale University Press, 1969.

Sypherd, Wilbur. *Jephthah and His Daughter: A Study in Comparative Literature*. Newark: University of Delaware Press, 1948.

Tacitus. *Dialogus*. Vol. 1. Trans. Sir W. Peterson, 1914. Rev. M. Winterbottom. Loeb Classical Library. Cambridge, MA: Harvard University Press, 1970.

Taplin, Oliver. *Greek Tragedy in Action*. Berkeley: University of California Press, 1979.

Taylor, Jeremy. *The Rule and Exercise of Holy Dying*. Vol. 2 of *Holy Living and Holy Dying*. 1651. Ed. P. G. Stanwood. Oxford: Clarendon Press, 1989.

Thomas, Keith. *Religion and the Decline of Magic*. New York: Charles Scribner's Sons, 1971.

Thompson, Ann. "*King Lear* and the Politics of Teaching Shakespeare." *Shakespeare Quarterly* 41 (1990): 139–46.

Traub, Valerie. "Prince Hal's Falstaff: Positioning Psychoanalysis and the Female Reproductive Body." *Shakespeare Quarterly* 40 (1989): 456–74.

Trimpi, Wesley. *Ben Jonson's Poems: A Study of the Plain Style*. Stanford, CA: Stanford University Press, 1963.

———. *Muses of One Mind: The Literary Analysis of Experience and Its Continuity*. Princeton, NJ: Princeton University Press, 1983.

The Troublesome Reign of King John. 1588. Ed. J. W. Sider. New York: Garland, 1979.

Udall, Nicholas. *Flowers for Latine Speakyng*. Ed. R. C. Alston. Menston, England: Scholar Press, 1972.

Veeser, H. Aram, ed. *Confessions of the Critics*. New York: Routledge, 1996.

Vernant, Jean-Pierre. "A General Theory of Sacrifice." In *Mortals and Immortals: Collected Essays*, ed. Froma I. Zeitlin. Princeton, NJ: Princeton University Press, 1991.

Waith, Eugene. "*Controversia* in the English Drama: Medwall and Massinger." *PMLA* 68 (1953): 268–303.

———. "John Fletcher and the Art of Declamation." *PMLA* 66 (1951): 226–34.

———. "The Metamorphosis of Violence in *Titus Andronicus*." *Shakespeare Survey* 10 (1957): 39–49.

———. *The Pattern of Tragicomedy in Beaumont and Fletcher, Yale Studies in English* 120. New Haven, CT: Yale University Press, 1959.

———. "*Pericles* and Seneca the Elder." *JEGP* 50 (1951): 180–82.

Walton, J. Michael. *The Greek Sense of Theatre*. London: Methuen, 1984.

Walys, Thomas. "De modo componendi sermones." In *Artes praedicandi: Contribution à l'histoire de la rhétorique au moyen âge*, ed. Th.-M. Charland. *Publications de l'institut d'études médiévales d'Ottawa* 7 (1936): 328–403.

———. "On the Method of Composing Sermons." Trans. Dorothy Grosser. Master's thesis, Cornell University, 1949.

Warner, Marina. *Alone of All Her Sex: The Myth and Cult of the Virgin Mary*. New York: Vintage, 1976.

Warnicke, Retha. *Women of the English Renaissance and Reformation*. Westport, CT: Greenwood, 1983.

Webbe, William. *A Discourse of English Poesy*. 1586. In *Elizabethan Critical Essays*, ed. G. Gregory Smith, 226–302. Oxford: Oxford University Press, 1904.

Webster, John [with Thomas Dekker]. *The Famous History of Sir Thomas Wyatt*. In *The Dramatic Works of John Webster*, vol. 1, ed. William Hazlitt. London: John Russell Smith, 1857.

Weever, John. *Ancient Funerall Monuments*. London, 1631.

Weimann, Robert. *Shakespeare and the Popular Tradition in the Theatre*. Ed. Robert Schwartz. Baltimore: Johns Hopkins University Press, 1987.

Weinberg, Bernard. *A History of Literary Criticism in the Italian Renaissance*. 2 vols. Chicago: University of Chicago Press, 1961.

Welsh, Andrew. "Heritage in *Pericles*." In *Shakespeare's Late Plays: Essays in Honor of Charles Crow*, ed. Richard C. Tobias and Paul G. Zolbrod, 89–113. Athens: Ohio University Press, 1974.

White, Helen C. *Tudor Books of Saints and Martyrs*. Madison: University of Wisconsin Press, 1963.

Wickham, Glynne. *Early English Stages*. 3 vols. in 4 parts. London: Routledge, 1958–81.

———. *Shakespeare's Dramatic Heritage: Collected Studies in Mediaeval, Tudor, and Shakespearean Drama*. London: Routledge, 1969.

Wiles, David. *Shakespeare's Clown: Actor and Text in the Elizabethan Playhouse*. Cambridge: Cambridge University Press, 1987.

Williams, Raymond. *Modern Tragedy*. Stanford, CA: Stanford University Press, 1966.

———. *Writing in Society*. London: Verso, n.d.

Wilson, Thomas. *The Art of Rhetorique*. 1560. Ed. G. H. Mair. Oxford: Clarendon Press, 1909.

Wood (Green), Mary Anne Everett. *Letters of Royal and Illustrious Ladies of Great Britain*. 3 vols. London: Henry Colburn, 1846.

Woolf, Rosemary. *The English Mystery Plays*. Berkeley: University of California Press, 1972.

Wright, F. Warren. *Cicero and the Theatre*. Smith College Classical Studies 11 (1931): 1–111.

Yachnin, Paul. "The Powerless Theatre." *English Literary Renaissance* 21:1 (Winter 1991): 49–74.

Zarilli, Phillip B. *Acting (Re)Considered*. London: Routledge, 1995.

Zeitlin, Froma I. "Playing the Other: Theater, Theatricality, and the Feminine in Greek Drama." In *Nothing to Do with Dionysus? Athenian Drama in Its Social Context*, ed. John J. Winkler and Froma I. Zeitlin, 63–96. Princeton, NJ: Princeton University Press, 1990.

Acknowledgments

THE CHAPTERS OF THIS BOOK, written in various times and places, are variously indebted. I am especially grateful to Wesley Trimpi, who, with the skill of Jonson's Camden in searching the most antique springs, introduced me to the questions I explore in the first chapter, "Seneca by Candlelight." David Riggs did all he could to guide me to sensible answers. Grants from The Mrs. Giles Whiting Foundation and the Mabelle McLeod Lewis Foundation provided financial assistance for the dissertation in which the central sections of the chapter originated.

"Iphigenia in Durham" owes much to Mary-Kay Gamel, who traveled all over the country to comment incisively on earlier versions. I am also grateful to Lynda Boose, Rebecca Mark, and Mary Elizabeth Perry, who offered timely suggestions, and to Lawrence L. Langer, whose championship secured the grant that enabled me to spend a summer among the Lumley manuscripts at the British Library.

Among those from whose comments "The Saint in the Brothel" especially benefited are Christopher A. Faraone, the late Jack Winkler, and pretty much the entire Classics Department of Stanford University, circa 1985. Kathy Gaca and Phyllis Gorfain were shrewd and sympathetic readers of later versions. I thank Kimberly Benston for the stalwart editorial support that led to the first published version of "Voluntary Wounds."

"Ethnicke Lamentations" would not have taken its present shape had I not heard Gail Holst-Warhaft's Sefaris Lecture at Harvard University shortly after I began work on women's lament in the Shakespearean chronicle plays. An invitation from Jean Howard and Phyllis Rackin to participate in an MLA panel allowed me to present my initial ideas on the topic, and later, an invitation from Robert S.

Knapp to address the Pacific Northwest Renaissance Conference enabled me not only to refine my historical inquiry but also to premiere its theatrical adaptation in a performance of what has now become the Queen Margaret section of my solo performance project, *Shakespeare by Heart*.

I am grateful to Michael Gorra, R. M. Robertson, and Helen Trimpi, all of whom read and commented helpfully on the manuscript. Jerome E. Singerman's cordial enthusiasm and editorial tact have withstood more serious tests of time and trouble than I ever intended. The readers for the press, while deftly pointing out errors of fact and vagaries of tone, were unfailingly magnanimous in their responses to my project. My thanks are also due to the editorial staff, both for their efficiency and for their courteous patience with my inefficiency.

Without the extraordinarily generous encouragement of Debora Shuger, this book would not have come to be. She has been the keenest of critics and the best of friends throughout the many years of its preparation.

Portions of "Voluntary Wounds" appeared in *PMLA*, and portions of "The Saint in the Brothel" appeared in *Shakespeare Quarterly*; both are reprinted by permission. Quotations from Shakespeare are from the Riverside edition; quotations from Jonson are from Herford and Simpson. Except for passages from Lattimore's translation of Aeschylus, quotations from Greek and Roman authors are cited according to the standard lineation of the Greek and Latin texts. Except in quotations of medieval verse (and one recalcitrant bit of Spenser), spelling and punctuation have been modernized.

Index